POLICING AT THE TOP

The roles, values and attitudes of chief police officers

Bryn Caless

First published in Great Britain in 2011 by

The Policy Press
University of Bristol
Fourth Floor
Beacon House
Queen's Road
Bristol BS8 1QU
UK

t: +44 (0)117 331 4054
f: +44 (0)117 331 4093
tpp-info@bristol.ac.uk
www.policypress.co.uk

North American office:
The Policy Press
c/o International Specialized Books Services
920 NE 58th Avenue, Suite 300
Portland, OR 97213-3786, USA
t: +1 503 287 3093
f: +1 503 280 8832
info@isbs.com

© The Policy Press 2011

British Library Cataloguing in Publication Data
A catalogue record for this book is available from the British Library.

Library of Congress Cataloging-in-Publication Data
A catalog record for this book has been requested.

ISBN 978 1 44730 015 1   paperback
ISBN 978 1 44730 016 8   hardcover

The right of Bryn Caless to be identified as author of this work has been asserted by
him in accordance with the Copyright, Designs and Patents Act 1988.

Cover design by The Policy Press.
Front cover: image kindly supplied by Wilson History & Research
Center.
Printed and bound in Great Britain by TJ International, Padstow.
The Policy Press uses environmentally responsible print partners.

This book is dedicated to Clarey,
without whom there is no meaning
with whom there is always joy

Contents

List of tables

Glossary

ACC	assistant chief constable (see chief officer)
ACPO	Association of Chief Police Officers; a limited company that claims to speak for the whole police service, membership of which is restricted to chief officers, but it is likely to mutate into a 'police institute' of some kind, aiming to speak for the whole police service.
APA	Association of Police Authorities
BCS	British Crime Survey; begun in 1982, this is an annual survey of the attitudes of victims to crime and the police. It is key to understanding the public's fear of crime.
BCU	Basic command unit; a local police group headed by a Superintendent or Chief Superintendent and based at one or more police stations. It is increasingly seen as an inefficient way of delivering local policing.
Bramshill	Residential police training site near Hook in Hampshire which houses the Police National Leadership College, the comprehensive National Police Library (but not for much longer apparently); and is where the SCC takes place. Bramshill is also called the National Police Staff College.
BTP	British Transport Police; despite its name this is the *railway* police force and has nothing to do with aircraft, motor vehicles or shipping.
CC	chief constable (see chief officer)
chief officer	A police officer who holds a formal *strategic command* rank, from ACC or commander (in the MPS), through DCC or deputy assistant commissioner (DAC) in the MPS, to CC or assistant commissioner in the MPS. Deputy commissioner and commissioner are two police ranks found only in London and should not be confused with the coalition government's creation of police crime commissioners.
CJS	Criminal justice system; the collective apparatus of police, courts, trials, sentencing, prisons and probation.
COMPSTAT	probably stands for 'comparative statistics' (no one is certain; some claim it is short for 'computer statistics',

	which makes less sense); imported from the US, it is a methodology to compare operational performance between police groups and to assess the efficacy of local command in terms of local targets set and met.
CPS	Crown Prosecution Service, retitled Public Prosecution Service in 2009
DCC	deputy chief constable (see chief officer)
DECC	directly elected crime commissioner (see PCC)
FOI	Freedom of Information (Act), basis for obtaining information from (often reluctant) public servants; the police refer to 'FOI requests'.
FTA	Fixed term appointment; usually of five years at a time, this is the basis for the employment of chief and deputy chief constables, and increasingly of ACCs too. FTAs are detested by ACPO and owned by police authorities, and, from mid-2012, PCCs.
'Gold'	Designation of the coordinating strategic commander in a crisis or operation, it is used by the police to describe the most senior on-call officer in a force; usually but not exclusively a chief officer.
HMIC	Her Majesty's Inspectorate of Constabulary
HMCIC	Her Majesty's Chief Inspector of Constabulary
HPDS	High Potential Development Scheme, revised (and sometimes reviled) method to 'fast track' those police officers allegedly with potential to become chief officers.
HR	human resources or people management
IPLDP	Initial Police Leadership Development Programme
MPA	Metropolitan Police Authority, the body chaired by the Deputy Mayor of London which oversees the MPS.
MPS	Metropolitan Police Service, serving all of London (except the City of London which has its own force) and headed by a commissioner. MPS has its own chief officer designations (see chief officer).
NCA	National Crime Agency, a massive structure which replaced the Serious Organised Crime Agency (SOCA) in 2011 and has taken parts of NPIA's functions, its aim is to challenge serious organised crime at levels above that of the individual police force, so acting regionally, nationally and internationally.

NOS	National Occupational Standards; sets of skills-based and behavioural competencies used to assess police officers at various ranks – some are generic to policing, others are rank or role based.
NPIA	National Policing Improvement Agency; among other things, the NPIA was responsible for all police learning and training. Its costs were high (£550 million each year) and it was abolished by the coalition government on assuming office in 2010.
NVQ	National Vocational Qualification, widely regarded in policing as an 'artisan' route to qualification.
OSPRE	Objective Structured Performance Related Examination for promotion to sergeant and inspector, now much criticised for its mechanistic approach to assessing the roles.
PA	Police authority; an oversight role normally performed by 17 people, (some elected, some appointed) under the Police Act 1964. The role is to be terminated in 2012.
PCC	Police crime commissioner, the person employed to hire and fire chief constables and to hold police forces to account, replacing police authorities. For a period, the 'crime commissioner' description was dropped in favour of 'directly elected individual' (DEI), but PCC seems now to be the accepted form.
PCSO	police community support officer
PDP	Personal development plan; used by chief officers (and others in the police) to record development needs and how they are met.
PDR	Performance development review; annual appraisal of an individual's performance and development needs (from which a PDP might emerge).
PNAC	Police National Assessment Centre, the formal 'gateway' process of interviews and exercises which aspirants to chief officer rank must pass in order to be accepted on the SCC.
QPM	Queen's Police Medal
SCC	Strategic Command Course; the mandatory programme for superintendents and chief superintendents who aim to become chief officers. All aspirant chief officers must 'pass' the SCC, (much as top-flight Army officers must pass the course at

the Joint Services Command and Staff College at
Camberley in Surrey), to be eligible for consideration
for chief officer posts.

Notes on the research methodology

My research into the roles, views and attitudes of chief officers of police in England and Wales began in late 2008 with an interview with the then President of the Association of Chief Police Officers (ACPO), Sir Ken Jones, QPM, and the work formally concluded in November 2009 in an interview with the newly appointed President of ACPO, Sir Hugh Orde, OBE. This gave a pleasing if slightly spurious cyclical framework to interviews across England and Wales in which chief officers were asked a series of questions about what they do, what they think about policing and how they got where they are. Some chief officers were spoken to again in 2010 to confirm, add to or clarify things they had said in 2009. A dialogue continued with some chief officers as this book was being written.

The formal tabled questions are to be found in the Appendix. Not all chief officers answered all questions (some indeed proved so loquacious that they did not get past question 16) and, while all officers' views were recorded in writing, not all have been used in this book. This is partly because some points of view between police officers were practically identical and no purpose would be served in replicating very similar statements and partly because a number of comments were such that the identity of the speaker could be established, but they could not easily be disguised without losing the flavour of what was being said.

Anonymity

All chief officers were given absolute guarantees of their anonymity, both in the face-to-face interviews and through the questionnaires. This follows a well-trodden academic path; indeed Robert Reiner in his seminal study of 1991 (see later), did the same. Where comments or references may have seemed to indicate the identity of the interlocutor, these have been depersonalised or disguised. There is, I think, little possibility of playing the game of 'spot the chief' in these pages, since some comments are conflated with others when they coincide and because the range of comment itself is across a considerable spectrum. Each interviewee or respondent to the questionnaire was allocated a number which is used throughout the book. The number allocated was arbitrary and bears no relation to the order in which the individual was interviewed. Six of the numbers between 1 and 100 are not allocated at all, because the total of respondents was 94. This avoids the (mistaken) supposition that 1 and 85 would be the 'interview numbers' for Sir Ken Jones and Sir Hugh Orde, who opened and closed the face-to-face interview sequence as noted above.

Interviews

Eighty-five interviews were conducted in person throughout 2008-10. The officers I saw know who they are, and, aside from noting that I spoke to the outgoing President of ACPO above and his successor, that is how it will stay. Sir Ken and Sir Hugh will recognise their words in the chapters that follow; you, dear reader, will not. I do not intend to identify any of my police interlocutors. The chief officers I spoke to would not have been so honest and forthcoming had their comments been attributable (certainly they would not about their own personal worries and concerns) and I want to reaffirm here that their trust in me is not misplaced.

The interviews themselves took place mostly in the respective force's headquarters, though some took place elsewhere for interviewees' private reasons. Each interview lasted between 90 minutes and two hours. Occasionally, chief officers would follow up what they told me with private emails or telephone calls; where necessary, their comments are used in the pages that follow, exactly as their statements made in interview are used. Such informal contacts have continued to this day. The interviews themselves were formal occasions and treated by both sides as such: they were not digitally recorded, but transcribed contemporaneously, and apart from occasional comments, questions or interpolations by me (indicated in square brackets), extracts reproduced in this book are in the words of the person(s) being interviewed.

Questionnaires

It was not possible to see some chief officers in person, either because of travel distances involved or because their diary dates kept slipping. If an interview could not be arranged, the 20 questions (Appendix) were sent instead, and the chief officer was given complete rein to answer in free text. Nine chief officers availed themselves of this, and a further seven agreed to do so (but at the time of writing there is no sign of the latter's returned questionnaires, though some claim to have sent them back to me). One chief officer in the Metropolitan Police rearranged his planned interview slot six times, agreed to fill in the questionnaire instead, but got diverted on to other things. I never did meet him and he never did complete the questionnaire. (If he reads this, I'd still like his comments on question 19, as he seems in need of some work–life balance; at least, that's what his colleagues say...)

Refusals

It is entirely proper that some chief officers should refuse to participate, as is their right. I expected that quite a few would refuse to be interviewed by me, but in the event only four did so, citing personal reasons, pressures of work or simply disinclination. Two of the four were promoted during the research (2008-10), which may explain their preoccupation with other matters and their belief that they needed to remain aloof from an often fraught process of intense questioning and challenge.

Summary statistics

There are 218 chief officers in England and Wales.[1] Direct interviews were held with 85 and 9 answered the questionnaire (very fully). Therefore 94 responses were obtained, which equates to 43.1%. The figure of 43% is statistically valid – by some margin – but it is not comprehensive, nor are all views of all chief officers necessarily represented in the pages that follow.[2]

However, I am confident that not only have I accurately sampled the opinions and views of a representative range of chief officers but also that many of those whom I spoke to are the genuine 'movers and shakers' in the police service, lending authority to considerations about what needs to be addressed in policing and what its future holds. Any subsequent editions of this book may entail further canvassing of chief officers' views, and it is hoped that more will participate on a subsequent occasion – now that the trust in me shown by their colleagues is honoured.

No analysis of the views and opinions of chief officers could fail to acknowledge the work of a pioneer in the field: Professor Robert Reiner, from the London School of Economics and Political Science,

---

[1] There were 217 at the end of 2008. Kent Police created a new ACC slot in 2009.

[2] I might note here that I approached the chair of the Association of Police Authorities (APA) for an on-the-record interview about some of the comments made by chief officers about police authorities and their approaches to policing (see Chapter Four). Unlike the Home Office and HMIC, each of whom granted me formal interviews and responded on the record to what chief officers said, the chair of the APA did not reply to any of my approaches by letter or by email.

then of the University of Bristol. He did his field research in 1986-87, and concentrated his gaze on 40 then-serving chief constables. Reiner's book, *Chief Constables: Bobbies, Bosses or Bureaucrats?* was published in 1991 and has not been reprinted. This is a pity, because Reiner had some good and comprehensive things to say about police culture and the selection of leaders at the time, and copies of his book are now fairly rare, even on Amazon.

It is worth pointing up some differences between Reiner's and my research, in addition to differences entailed in the elapse of a complete generation of police officers. First, Reiner restricted himself to chief constables, whereas I have deliberately widened the range to include *all* chief officer ranks (see Glossary). My reasons for broadening the scope of the research were many; chief among them the wish to encapsulate a representative sample of views from ACPO ranks, a need to understand what the *future* chief constables were thinking and saying, and the fact that ACCs and commanders are often the implementers, innovators and planners in chief officer teams, putting into effect the visions created by the chief constable or commissioner. Such people are often refreshingly innovative and iconoclastic in their views, even, or perhaps especially, when new to command. Further, though the time from my field research to writing this book was quicker (by two years) than Reiner's, a few of the chief constables I spoke to have already retired or moved to other things. I feel that, had I concentrated solely on them rather than including *all* chief officers, some of the work in this book would already be close to redundant. As it is, I have canvassed opinions from those very young in chief officer service as well as those who are seasoned and whose pedigree is impressive. Therefore I am confident that the chief officers' views are not only representative; they are also durable.

However, where Reiner claims his book as a 'virtual census' of chief constables' views, mine is more circumspect and more modest. I am not trying to emulate Reiner and certainly am not attempting to place chief officer origins in some kind of socio-political matrix, as he did. Some of what Reiner did is now passé, much of what he did was estimable, but I do not feel that I had to follow his path, well beaten though it is. For example, Reiner made a point of asking chief constables about contemporary events (which now give his book a dated feel; the riots in Brixton in 1981 seem a very long time ago), but he did not question them about a more contemporary phenomenon: how hard and how long they worked. I did so quite deliberately, not only to elicit some interesting 'workaholic' and anti-workaholic responses about work–life balance, but also because the portfolios of chief officers have demonstrably increased in the 25 or so years since Reiner embarked on his work. I note contemporary events only in passing and as they affect policing specifically, and consign most of them to footnotes.

Finally, I did not particularly want to write a book purely either of social science or of criminology, but one which reflected the views and attitudes of police leaders, at a time when policing seems to be in flux and when media attention on law, order and society has never been more intense. Chief officers of police have opinions that matter and they are in positions of considerable authority and power,[3] whatever the checks and balances with which governments and local authorities hedge them – quite properly – in the name of democracy.

What I offer, for the first time, is rich detail of chief officers' views across much of the policing piece, from how they became chief officers in the first place, to what they think of the Home Office, their police authorities, and HM Inspectorate of Constabulary. The chief officers speaking in this book determine the operational effectiveness of police forces across England and Wales, and it is timely to consider what they do, what they think of policing, of each other and about those who oversee them. There are also internal controversies to be aired, such as the appointment of non-police officers to chief officer roles, the suggestion that the police service adopts multiple entry at ranks above sergeant, the creation of a national police force and chief officers' views on how the police should be measured or assessed, as well as what they think of oversight and accountability. Some of these things walk in parallel with Robert Reiner's pioneering footsteps; others leave his path entirely, and some explore very different parts of the landscape.

A couple of stylistic points, which may irritate you if I don't explain them, are:

- the convention of referring generically to all ACPO ranks as 'chief officers' in lower case, together with ranks such as assistant chief constable. Capitals are only used for the abbreviated forms (ACC) or for specific posts (Commissioner of the Metropolitan Police). This tries to be consistent and avoids the lush jungle of capitals.

---

[3] The chair of the Metropolitan Police Authority and Deputy Mayor of London, Kit Malthouse, in August 2010 called for greater curbs on the power of chief constables, saying "They are incredibly powerful individuals. Each one controls a standing army, they have extreme powers to incarcerate you and me and to use force against us when they see fit. Yet none of their beliefs, prejudices or views that may affect their policing style are ever examined in a public arena." Well, they are now. See O'Neill (2010).

- the number of acronyms and seemingly endless sets of initials used throughout this book, are inherent within policing and part of its language. See the Glossary earlier.
- the proliferation of footnotes. In a post-modern, ironic way, I apologise for them, but I know no better way of including the interesting aside, the textual comment or the *locus* for material than in a footnote, without disrupting the continuous flow of the main narrative. Such immediacy is lost if the footnotes are merely appended at the end of the chapter, so I hope you will find their inclusion on the page both relevant and stimulating.

About the author

Bryn Caless had both an academic and a military career together spanning some 25 years before being appointed as director of human resources for Kent Police. He served on several strategic national committees for the police, which stimulated his interest in the role of chief officers. After 10 years' service, he now lectures on policing in the Law and Criminal Justice Studies Department of Canterbury Christ Church University.

Acknowledgements

I thank warmly every one of those chief officers who spoke so frankly, cheerfully and trustingly to me, and I assure them of my continuing commitment to two things: the good of the police service and their anonymity;

to **Helen and Wez Jacobs** for their hospitality and interest during some of the researches, travels and interviews for this book (and, much more, for being part of my family);

to those **chief officers** who promised me space in their frantic schedules, but couldn't do it, and to those who promised to fill in the questionnaire and never did, and also those who claimed to have sent completed questionnaires back to me but which never arrived;

my very grateful thanks are owing to Dr **Stephen Tong**, Director of Policing Studies (Broadstairs Campus) at Canterbury Christ Church University, a valued friend and colleague, for his encouragement, belief in the book, for advising and reading the drafts and for saying "Go for it!" a lot;

to **Scott Farrant**, whose bright ideas and insights were always pleasurable and who read the script assiduously;

to **Mark Simpson**, who read my early drafts and whose advice was sane and measured;

to **Ian Pointon** of the Police Federation who gave freely of his experience and expertise, particularly in the arcana of police pensions;

to **Robin Bryant**, statistician and polymath, for expert reassurance over the statistical analyses and for softening my iron fist with some velvet from time to time;

to **Barry Spruce**, friend and seasoned debater, who read parts of this book and cogently argued with me;

to former Chief Superintendent **Mark Salisbury**, an encouraging and enthusiastic friend who, for upwards of 15 years, has helped me understand policing from the inside;

to Major **Chris Farley**, lately Royal Military Police, and Mrs **Lizzie Farley** for always encouraging this scribbler and who couldn't wait for the book to come out;

to **Andrew Wren**, Head of the Police Productivity Unit at the Home Office for fielding questions on the record, on behalf of his political masters;

to **Alf Hitchcock** lately Director of the National Police Leadership College and now Chief Constable of Bedfordshire, for his willingness to answer very searching (and occasionally leading) questions about the selection, learning and development of chief officers;

to **Sir Denis O'Connor**, CB, QPM, HM Chief Inspector of Constabulary, for a stimulating discussion that went on longer than either of us realised;

to all the **personal assistants** of these busy people, who found time in diaries for a dishevelled writer and never (well, seldom) voiced their disappointment that I was not George Clooney;

to the **staff at the former Bramshill Police National Library**, for their unfailing interest and knowledge (even when the Manor House building was being shored up around them);

to the **Office of Public Service Information** (OPSI), for permission to quote extensively from government and public service publications under licence C2007000322;

to colleagues in **Kent Police**, who first engaged my interest in chief officers and how they got that way, particularly Chief Constable **Sir David Phillips**, KBE, QPM, Chief Constable **Jim Barker-McCardle**, QPM, and Assistant Chief Constables Dr **Allyn Thomas and Gary Beautridge**;

to **Karen Bowler**, **Kathryn King** and **Laura Greaves** and all the supportive and knowledgeable staff at **The Policy Press**, who believed in this project when many elsewhere were nervous about it;

to all my lovely family: **Helen**, **Wez**, **Sally**, **Johnny**, **Kit**, **Meghna** and **Maddy**,

but most of all and the biggest debt of all to darling **Clarey**, who *always* found time in her own busy professional life to encourage, to coax, to reassure, to listen to my ideas and to read my words. Never was a man so truly blessed.

The notion of the 'top cop'

> **Interviewee 91:** When you come to write your book, don't downplay the job we do. We have enough critics; it would be nice for once to have a champion.

In 1968, Lord Denning thought that a chief officer occupied a unique position in relation to both politics and the law. Delivering a weighty judgement in the matter of a dispute of authority between the state and the Commissioner of the Metropolitan Police, Lord Denning observed that:

> [A chief constable] … is not the servant of anyone, save of the law itself. No minister of the Crown can tell him that he must or must not prosecute this man or that one. Nor can any police authority tell him so. […] he is answerable to the law and to the law alone. (Denning, 1968)

It is unlikely that many would now espouse such purity of purpose and certainly, Ministers of the Crown have long regarded 'law and order' as something where politics is embedded. In 50 years, we have come a long way from the notion that chief constables, and by extension all other chief officers, were answerable to the law and to nothing else. A modern observer of the police would probably add that chief officers are answerable to the public, through consultative bodies and as a member of a series of partnerships. It is likely too that a list of 'accountabilities' would include being responsive to the media (if not directly answerable to them), to Her Majesty's Inspectorate of Constabulary (HMIC), to the Home Office and the Home Secretary, and latterly to the 'police crime commissioner' who replaces Police Authorities in 2012 in providing oversight of a chief officer's function.

What this means essentially is that Denning's view of the role of a chief constable now sounds curiously old-fashioned and incomplete, but actually, it was not wholly accurate even when he wrote it. For all that there is scrutiny, and for all that there is oversight of what he or she does, the chief officer of police remains a quite unknown and elusive factor in criminology and in the analysis of policing. My concern in this book is not with the tactical or operational leadership shown at a parochial level, but with the strategic command level leadership in the police. These 'chief officer' ranks are known synonymously as 'ACPO ranks' (after the Association of Chief Police Officers to which all chief officers belong on attainment of the first chief officer rank of assistant chief constable. ACPO purports to speak on behalf of the whole police service).[1]

> **Interviewee 65:** It is a constant surprise to people outside the police just how responsive a chief officer has to be to all shades and sorts of opinion and it is a constant surprise to *me* how little those who have opinions to pass on the quality of those who lead the police, actually know about the job. The chief officer is glared at by the media, sneered at by politicians, picked at by HMIC, sniped at by lawyers, dissed[2] by criminals, analysed by courts, criticised by the IPCC and often wilfully misunderstood by government officials. What is more surprising than anything else is that the chief officers keep their tempers in the face of this spurious know-all oversight.

Allowing for the chief officer's disenchantment when she said this to me, there is nonetheless some resonance in the suggestion that chief officers can feel unfairly beleaguered and besieged and that there are

---

[1] ACPO is not a police union, it is actually a limited company which is financed by the police service itself, but it features prominently in any discussion about chief officers, command and leadership in the police. It is led by a president who was a serving chief constable until appointment and who has been elected by his peers (no woman has yet attained the post), for a term up to five years. In practice, the president serves about three years. He chairs a number of strategic groups, chief among which is the Chief Constables' Council, and he leads on the business areas of specialist police knowledge. The president is influential among politicians and Whitehall committees and the media. ACPO's own mission statement is:

> ACPO is an independent, professionally led strategic body. In the public interest and, in equal and active partnership with Government and the Association of Police Authorities, ACPO leads and coordinates the direction and development of the police service in England, Wales and Northern Ireland. In times of national need, ACPO, on behalf of all chief officers, coordinates the strategic policing response. (ACPO, 2009)

It seems likely, following recommendations in the Neyroud Review (2011) that ACPO will seek a form of 'chartered institute' status, commensurate with its increased role as guardian of police leadership and of aspects of learning and development within policing, though in January 2011 its oversight of covert policing was handed to the Metropolitan Police Service.

[2] Disrespected.

days when nothing they do is right. I know; I have observed such things at first hand for more than 10 years. At the same time, I can acknowledge that some chief officers are adept at 'special pleading' and at engendering alarm by focusing on worst-case scenarios when threatened, for example, by budget reductions. A balance is needed between seeing chief officers in an objectified work context and allowing them free rein to speak. By locating the chief officer role in contemporary policing, and by systematic reference to the academic literature, I hope to provide precisely that context in which chief officers' views can be accorded proper weight and consideration. Make no mistake, their views are important and their conceptions of policing are central to the future of the service. It is just that sometimes we need to be wary of taking what they say literally, and occasionally we need to be convinced that there is a sound basis for their world view.

As a contemporary background, there has been a progressive decline in the availability of candidates for some chief officer posts: in one instance, the vacant chief constable's job in Lincolnshire in 2009 attracted a single applicant. Some chief officers, certainly those above the rank of assistant chief constable (commander in the Metropolitan Police), appear reluctant to move any great distance across England and Wales to compete for jobs, with all the attendant disruption of uprooting settled families or partners' careers, when their basic salaries would be the same if they succeeded in obtaining posts nearer to home.

Some police authorities have paid large retainers to some chief constables to keep them. (*The Times* investigated some examples under Freedom of Information protocols in 2009, and revealed that some chief officers received in excess of £70,000 above their set salaries to induce them to remain with their forces.[3]) Peering into this world of police leaders is not easy, and there are few sources of illumination. The questions, though, are many.

How are police leaders, at this high level, identified and developed? What motivates them to attain such rank? What sort of people are they? How do they get on with each other? What worries or concerns them? What do they think about policing and society? What future

---

[3] See O'Neill, S. (2009), 'Secret pay deals give top police thousands extra', *The Times*, 6 July 2009, and a further article the following day, also by Sean O'Neill, titled 'Police Forces go Over the Top to get Right Man for Job'. One of the chief constables featured in *The Times*' articles was Sir Norman Bettison from West Yorkshire who reportedly received £50,000 above his official salary. Quixotically, Sir Norman subsequently wrote a piece for *The Times* in which he said that he was paid too much: 'I'm not worth £213,000. This wage bill is mad. My Micawber Plan will help to cut Britain's debt by freezing public sector pay, starting with those at the top' (Bettison, 2010).

do they envisage for policing? How do they respond to oversight respectively from the Home Secretary, HMIC and locally from their police authority/'police crime commissioner'? What do they think about direct entry into higher police ranks, since all police officers currently have to begin as constables? What do they think about the things that politicians say about law and order? These are some of the questions which this book tries to answer, through the chief officers' own words as well as through critical analysis. It is not at all well-trodden ground,[4] and this is the first study of its kind that includes *all* ranks of chief officers. Even those studies concerning chief constables alone are pretty rare, even arcane.

It is now 25 years since Professor Robert Reiner undertook his research for his 1991 book *Chief Constables: Bobbies, Bosses, or Bureaucrats?* Reiner interviewed 40 chief constables during 1986-87, and found them people who combined 'street wisdom with intellectual potential' (Reiner, 1991, preface) and who formed 'a powerful elite group of growing importance' (p 3). Since that time, policing has changed greatly, as have expectations of what police forces (increasingly police *services*) can do. From 1992, we have seen 'new public management' come and go, along with COMPSTAT, problem-oriented policing, intelligence-led policing and many other initiatives.[5] During the research phase

---

[4] Though we might note Roger Graef's ground-breaking work *Talking Blues: The Police in Their Own Words* (1989) and Robert Reiner's *The Blue-Coated Worker* (1978), which each gave space for the voices of 'rank-and-file' police officers.

[5] (a) 'New public management' (NPM) was an importation from private industry pioneered by the Conservative government under John Major in 1994, enthusiastically adopted by the Labour government under Tony Blair in 1997, and then applied to public services generally and subsequently to policing. The idea behind NPM was that the public sector should demonstrate a return on the investment of taxpayers' money by reaching a series of targets. It was too simple a measurement to survive the complexities of policing (see Wright, 2002). (b) An operational performance review framework known as COMPSTAT (comparative statistics) was introduced in 1994 by William (Bill) Bratton, the Chief of the New York Police Department. COMPSTAT involved analysts obtaining statistical data relating to different police divisions in the city, which were then used to challenge local commanders about their performance in an open forum. Performance statistics dramatically improved following this innovation, but a detailed analysis of longer-term crime trends in New York revealed that crimes per 100,000 in population had in any case been falling since 1991. For all that, COMPSTAT spread rapidly throughout the world as a tool to improve performance, but in the UK it was often seen as a form of institutionalised bullying or a ritualised public humiliation of police commanders, and the practice has largely been dropped. (c) Problem-oriented policing (POP) developed from work by an American academic called Herman Goldstein, who posited in 1979 that social degeneration and urban decay

for this book, the Police Performance Assessment Framework (PPAF) with its many measurable targets for policing, was cut at a stroke and a new 'single confidence measure', that of the public in the police, was introduced. This was linked with undertakings by the police to sustain agreed standards (10 were specified) in dealing with the public and with crime, and the public was to be consulted about its confidence in the police through the policing pledge.

Forces certainly found it an abrupt and largely unheralded change. There had been much internal criticism of PPAF performance measures because a 'what gets measured gets done' philosophy replaced traditional outcomes, and because only narrow segments of policing were measured at all. There was no measure for police discretion, for example, and no qualitative distinction between complex or simple robberies or categories of homicide. The arrival of the policing pledge and the 'single confidence measure' is itself now criticised as reflecting only one part of policing – the interface with local communities – leaving swathes of policing unconsidered. What this rather piecemeal and unhappy history suggests is that policing is too complex and wide ranging to be easily captured by systematised quantitative performance measurement alone.

Forces were assessed for the first time by HMIC against implementation of the policing pledge in October 2009 and many were found to be performing below expectations. For their part, the police noted that measuring public satisfaction with the police in terms of

begat crime and so police officers should respond to social ills and deprivation as much as to crime. This 'broken windows' model foundered on the notion that the police were also social workers, though later, local structural degeneration was reinterpreted as a part of 'signal crime'. Partnership working at the neighbourhood policing level addresses such issues as damaged property and vandalised infrastructures, but it is in a team sense rather than being seen as a police prerogative, so POP has dropped away as a model, while 'signal crime' has gained in stature (Innes, 2005). (d) Intelligence-led policing (ILP) was pioneered from about 1994 by Sir David Phillips, then Chief Constable of Kent Police and subsequently President of ACPO. This took as its basis that the police should target crime types rather than individual criminals and they should amass information covertly to disrupt criminality and arrest offenders. ILP achieved considerable early success, but has been hard to sustain across all police forces particularly because the national intelligence model (NIM) has become somewhat rigid and compartmentalised and does not cater for policing which is not crime based. Attempts have been made (Harfield et al, 2008), to uprate NIM to a more embracing 'knowledge management model' without much evident enthusiasm from police forces. While in many ways ILP is still a model for both serious and volume crime investigation, community and neighbourhood policing has claimed higher priorities in forces, especially since central (government) funding accompanied local policing.

community relations and local targets in neighbourhood policing was all very well, but the police did more than this. Policing is about crime investigation, public order, civil emergency and counter terrorism as well as about ASBOs (anti-social behaviour orders), vandalism and street crime. Then, in June 2010, the incoming Home Secretary Theresa May promptly announced the end of the policing pledge and the 'single confidence measure'. The police should concentrate only on cutting crime, she said (Fresco, 2010).

At the time of writing, it is not yet clear what, if any, performance regime will measure what the police do, but assessments are likely to focus on serious and organised crime as much as on neighbourhood policing and may concentrate on reducing the incidence of crime (and thus try to allay the public's fear of crime). As I will note in more detail later, the latest organisational changes in policing, which include the abolition or mutation of the National Policing Improvement Agency into the National Crime Agency,[6] the latter's absorption of the Serious Organised Crime Agency and the ownership by ACPO itself of the identification, selection and training of new chief officers, present a police service in considerable flux. That pattern of change has to be seen very much in a context of financial stringency and intensely increased pressure on resources.

As the nature of 'post-modern' policing has mutated into different forms, and as measurement of the delivery of policing has changed, so, I believe, have the kinds of people who lead the police. They no longer have what Reiner rather condescendingly called 'intellectual potential', they have instead solid intellectual achievement. Nearly every chief officer of police has a degree, most have more than one; nearly all have postgraduate diplomas in subjects like criminology or business. PhDs are not uncommon, several chiefs are published authors,[7] a number contribute closely argued, stimulating and well-researched academic papers to learned journals. Nearly 40% of police officers now entering the job as constables have first degrees. Some of those who do not have degrees may expect their forces to fund them to get one. This is a very different policing world from that encountered by Robert Reiner in 1986; all the chief constables from that time have long since left the service (they had entered policing in the 1950s, with one or two from the early 1960s). Some of those who are now chief officers were not even born then, and some did not enter policing until 1994: a whole generation of police officers has passed through in the interim.

---

[6] An initiative of the coalition government in 2011, due for completion in 2013.

[7] Some pseudonymously.

There has also been a sea-change in the range and complexity of policing since the late 1980s; there is now an expectation that chief officers have the intellectual skills and business competencies to respond ably and efficiently to that range and complexity. There is a distinct sense in which today's chief officer grapples with problems and pressures which Reiner's generation of chief constables could only have guessed at (diversity and 'freedom of information' being two obvious examples). And yet, it is probable that there will always be a duality or paradox within policing between the need for brains and the need for physical and moral courage, much as there is in the armed forces. The characteristics which make a good constable or sergeant are not necessarily those which make a good assistant chief constable. Organisational capabilities themselves vary according to rank as well: an inspector deploying uniformed officers in a volatile public order situation uses very different leadership skills from those of a chief officer implementing a system for public consultation.

The media 'image' of chief officers

What about the 'image' of chief officers? How familiar are we with the police strategic command role, for example through television, radio or the printed word? The public is familiar with the fictionalised detective policeman and woman, but much less so with a fictionalised 'top cop'. The fictional portrayal of senior police officers is often negative.[8] On television, the recurrent cliché is of the maverick but loveable detective pitted against symbols of orthodox authority; thus DCI Morse is restive under the rule of Detective Chief Superintendent Strange and DI Frost subverts Superintendent Mullet. This seldom registers the paradox that the maverick is often himself or herself authoritarian. Portrayal of police senior ranks in fiction seldom goes above detective chief superintendent (*Foyle's War*), but when it does, the chief officers concerned are either well-meaning buffoons (Chief Constable Melchett in Agatha Christie's *Miss Marple* stories), career opportunists (the nameless assistant commissioner in ITV's *Identity*) or political weasels (Assistant Commissioner Harkness in PD James' *Adam Dalgleish* series). A relishable irony in the last of these is that Dalgleish is himself a chief officer (a commander in the Metropolitan Police, equivalent to an assistant chief constable) but he seldom does anything strategic or recognisably related to ACPO.

---

[8] Few references to top cops exist in the critical literature about the media and the police either. See, for example, Reiner (2003) or Leishman and Mason (2003).

From 1990 until 1995 there was a series on TV called *The Chief* which was about chief police officers, and was familiar enough at the time for Robert Reiner to refer to it (Reiner, 1991, p 3), but it has long since gone off the TV radar.[9] Since that time, one would be hard pushed to recall a single portrayal of a chief officer on stage, screen or novel which either approximates to contemporary reality or which evokes sympathetic identification – and this at a time when the fictional depiction of the police has never been more prolific.[10] The primary reason for this, other than writers' ignorance, probably lies in the absence of conflict (and therefore good drama, which in turn makes good television) in chief officers' portfolios. There is seldom scope for dramatic chases, tense investigations, backings of hunches, interfaces with witnesses, victims and suspects or the parallel paradings of neuroses and failed relationships. There is little scope in the portrayal of chief officers of what Robert Reiner calls 'newsworthiness' – from which we may presume 'fictionworthiness' – of 'individualisation, immediacy, drama, titillation [and] novelty' (Reiner, 2003, p 270). This leaves most police fiction with a black hole in its command ranks and it is therefore not surprising that people have few or negative opinions about fictional chief officers compared with the often lively debates about the fictional 'detective investigator' as represented by DCI Gene Hunt (*Life on Mars, Ashes to Ashes*) or the eponymous DI John Rebus.[11] The character of Gene Hunt even featured in rival party posters during the 2010 General Election.[12]

---

[9] It does not feature on the interminable 'cop series' of dated TV programmes/films which are listed in DVD catalogues, or even on the Dave ja vu Freeview channel.

[10] A random search through TV and radio listings for the week of 17-23 April 2010, shows that across satellite and terrestrial broadcasting for the period there were 68 screenings of TV police fiction programmes with a British basis and 71 screenings of TV police fiction programmes from the US. There were 14 full-length 'cop' feature films, nine of which were from the US, five from Britain and 14 radio programmes featuring British police fiction. Very, very few of the 68 British-based screenings portrayed a chief officer. The TV screenings added up to something like 237 hours featuring fictional police work. That is not much in the total scheme of broadcasting things, perhaps, but it is a persistent diet ranging from *Inspector Wexford* repeats, through *Midsomer Murders, Taggart, Morse, Wycliff, Foyle's War, Ashes to Ashes* and *New Tricks* on the British TV side, with *CSI New York, NCIS, Criminal Minds* and *Red Heat* (1988) from the US (source: *The Times' Playlist*, 17-23 April 2010, pp 29–55, London: *The Times*).

[11] A good analysis of the fictional representation of the police is in the old but still incisive article by Clarke, A., '"You're nicked!" Television Police Series and Definitions of Law and Order' (1992).

[12] Where the face of the leader of the Conservative Party (and later coalition Prime Minister), David Cameron, was substituted on the keynote Quattro car.

This book, I hope, is an illumination of a part of policing that – often through no fault of its own – has been mired in obscurity and incomprehension. Many chief police officers have strong profiles within their own forces, and some have had profiles in the world at large (an unhappy example perhaps was Sir Ian, now Lord Blair, former Commissioner of the Metropolitan Police), but the person who becomes a chief officer, what he or she wants and how he or she does the job is not always clear to those outside policing. Even to those inside the police, the 'top corridor' and the sometimes remote figures there who direct the police, can appear enigmatic and elusive.

The numbers game

Table I.1 (overleaf), based on Home Office data for 2009-2010, shows the relative ACPO (chief officer) strength by police forces across England and Wales. It may be noted that there are some disparities: the Metropolitan Police, for instance, is about ten times the size of the average 'shire force' in terms of chief officer strength, while some small forces, such as Hertfordshire, have as many chief officers as a major conurbation like Greater Manchester or Merseyside. Explanations of these apparent disparities are wanting, since the chief officer strength of any given force is decided between its chief constable and the police authority or the directly elected 'police crime commissioner' of that force, and numbers will be determined by available budgets and perceived need.

From this it may be seen that, even when restricted to the 43 home forces in England and Wales, the collective body of chief officers is sizeable and carries considerable political and strategic weight.

This book, based on confidential interviews with a large number of these chief officers and containing many of their own words and individual views, is an attempt to bring the neglected profile of the chief officer of police into sharper focus. This is a good thing: the current generation of chief police officers and that immediately to come, will have profound effects on how our society deals with crime, disaffection and marginalisation and what sort of security and safety we want. It is important that we understand at least some of how they perceive the world, British society and what they do, so that we the public may in turn influence how they approach the business of policing.

Table 1.1: Chief officer strength in England and Wales by police force

Force	Number of chief officers	Force	Number of chief officers
Avon & Somerset	6	Lincolnshire	3
Bedfordshire	4	Merseyside	6
Cambridgeshire	3	Metropolitan	36
Cheshire	4	Norfolk	4
City of London	3	North Wales	3
Cleveland	4	North Yorkshire	4
Cumbria	3	Northamptonshire	4
Derbyshire	4	Northumbria	5
Devon & Cornwall	6	Nottinghamshire	4
Dorset	4	South Wales	5
Durham	3	South Yorkshire	5
Dyfed-Powys	3	Staffordshire	4
Essex	5	Suffolk	3
Gloucestershire	4	Surrey	4
Greater Manchester	6	Sussex	5
Gwent	3	Thames Valley	4
Hampshire	5	Warwickshire	4
Hertfordshire	6	West Mercia	5
Humberside	4	West Midlands	7
Kent	5	West Yorkshire	5
Lancashire	5	Wiltshire	4
Leicestershire	4	**Total for England and Wales**	**218***

Note: *0.15% of total police strength; chief officer numbers fluctuate continuously, especially at ACC/commander ranks.

Source: adapted from Sigurdsson and Dhani (2010)

ONE

Cloning or culture? The selection and appointment of chief officers

> **Interviewee 37:** I tell you what, the most terrified I have ever been was on the PNAC. All that intense scrutiny, and I went twice! By comparison, the SCC was a stroll in the park and even the weary round of interviews to land my first ACC [assistant chief constable] job was nowhere near as nerve racking. Actually, I really enjoyed the SCC – the first time I had enough leisure really to think about policing and why we do what we do. I'd rather have teeth out than go through PNAC again, though.

Chief officers of police, with very rare exceptions, begin as patrol constables and come up through the ranks of a police force to superintendent or chief superintendent, at which point (or sometimes before) they begin to think about entering the process to be selected as a chief officer. This can be comparatively short or quite prolonged: experiences vary. But all aspirant chief officers have to be recommended by their chief constables,[1] have to pass the successive 'gateway' stages of the (Senior) Police National Assessment Centre (PNAC), and the Senior Command Course (SCC) with its modular programmes and additional academic studies, before being eligible to apply for vacancies at the first chief officer rank of assistant chief constable.[2] It is a process that is extensive – the longest continuous attempt I heard about lasted six years and four months from obtaining a recommendation to being

---

[1] There are other provisions for officers on secondment, but the first of many hurdles to becoming a chief officer is the recommendation by a serving chief officer, together with evidence of competences and potential. This, as we shall see, is both objective and subjective: no one succeeds in entering PNAC without dispassionate evidence of competence and experience, but equally, the subjective opinion of a chief constable is key to acceptance. There are a number of instances where candidates have been held back because the chief constable had a low or unfavourable opinion of the candidate's worth. It is difficult to see how this can be avoided, since favourable estimation of a person is often central to his or her endorsement for further development in any walk of life, not just in policing. However, that is not the same as claiming that the system to enter PNAC is utterly disinterested; it is not.

[2] Or commander in the Metropolitan Police.

appointed as ACC – and rigorous (its proponents claim), where the faint-hearted drop out early and only the most robust, and therefore in Darwinian terms the best fitted, achieve success.

This chapter will look in detail at the main processes for selection to chief officer in the UK, using both published material and the private reflections of chief officers themselves as they recount their own experiences of being involved in the learning and selection procedures. Inevitably, there are some differences between private recollection and public description, but the overwhelmingly consistent impression of those who have undergone selection is of *pressure*: to get the application right; to secure the requisite endorsement; to get selected for PNAC; to learn as much as possible about the testing and interviewing at PNAC before attending; to perform well across all the tests and interviews on the day and thus make it to selection for the SCC; to do well on the SCC and come to notice; to use the SCC opportunities for extensive networking; to select an appropriate vacancy, apply, be short-listed and to succeed at interview with the relevant police authority and chief constable. No one pretends that this is easy:

> **Interviewee 8:** Anyone who tells you that selection is fixed or that you can get through on the nod is talking complete rubbish. Everyone I know who has been through PNAC and the SCC deserved to be there and worked bloody hard to get over all the hurdles. You discover a lot about yourself during these processes, including things that are not very nice, such as coming to terms with what really motivates you, and you really have to want to be a chief officer to carry on sometimes. There were days when I felt just wrung out.

This comment may stand for a number of others; the recollection of many chief officers of the whole selection process is one where they felt exposed, challenged, inadequate, nervous, stimulated, stretched, downcast, exhilarated and a bit raw by turns, but none would have missed it and none who spoke to me regretted embarking on it.

'Fast tracking'

Within the past 10 years or so, another element has been introduced to try to identify much earlier those police officers with leadership potential, and which may be used as a 'fast-track' option to attract high quality candidates into the police force in the first instance.[3] The mechanism in widespread use to do this is the High Potential Development Scheme or HPDS. The National Policing Improvement Agency (NPIA) described the purpose of the HPDS like this:

> The HPDS is designed to attract and develop the most talented individuals in the police service to become the next generation of police leaders. It is the first initiative to be delivered under the police leadership strategy, Leading Policing, which was produced by the NPIA on behalf of the Association of Chief Police Officers (ACPO), the Association of police authorities (APA) and the Home Office following an extensive national debate within the service. (NPIA, 2009)

The initial HPDS, launched in 2001–02, allowed individuals to put themselves forward for fast-track development, with odd results whereby some, not identified by their forces as having any potential, joined the programme and emerged with a Master's degree and an automatic right to promotion. These less worldly elements of the HPDS were modified by the Home Office in 2006 and a revised system emerged about a year later where a force's recommendation was again central to an individual's place on the scheme.

With some tweaking around competences and aptitude, as well as a formal partnership with an academic provider (see later); this is more or less where the HPDS stands now.[4] There were 54 police officers accepted on to the HPDS in December 2009 following assessment made through written, interactive and group exercises, an 'oral' (verbal) briefing and a competency-based interview. Standards appear to be exacting, since 109 candidates did not make the cut.[5] The bonus for the successful candidate is virtually guaranteed promotion:

---

[3] In January 2011, the Minister for Policing announced that a fast track recruitment scheme was necessary because joining the police at the lowest constable level was no longer 'fit for purpose'. ACPO pointed out rather wearily that the HPDS already existed and that police officers needed the experience of being constables, 'using professional discretion on the streets' (www.bbc.co.uk/news/uk-12170502; accessed 1 February, 2011).

[4] There are other routes to chief officer, however, including formal leadership modules offered at various ranks by the NPIA. ACPO formally received the remit for police leadership development in mid-2010 from the incoming Home Secretary, when NPIA and other quangos were abolished.

[5] According to reports in *Police Review*, 25 December, 2009, p 6.

HPDS officers are subject to a specific provision in the police promotion regulations which means that *they are to be promoted as soon as they satisfy the Chief Officer that they are competent in the new rank.* This can speed up their progression as they do not have to wait for a vacancy to become available. (NPIA, 2009,[6] my italics)

The central HPDS programme consists of six three-day modules, which are delivered either at Warwick University's Business School campus or at selected police training sites. Each of the modules noted below requires an assessed piece of work that relates to experience in the police:

- Leadership and public value
- Managing people and change
- Operations and performance management
- Partnership working, stakeholder management and community engagement
- Policy making and strategy
- Managing and using resources (NPIA, 2009)

These are generic management and leadership topics and none is unique to the police. All can be *applied* to policing of course, and I look in more detail in Chapter Three at how the leadership competencies for chief officers are used. After about two years' periodic learning and assessment, HPDS students write a workplace-related dissertation, successful completion of which is rewarded with a Post Graduate Diploma in Police Leadership. Then over two or three more years, there is 'professional consolidation' of what has been learned (or what is called elsewhere continuous professional development), during which HPDS students are assessed for police leadership potential. NPIA put this phase succinctly:

The nature and duration of this part of the programme will vary according to the needs of delegates but it will ensure that they experience alternative approaches to leadership and management issues. The highest performers will be invited to progress to a Master's qualification. (NPIA, 2009)

---

[6] Available from npia.police.uk, High Potential Development Scheme website entry www.npia.police.uk/en/10634.htm; accessed 12 July 2010.

At the end of five years, students leave the HPDS. Currently, the scheme is restricted to constables and sergeants (it used to include inspectors), and this has provoked some criticism from chief officers and others such as police authorities, who have argued that middle-ranking police officers have no opportunity to show their potential for leadership, that HPDS does not cater adequately for officers from a minority ethnic background and that those who complete the programme do not seem fitted to advance beyond superintendent.[7] That said, in late 2010 it was reported that HPDS graduates dominated the field for promotion from sergeant to inspector: 95% of former HPDS students passed selection, compared with 41% for the norm.[8]

Disaffection with HPDS as a means of identifying potential police leaders is articulated by the Metropolitan Police Authority, which has noted that HPDS does not embrace the inspector and chief inspector ranks and that it appears not to prepare officers 'sufficiently for chief officer rank' (Crawford, 2010). The Metropolitan Police Service, supported by its police authority, has characteristically developed its own scheme for inspectors and chief inspectors, called the Emerging Leaders Programme, run in partnership with other initiatives and attracting an application by 72.[9] Twenty-seven police officers and four police staff[10] began the programme in January 2010. Sheer numbers play their part in allowing this departure from the norm: the Metropolitan Police draws from a total strength of some 36,000 police officers (10 times the 'average' police force). This compares with spaces available for slightly more than 50 officers for the whole of England and Wales on each annual HPDS. Indeed the Metropolitan Police Service fielded 31 candidates for the 2009 HPDS intake but only six were accepted (MPA, 2010, p 5, para 15), which underpins some of

---

[7] Among others, criticism has come from Ian Johnston, President of the Superintendents' Association, in September 2008, available from: www.policesupers.com/news/full. asp?id=77&news=345; accessed 12 July 2010.

[8] Vooght, C., 'Fast track candidates make the top grade in inspectors' exams', *Police Review*, 29 October, 2010, p 10.

[9] Ibid., p 7, para 25: 'The Emerging Leaders Programme had a high level of interest with 120 members of staff attending briefings regarding the scheme. In total, 104 applications for the programme were received at Stage One. Of these, 79 were male (76%), 25 were female (24%), 82 were white (79%) and 22 were BME (21%)'; para 26: '72 candidates were selected at the Stage One application form papersift to progress to the final stage assessment centre. Of these, 52 were male (72%), 20 were female (28%), 55 were white (76%) and 17 were BME (24%).'

[10] Police staff are non-police officers performing a police support role.

the frustrations felt by the Metropolitan Police Authority and chief officers alike:

> **Interviewee 10:** We struggle to get people on to the HPDS and then they're on it for absolute ages. You lose them, really, and there aren't very many opportunities each time the scheme opens. We should be thinking about spotting potential far earlier – like at recruitment – and tailoring our requirements accordingly. Hell, policing could be a very attractive option at a time when graduates can't find work.

In fact, fewer and fewer forces are recruiting as the squeeze on public expenditure tightens and currently not many are accepting even outstanding candidates.[11] Nonetheless, Interviewee 10 speaks for many chief officers when suggesting that the quest for potential chief officers could be focused much more at the stage of initial candidacy. The Metropolitan Police Authority agrees, because part of its thrust to identify potential leaders is aimed at the Russell Group of universities[12] in an attempt to attract good applicants. Other, smaller, police forces are more likely to develop relationships with one or two universities within their policing area. Such partnerships may further develop in the light of initiatives around 'pre-joiner' learning.[13] It is too early fully to evaluate the pre-joiner scheme and to establish whether or not it has a long-term future, but initial developments look promising. What this collaborative venture may do is attract a quality candidate to consider the police as a career and consequently enrich the available

---

[11] Indeed, in January 2011, figures released by the Home Office showed that police officer strength had declined by more than 2,000 in September 2010 (see Dhani and Kaiza, 2011).

[12] The Russell Group consists of 20 British universities with international reputations which attract high research funding, prestigious teaching/research staff and elite students.

[13] This is a scheme whereby the National Occupational Standards for constables can be partly taught at universities which register their relevant students as special constables, thus the latter obtain practical experience as well as academic study, producing 'applied' policing studies, in concert with NPIA's Initial Police Leadership Development Programme (IPLDP). At the time of writing, these initiatives are emerging quite slowly (though endorsed by the Neyroud *Review*, 2011), but universities see a percentage in offering an HE Diploma that can convert later to a foundation (fd) or Honours degree, while police forces see huge financial benefits in having universities do the bulk of initial teaching.

pool of future leaders.[14] In his *Review* to the Home Secretary on police leadership and training, Peter Neyroud specifically advocated this 'pre-joiner' route as the necessary way ahead for police recruitment, while also suggesting that academic partners in further and higher education might provide the appropriate routes and the means for learning (Neyroud, 2011). But there are critics of the constant scurry for promotion and the general trend towards upward movement in the police service. One comment was made by Derek Barham of the Metropolitan Police, acidly characterising the aspirant chief officer like this:

> Police progress [...] arguably favours style over substance, promoting the brave, the bold, the brash, the politically astute and the steadfastly ambitious. (Barham, 2010a)

Again, we might note that there is nothing in this criticism that is necessarily specific to policing; such comments could equally be made of ambitious doctors, soldiers, lawyers, academics, engineers, actors or politicians. Those who rise in any organisation have ambition and energy in common. The real question is whether those who rise are the ones who best benefit the organisation, and that's as hard to answer in policing as it is in any other walk of life.

The Senior Police National Assessment Centre: Senior PNAC

The actual move from superintendent or chief superintendent to chief officer is determined by the individual's attendance on the SCC. As Sir Ian put it (in his oddly clunky prose):

> The main hurdle for those who aspire to senior rank in the police [...] is to pass the extended interview process controlling access to the Strategic [...] Command Course at Bramshill. Without attending this course, it is not possible to become a chief Officer. (Blair, 2009, p 87)

He could have mentioned that access to the 'extended interview process' itself (now called 'Senior PNAC') is initiated by a chief officer recommendation. I explore chief officers' more detailed personal

---

[14] Though in Chapter Five, I explore with chief officers the possibility of other routes into the police, and whether experience in policing is a prerequisite for command.

experiences of this in Chapter Two, but briefly a serving chief officer (usually, but not exclusively, the chief constable of the force in which the aspirant is serving), endorses the candidate's application form for PNAC to the effect that s/he has undertaken the experiences detailed in examples, and shows requisite skills, competency and potential. There is a lengthy process to be gone through in an application booklet where the candidate evidences each of his or her competencies and recounts his or her operational and experiential track record in support of those competencies. Each of the entries containing evidence is confirmed (and sometimes augmented) by the candidate's line manager – endorsed overall by the chief officer if different – who then recommends (or does not) that the candidate is 'ready now' to become an ACC or commander. In part of the application booklet, candidates are expected to show that they are competent in three leadership domains and that they satisfy four core criteria. These are:

> Executive policing evidenced and verified through the core criterion (1) *Substantial and challenging command in a significant role*.
> Professional policing evidenced and verified through the core criterion (2) *policing operations*.
> Business policing evidenced and verified through the core criteria (3) *organisational strategy*, and (4) *experience of handling finance and budgets*.[15]

It is expected that candidates will have substantial and varied experience in police operational and strategic command positions prior to applying and it is equally likely that only in the superintendent and chief superintendent ranks is such 'substantial and varied experience' to be found. This application, complete with signatures of candidate and verifier at key points and with signed declarations,[16] forms the basis for the paper sift for the Senior PNAC. One candidate's rueful experience may be indicative:

---

[15] The full application form and detail about evidencing competence and experience may be seen at www.npia.police.uk/en/docs/SPNAC2010ApplicationForm.doc; accessed 12 July 2010. Commentary in the main text is based on the application form for 2010, which was published by NPIA in April 2010. ACPO has since taken responsibility for this process.

[16] Including that for the line manager who is asked to identify three strengths for the candidate and three areas for development.

Interviewee 49: I roughed out my application form about six times before committing myself to the examples which evidenced my competencies, only for the chief to call me in a day or so later and say 'This application of yours is bollocks!' which scared me before he went on to say 'You've forgotten what you did in the [...] operation in the spring and that's a far better example than the one you've chosen.' And he went on and gave me better examples to use in other parts of the application. I had to rewrite the whole thing. It was quite clear that he had a very informed view of my work and what I had achieved – far better than mine – and that he knew what the PNAC assessors wanted, because I was then called up for that year's tranche.

Not all candidates are as fortunate as this one, and a number of chief officers noted to me that it was always possible for a line manager to damn a Senior PNAC candidate with 'faint praise'. The apparent endorsement can turn out to be anything but, and applicants, like assessors, have to be skilled at reading between the lines of what the bosses have written. To reinforce the point, chief officers who themselves now endorse candidates to PNAC, comment that the examples chosen in the application are absolutely key to whether a candidate stands out or not. There are too many instances of 'operational experience' for example that are

Interviewee 30: [...] a bit thin to be honest. I had one not too long ago where the candidate used a public order event to evidence operational command and hadn't thought through the effect on the assessors of choosing an example which had gone hopelessly wrong and in which the candidate was shown as utterly ineffective. Sometimes people aren't very self-critical.

There are no published data available on the proportion who successfully pass the paper sift, but it is likely to be between half and a third of applicants if the success rates at PNAC itself are used as a measure (see later). The annual PNAC is always directed by a senior chief officer; in 2009 for example, it was directed by Sir Hugh Orde, the former Chief Constable of the Police Service of Northern Ireland (PSNI)[17], with other chief constables serving as co-directors on one of

---

[17] Appointed President of ACPO in 2009; his successor as CC in PSNI was Matt Baggott, then Chief Constable of Leicestershire Constabulary.

the three intakes.[18] A number of assistant directors, drawn from police forces, agencies and other organisations such as the Fire and Rescue Service, support the process; bringing a non-policing perspective to bear. All the 'directing staff' have responsibility for some interviewing and assessment. There is no doubt, though, that the police own and run the process, both as lead directing staff and through ACPO support. Indeed, ACPO made this position explicit to the government in 2008, when it asserted that

> [...] there is now a real opportunity to deliver what has arguably been lacking: *a truly police owned and led* focus on professional development which is one of the Service's most critical spheres of operation.[19] (my italics)

This has been further developed by the coalition government; in July 2010 the incoming Home Secretary passed responsibility for police leadership and development to ACPO itself, and this is reflected fully in the *Review of Police Leadership and Training* (Neyroud, 2011). Whether the process is now balanced, objective and transparent is less obvious. I should note in passing that PNAC is a UK-based process, assessing candidates from PSNI and Scotland as well as from England and Wales.

Senior PNAC's purpose is to assess whether the candidate who showed promise as a leader in his or her application booklet can demonstrate both leadership potential and readiness to command through a series of job-related scenarios and exercises. A team of assessors is allocated to observe and evaluate each candidate's performance through the exercises; there are usually four assessors for every group of five candidates. The assessors' observations and evaluations are later collated and a composite judgement arrived at.[20] The exercises themselves are:

- A management exercise (2 hours, 30 minutes)
- A chief officer briefing (2 hours, 30 minutes)

---

[18] See *Senior PNAC, Results and Analysis Report*, Executive Summary, November 2009, NPIA, available from www.npia.police.uk/en/docs/ SPNACResultsandAnalysisExecSummary2009.pdf; accessed 10 June 2010 and 12 July 2010.

[19] ACPO *Response to the Government's Green Paper on Police*, 2008, London: ACPO, para 5.7.

[20] Though the NPIA insists in its literature that 'an *objective assessment* of the candidate is reached'(my italics); see www.npia.police.uk/en/docs/SPNACPresentation2010. pdf; accessed 12 July 2010. It remains to be seen whether ACPO succumbs to the same hubris.

- A negotiating exercise (1 hour, 30 minutes)
- A media exercise (30 minutes)
- A policing presentation and interview (1 hour)
- A non–service interview (45 minutes)

The total amount of time taken by each candidate in these exercises is *eight hours and 45 minutes*, which means that successful performance can be as much about stamina and concentration as it is about knowledge and competency. The process appears to be deliberately intense, heavily scrutinised and rigorous in order to screen out those not ready for chief officer rank:

> **Interviewee 16:** I got through on my first attempt but I can still remember how I felt at the end of the PNAC assessment day: I was utterly and completely drained, and I had nothing left to give. If they'd asked me to come back or to do another exercise I would have burst into tears. I was running on empty, no question.

We can unpick one or two of the exercises a little further to see what candidates are expected to do. The media exercise, for example, entails candidates undertaking 'a live "mock" interview with a professional journalist'.[21] The interview itself takes only five minutes or so, but can be as much as 10 if there is a vigorous exchange. The first 20 minutes is allocated as preparation time for the candidate who has to read a series of documents and plan how to deal with the media as a result. Invariably, this is an exercise that involves defending police action in some way and trying to put across a positive message. This can be testing for candidates who have no prior experience of dealing with the media, especially with professional journalists asking intrusive questions.

Another pressured experience is the policing presentation and interview, where each candidate is judged for competence-related skills by two experienced police assessors. The candidate is given half an hour to prepare a presentation lasting 10 minutes on a topic to do with policing, following which the assessors ask questions. The candidate then has a competency-related interview with the same assessors lasting a further 30 minutes. A similar shorter exercise later involves non-police assessors with candidates interviewed for three

---

[21] See Appendix B, pp 13–16 of the NPIA document www.npia.police.uk/en/docs/ SPNAC_Reasonable_Adjustment_Policy_2009.pdf; accessed 12 July 2010.

quarters of an hour about how they dealt with situations in the past and how they might deal with them in the future.

A final example of the exercises is a strategic review, which entails a written exercise based on a series of papers relating to an imaginary police incident. Candidates working alone prepare a strategic paper about the incident, which not only tests their abilities to digest large amounts of written material but also how well they can present in writing their analysis and understanding of what they have read.

The composite (that is, the overall) assessment for each candidate is graded according to the competencies demonstrated[22] and there are four grades of evidence: 'A' denotes 'substantial positive evidence of the competency' with 'few or no' areas of development; 'B' demonstrates 'positive evidence' of the competency, with 'some' areas for development, 'but on balance more positive evidence'; 'C' reveals 'some positive evidence' but on balance 'more areas for development', while 'D' is given when 'substantial areas of development' are identified with 'little or no positive evidence of the competency'. These final assessments are aggregated from marking across all the exercises and have three possible designations:

S = 'successful demonstration of readiness' which is an invitation to attend the Strategic Command Course.

UE = unsuccessful on the occasion of this PNAC but the candidate is encouraged to return, having addressed identified development needs.

UQ = unsuccessful on the occasion of this PNAC but the question of the candidate's return to a future PNAC is left open.[23]

We have a good idea how many candidates make the cut. NPIA's report in November 2009 of that year's PNAC noted that 89 candidates attended the PNAC across three intakes, and 44 were successful (representing 49%); 15 (17%) of those who were unsuccessful were graded UE and encouraged to return, while 30 (34%) were graded UQ where the question of a return to PNAC was 'left open'.[24] Other

---

[22] Performance in some exercises is marked to a set of six numeric standards, which is mildly confusing. The letter grades mentioned above are used only for the candidate's overall performance on PNAC.

[23] See 'Senior PNAC Presentation: Overall Result', www.npia.police.uk/en/docs/SPNACPresentation2010.pdf; accessed 12 July 2010.

[24] See *Senior Police National Assessment Centre, 2009, Results and Analysis Report*, November 2009, available from: www.npia.police.uk/en/docs/SPNACResultsand AnalysisExecSummary2009.pdf; accessed 12 July 2010.

---

indicators (no stronger claim than this may be made on such partial and numerically slight evidence) suggest that those candidates with fewer years' service are likely to do better than those with long service, while those with degrees predictably perform better than those who have no higher education qualification.[25] Most candidates (92%) were chief superintendents and just over half of these were successful; while one of the seven superintendents attending was successful.

The statistics given in the paragraphs above do not permit me to make large generalisations either about the nature of the candidates' experience of PNAC nor about the accuracy with which the exercises indicate candidates' readiness for chief officer rank. That would need a longer span of results spread over a number of years, which would also have to be mapped against the subsequent careers of the chief officers concerned. Since there are other hurdles involved (completion of the SCC and appointment to a chief officer post), it might not be possible to assign any success in subsequent careers specifically to performance on the PNAC. All one can really say is that the candidate would never have become a chief officer had s/he not passed the PNAC. It would also be necessary as a 'control' perhaps, to map and analyse in the same way the subsequent careers of those who never made the cut to PNAC, but it seems unlikely that such data are collected.[26]

What this means in essence is that although PNAC acts as a gateway to the rest of the chief officer development process, there are no objective correlatives through which it can be assessed as a distinct process. This is research that should be done, if only to sustain confidence in what *appears* to be rigorous, independent and fair. Greater transparency about the process would enable any judgements to be made more reliably, of course.[27]

---

[25] Ibid., paras 14, 15 and 16. There are other (slighter) indicators about age ranges and service as well as black and minority ethnic (BME) and gender statistical analyses in the report.

[26] The Home Office told me that it did not collect such data and NPIA appeared not to. ACPO certainly does not. Therefore I am unable to prove any negatives. Equally, we cannot arrive at 'objective assessment' of PNAC without access to such control data.

[27] For example, many of NPIA's data were not available to the non-police enquirer and NPIA itself exhibited unnecessarily fussy protectiveness of its published material. It is not yet clear whether ACPO will be more open or more protective, since it is a limited company and not a public service department.

The Strategic Command Course

The Strategic Command Course (SCC) used to be a six month-long residential programme where aspirant chief officers were housed at the National Police Staff College at Bramshill, near Hook in Hampshire. There, they followed (as now) an intensive programme of development and exposure to high-level police thinking, including meeting captains of industry, academics, businessmen, civil servants, politicians and senior police officers. Much emphasis was put on the intensity of the programme and for many candidates it was a life-changing if unremitting experience:

> **Interviewee 89:** I went on the SCC in the days when it was residential and you were in each other's pockets all day, all week and I had never experienced anything like it. It was so intense, so focused that you start to forget about family, force, friends and everything except the exercise you're doing or the topic you're researching. It was all the experience of a university pressed down and concentrated into half a year. Awesome.

Others did not find it so congenial:

> **Interviewee 38:** The course content was fine but it was geared to those without family responsibilities. I had a young family then and a sick father and there was no way that I could calmly abandon them for six months, seeing them only briefly at weekends and hoping my husband could cope on his own. I did not want to be monastic in this way, though I was quite prepared to do the learning.

Complaints about the residential structure of the course led to its modification into a modular form in 2003, so that SCC students now attend for a particular topic and then go back to their forces. The intensity of the learning does not appear to have changed, but the experience is no longer as concentrated. Some chief officers believe that this has made networking more difficult than it used to be when everyone lived at Bramshill for the duration; others think it has made the SCC more appealing and more accessible.

There is a considerable amount of prior preparation. Students are 'expected to have completed a Hay ECI and Myers Briggs Type Indicator Step II' as developmental tools, and to have a personal development plan (PDP) in place before attending. The Myers Briggs Type Indicator is a well-known psychometric indicator of 'personality', which is broadly based on Jung's exploration of 'types' in his psychological study of 1921 (see Bibliography). The Hay ECI or Emotional Competence Indicator, is based on the work by Daniel Goleman in emotional intelligence and focuses on those competences which leaders use to get improved results (Goleman and Boyatizis, 2002). Guidance for SCC candidates is at pains to point out that:

> These [tools] do not form part of the decision making process and are for developmental purposes only.

A personal development plan is designed to help the individual officer map, analyse and reflect on learning needs and development.[28] It gives a structure and direction to individual study and is familiar to most police officers since it is widely used with student constables on first entry to a force and on learning programmes thereafter. Additionally, an extensive initial reading list is provided to candidates for the SCC, with the admonition that they are 'expected to have read' the texts specified. This is a bit of a tall order. The typical list for 2008, for example, was structured like this:

- Leadership and emotional intelligence: 14 texts including seminal books by Bennis and Thomas (2003) and by Goleman et al (2002a).
- Culture: four texts, including a full-length police study by McLaughlin (2007).
- Ethics and values: eight texts, including *Policing, Ethics and Human Rights*, the standard treatment by Neyroud and Buckley (2001).
- Knowledge: three texts including Tim Newburn's massive *Handbook of Policing* (2003).
- Equality diversity and human rights: 13 texts including the Report of the Stephen Lawrence Inquiry (Macpherson, 1999) and the Victoria Climbié Inquiry (Laming, 2003).

---

[28] Interestingly, the National Senior Careers Advisory Service (NSCAS) advises SCC candidates on how to construct a PDP and how to get the best out of one. NSCAS ranges across senior public appointments in general, not just the police. See NPIA commentary on the SCC 2010, available from www.npia.police.uk/en/6973.htm, Code 124, accessed 13 July 2010, and outline advice in Home Office, *Performance and Development Reviews* [PDRs] *for Chief Police Officers*, 2003, HO Circular 27/2003, London: Home Office.

• Futures: two texts, one of which is Charles Handy's *The Empty Raincoat*.[29]

This totals 44 texts, ranging from selected 10-page extracts to publications of 300 pages or more and there are a further 14 websites specified, ranging from the Institute for Public Policy Research to Greenpeace, which candidates are expected to visit. There are averagely about two and a half months (including Christmas) between PNAC and the start of the SCC, which led one chief officer to remark:

> **Interviewee 70:** I expected that everyone else on the SCC would be a complete whizz. I really struggled to get all the reading done in advance and laboured for weeks trying to make sense of some of these academic studies – on leadership for example. When I got to Bramshill in the New Year, I found I was the only one who had read the complete list in my 'set'. The others weren't such whizzes after all. Glad I did it though because it prepared me for what was to follow.

The *12 ACPO Competences for Chief Officers* (which I analyse in detail in Chapter Three) form the general basis for the Strategic Command Course itself, which is not a conventional teaching programme. Rather, it is about providing 'a wide range of learning opportunities and high levels of choice based upon individual learning needs' (NPIA, 2010b). The fact that the modular SCC programme nominally costs £15,000 (for non-Home Office forces and police forces from overseas) and that organisations appear willingly to pay this amount in order for their officers to attend, suggests that the SCC is respected and sought after. An overview of the course avers that it is intended

> to enable participants to reflect upon their achievements, share experiences and ideas with other leaders, reflect upon and refine their leadership platform [sic] and enhance their operational and strategic capability[sic] in preparation for their new role. (NPIA, 2010b)

---

[29] Source: NPIA, *Strategic Command Course 2008*, 'Initial Reading List', available from www.npia.police.uk/en/2211.htm; accessed 6 July 2010. Some of the leadership texts are cited in Chapter Three.

The delivery of the learning is structured in a similar way to the top management programmes for the public service,[30] so that police officers on the SCC

> attend seminars and lectures, engage in coaching and mentoring, directed learning, exercises and action research, explore their future working environment and present their findings to panels drawn from the Police Service, academia and public and private sector executives. (NPIA, 2010b)

Many serving chief officers look back on their time on the SCC with great affection:

> **Interviewee 74:** It was great, it really was. Here you were, freed from the daily hassle and away from all the pressure on performance in your force and able to really think about what we do and more importantly, whether there are other ways to do it. We met chiefs who were legends and some household names from industry. Where else could I do that? The discussions we used to have about operational resilience for instance would get quite heated and there were lots of different points of view. It was stimulating but it was also bloody hard work. Different sort of pressure, of course.

Others have more mixed views:

> **Interviewee 16:** It's often represented as the 'Police University'. It isn't of course because that detached, research-based rigour of a university simply isn't there and although there is challenge and debate, there is seldom a deep, independent questioning of the need for policing at all, if you see what I mean. It isn't 'no holds barred' in any sense. There is still consensus about basic meanings.

Another chief officer found a different kind of pressure:

> **Interviewee 36:** I can write well and have a shrewd grasp of strategy and how things work in government and what used to be

---

[30] Such as those delivered by the 'Government National School' for *Top Management Programme*, see www.nationalschool.gov.uk/programmes/programme.asp?id=17751; accessed 13 July 2010. The Programme is described on its web-page as 'the Cabinet Secretary's flagship leadership development programme. It is designed for the top slice of leaders in the civil service and the private, third and wider public sectors, who must all be in senior executive management positions and delivering critical outcomes for their organisations.'

called 'the corridors of power'. There was one student on the SCC with me who used to wheedle stuff out of me all the time because he hadn't the faintest idea about strategy, didn't care about writing at all and concentrated more on brown-nosing [cultivating] the visiting speakers. And then he'd pass my ideas off as his own. The irony was that he then got quite a reputation as a thinker and even got a job before I did. He was, and is, a fucking moron.

There is neither time nor space to undertake a full analysis of the SCC programme content, nor am I convinced that such an exercise would be particularly useful, given that a lot of the value of the SCC comes from

Interviewee 40: [...] outside the formal classroom – you know, arguing over a drink, sitting with the guest speaker and really picking their brains, talking informally to high profile chief constables, top people in industry and media figures, and putting together networks of contacts and people who might help later in your career. It's all informal, unscripted and depends on the social skills of the individual whether they can make use of that time.

Nonetheless, it is worth a brief look at the indicative formal learning outcomes (what are called 'learning objectives' in the rubric for the SCC programme), which sit alongside the *12 ACPO Chief Officer Competences*. There are three parts to the learning outcomes: professional policing skills, executive skills and business skills. If we look at one outcome in detail from each of the sections, we can see how the outcomes are tailored to have relevance to police command. This, for example, is from professional policing skills:

Take on the challenges and responsibilities of leadership in Gold (Strategic) Command in high risk operations, e.g. counter terrorism, major international events (Olympics 2012), firearms, public order, predatory criminality and CBRN.[31] Demonstrate the awareness of how and when to intervene in order to secure appropriate outcomes. (NPIA, 2010b)

---

[31] CBRN is chemical, biological, radiological and nuclear agents, the means by which mass terror might be engendered by terrorists or international criminals. Specific examples are few, but Saddam Hussein's regime used chemical agents against Kurdish civilians in Iraq in 1988 (see BBC report at http://news.bbc.co.uk/1/hi/1877161.stm; accessed 13 July 2010) and an apocalyptic terrorist group, *Aum Shinri Kyo*, released Sarin gas on the Tokyo subway system in March 1995 (see Brackett, 1996).

These are the really big policing events, such as had to be handled in July 2005 when 'home-grown' (Al-Qaeda-inspired) extremists attacked London's transport structure or in June 2010 when Northumbria Police had to contain the threat of the use of firearms by Raoul Moat,[32] and which require leaders to focus on ends as well as means, and makes partnerships and consensus vital components of effective strategic working.

Here is a different kind of outcome, from executive skills:

> Describe and be fully conversant with the governance, accountability and working of police authorities (Scottish Executive). Demonstrate the ability to positively influence business collaboration with a view to achieving targeted outcomes, whilst ensuring appropriate accountability. (NPIA, 2010b)

I explore the private views of chief officers in relation to the oversight mechanisms of police authorities, directly elected police crime commissioners, HMIC and the Home Office in Chapter Four, and it is enough here to observe that the student officer on the SCC is not required merely to understand how police authorities/PCCs function (or in Scotland, the Executive), but also to be able to show how individual chief officers can influence those who hold them accountable as well as affecting other business partnerships. These will be important skills-sets in the student's future posts.

A final example of a learning outcome is from business skills:

> Demonstrate an understanding of the principles of finance, HR and IT at [a] strategic level. Be able to negotiate on all aspects of organisational capability – in particular effective resource utilisation. (NPIA, 2010b)

This may be the student chief officer's first encounter with *strategic* level human resource management, finance or information technology which are specialisms in their own right and which a newly appointed chief officer would be expected to have an intelligent interest in, and,

---

[32] See BBC reports of June 2010 on the police hunt for and containment of Raoul Thomas Moat who shot his ex-girlfriend, killed her lover and seriously injured a police officer and then went to ground for days before he finally killed himself when surrounded. The events generated immense national interest and a massive police operation involving several police forces and the Army; see http://news.bbc.co.uk/1/hi/uk/10583839.stm; accessed 13 July 2010.

sometimes, to direct. The two principal factors here are that, despite the cliché of 'organisational capability', this is actually about handling people, equipment and money and about doing so in an increasingly stringent economic climate, as central funding for policing is progressively reduced. The strategic aspect to all this means that officers have to be focused on the bigger picture rather than the individual department or portfolio of work, and there is implicit in this learning outcome an understanding of the nature of collaboration between forces and of potential merger or amalgamation, some elements of which I explore further in Chapter Five.

A brief flavour of other learning outcomes from the SCC includes: operate 'as an effective leader' in a 'complex business environment', 'articulate a vision of the service', 'demonstrate the key characteristics of a transformational leader', 'operate effectively in an environment of 'continuous change' while improving public engagement', 'manage the complex and competing needs of stakeholders (including victims of crime)' and 'develop high level competence in critical incident assessment'. These are complex matters, many of which are explored in more detail in the chapters that follow, but they serve collectively to remind us that strategic level policing is now exposed to scrutiny as never before and that effective chief officers have to be as sure-footed in handling public order or staff morale as they have to be in handling police authorities/directly elected police crime commissioners, or the media and the wider public. This learning sequence is probably the nearest that the police service gets to applied police studies where what is learned in the 'safe' environment of Bramshill may very soon thereafter be applied to real life situations:

> **Interviewee 54:** It was amazing really. On the Friday morning we had been talking together about what a 'Gold' commander does when faced with the need to authorise an armed response and by Saturday afternoon, back in force, I was called in to deal with just such an incident. Fortunately, I had excellent support and had no time to panic, but I kept thinking that any minute one of the directing staff would come in and say 'OK, exercise over. Now how do you think you did?' Sadly, this incident was live and real, and the outcome was a death by suicide.

About 400 hours of formal learning, spread over 45 days, plus about the same again in private study and active research, constitute the SCC experience for the majority of police officers, but, as some of them have noted, the informal mechanisms and contacts as well as what each individual has learned, both about themselves and about the police service, persist far beyond the confines of the programme itself. Most will have embarked in a parallel academic programme to obtain a post-graduate diploma or a master's degree on a policing-related or business topic, and therefore the reflectiveness that characterised the SCC will persist into other forms of learning about the police. Indeed, there is a programme of continuous professional development (CPD) that is available for individual chief officers during the remainder of their ACPO careers. One strand of CPD is linked with the Institute of Directors, and another is through the government's Top Management programmes noted above. The expenditure on these CPD initiatives was the focus for comment in late 2010.[33]

'The weary round of interviews': appointment as a chief officer

The next hurdle that graduates of the SCC face is appointment itself and consequent membership of ACPO, but that can be months or years away:

> **Interviewee 49:** So I came out from the SCC bright-eyed and bushy-tailed, finishing off a dissertation on [a policing topic] for my diploma and expecting that I'd be off to another force, complete with shiny epaulettes, within weeks. The reality was a bit of a let-down. It took nine more months, five interviews, 'nothing' jobs in my own force and a lot of travelling before I finally got a post as an ACC, and that in a force that was never on my original list!

One police officer (whom I did not interview but who is regarded among fellow chief officers as a bit of a legend), went to *17 interviews* with different police authorities before eventual acceptance as an ACC. His nickname, predictably, is 'Make-weight'.

Advertisements of ACC/commander posts are more often carried in specialist police publications[34] than in national newspapers. Many appear on force websites as well. The normal format runs something like this.

---

[33] Chief officers receive coaching and mentoring which a freedom of information request in late 2010 revealed as costing nearly £200,000 from 2007–08 to 2008–09. In the same period, NPIA spent £3.822 million on the National Senior Careers Advisory Service; see 'Policing Leaders Face Scrutiny over Soaring Mentoring Costs' (no by-line), *Police Review*, 12 November 2010, p 4.

[34] Particularly, but not exclusively, in the back pages of the fortnightly *Police Review*, published by Jane's.

Assistant Chief Constable

Blankshire Police Authority wishes to appoint an **Assistant Chief Constable**
by the end of September to join the Top Team in driving the delivery of a
quality service to local communities. We're looking for a leader who can see
things from a different perspective and who has a complete set of leadership
skills and who understands the strategic direction of our Force.

As a key member of the Chief Officer Board you will believe passionately
in making the best possible service available to our local and diverse
communities and you will help to make a measurable difference to public
confidence. You will be joining us at a time when the Chief Officer team and
the authority face a number of challenges. We are restructuring our divisions
and reviewing our back office functions. Our challenging financial situation
is well known. You will have the drive and determination to contribute
strategically to our business while also focusing on achieving goals and making
the most of our people and our resources. We're looking to you to act as a
motivational leader – implementing improvements and developing new ways
of doing things.

**If you're made of the right material, we want you to focus all your
formidable energies and passion for excellence in our new era
of policing.**

For full details and to apply, contact Dr Elizabeth Watson, the Police and
Crime Commissioner for Blankshire Police (06827 912477). You are also
invited to ring Mycroft Moriarty, OBE, QPM, MSt., the Chief Constable,
for an informal chat about the post and his expectations of the incumbent
(06827 380651, Extn. 201).

Closing date for applications: 12 noon on 21 June 2013

Previous applicants need not re-apply[35]

Skilled readers of police language will have no difficulty in recognising
what is being suggested in this advertisement. The force is strapped
for cash, and any incoming ACC can expect to have to do more

---

[35] This is a composite of six different advertisements for ACC posts across the UK
culled from various sources in 2010; and, though the post and contact details are
fictitious, the language used throughout is absolutely genuine. This is very typical
of the conventional ad for a chief officer post. In July 2010, NPIA actually ran a
'portmanteau' advertisement, featuring chief officer vacancies in eight forces (*Police
Review*, 23 July 2010).

with less, and will probably be tasked to identify additional savings. The professional 'portfolio' on offer is principally neighbourhood and area/district policing and the incumbent is likely to be tested in delivering services to some challenging places – not just in engaging with communities in deprived urban areas, but also in meeting the expectations of those living in more prosperous districts. The appointee will be expected very quickly to make a positive impact on public confidence in the police, while helping colleagues restructure the force and develop plans for redundancies among police support staff in HR, finance, administration, IT and estates. More than that, the police crime commissioner (PCC) and the chief constable expect the successful candidate to be a powerhouse of new ideas to save money and to push for new and cost-effective ways of policing (perhaps through extensive use of special constables and other volunteers). Evidently, the PCC has advertised something like this post before and she was unimpressed with the quality of previous applicants – hence the suggestion that no one should reapply. The invitation to ring the chief constable strongly suggests that he has views that must be taken into account, especially as he will sit on any interview panel (see later).

In other words, this is a challenging post, likely to be fraught with difficulties over resources and economies and there is also a hint of some friction between the PCC and the chief constable, which it would be as well for applicants to be aware of at the outset. Only in the 2008 Green Paper, was it formalised that chief constables could have a say in the appointment of their subordinate chief officers.[36] Previously, they generally had to put up with whomever the police authority chose to appoint, unless they had particularly strong influence with the authority concerned.

But there is still some way to go before the vacant post is filled. Most prospective ACCs draw up a list of where they would like to go and what sort of work they want to do:

> **Interviewee 23:** I knew exactly where I wanted to go and reckoned that any of four forces in the [...] area would suit. I listed out the factors: my partner was happy to work there because the travel was easy and it was a nice part of the world and there were good schools. I was unsuccessful with the first choice but got the

---

[36] The lugubrious Derek Barham, whose cynicism about promotion we encountered earlier, said in the same article (Barham, 2010a) that 'Allowing a police leader to arbitrarily pick their [sic] top team, will open the door to claims of nepotism, discrimination and patronage.'

second and settled very quickly. I wanted to have the portfolio for Serious Organised Crime or Crime Operations and that's what I got. It was also a long way from my 'parent' force, which helped too.

The paper–sift stage takes several weeks and a short list is prepared by the police authority or PCC of those whom they wish to interview. Individuals are invited to the force, often the night before the interview round, in order to informally meet those making the assessment.[37] For some, it was not a happy experience:

Interviewee 36: Oh, I can remember it well. Six of us, who would be contending the next day, had to make small talk and then have tea with members of the authority, each of whom seemed to have an agenda which involved enlisting your support for some mad scheme such as covert air-borne surveillance of fly-tippers. You learned a lot from the encounter: what preoccupations the authority members have, who was going to be on the panel next day and who the favoured candidate was (one of their own force, of course). It was artificial, strained and nerve-racking, and I hated every minute of it.

[Interviewer: Did you get the job?]

Did I hell! No, it went to the local candidate. I was there to make up the numbers, that much was obvious. Fortunately, I got a job shortly afterwards with a force that didn't go in for these pre-meets and I felt much more comfortable.

For others, the 'pre-meet' could be helpful:

Interviewee 30: It was OK actually. I liked meeting some of the police authority characters and hearing what they were interested in. They were interested in me too. I learned a lot informally about shortcomings in the force and about how dysfunctional the top team was, in a very short time. That didn't stop me accepting when I was offered the post next day.

---

[37] The appointment of a single person, a 'police crime commissioner', replacing the 17-member police authority, to hold a force to account (and who can 'hire and fire' the chief constable) has been cautiously received by ACPO and civil libertarians alike. I discuss this in greater detail in Chapter Four. See also Brain, T. 'You're Fired!' in *Police Review*, 22 October 2010, pp 26–7.

Structures for interview vary, as one might expect, from force to force. Sometimes, short-listed candidates might attend a series of force briefings a day before the interviews, where department heads explain constraints or initiatives in progress, and there is a general thrust to describe the force. Other forces may rely more on informal contact with chief officers. Many police authorities/PCCs ask short-listed candidates to prepare short presentations to be given before the panel interview on current topics:

> **Interviewee 8:** I was asked how I would save a million pounds. So I got up on my hind legs, went through what I knew of the force's budget, shot down two ludicrous projects which I'd learned about the night before, and triumphantly saved the force £1.5 million, only to discover that the two projects were the cherished ideas of the authority chair. No, I didn't get the job!

Some forces have their human resources director attending interviews *ex officio*, to ensure fairness and a consistent process, and to advise members of the interview panel. Panels can have as many as seven members or as few as three. Practice varies, although HMIC has helped to standardise some of the interview procedures and is available to advise chairs of police authorities/PCCs:

> **Interviewee 21:** The appointments process is designed to be tough – HMIC designs the structure and can suggest some of the questions [...] so that there is rigour. That can be very stressful, but since we are all volunteers for the appointment, we can't complain if it is hard to get.

The usual format is that the chair/PCC will lead the questioning, followed in turn by each of the panel members. The chief constable is likely to focus on the policing duties of the post and how the candidate will be expected to perform them. However it is not possible to predict questions with any accuracy, and each authority/PCC will have its own predilections, interests and worries. The best-prepared interview candidates will have researched the force thoroughly beforehand:

> **Interviewee 64:** I so wanted this job – it was me all the way through. I spent weeks reading PA blogs, minutes of planning committees and PA public reports. I'd noticed that the authority

had had problems with FOI requests,[38] and this was something I knew a lot about. I studied each member of the authority and the chief and her deputy until I felt I could identify each one in the dark. When it came to the interview, almost the first question was about FOI and I launched into my 'expert' reply. You could almost feel the tension go out of the room. I got the job and for the next year or so, the chief used me to front all 'hard' media encounters. It was all down to that prior preparation: I knew what was coming and I knew how to deal with it. As a result I was relaxed and beat the local man out of sight.

As I noted above, some candidates need to experience a number of interviews before they are as well prepared as Interviewee 64. Surprisingly, only a very few aspirants are *never* appointed. In the source of my research, I came across only two instances of an SCC graduate *not* getting an ACC/commander post at all, and one of those was later able to take an ex-officio appointment in the rank.

The general reservation that chief officers have about the interview process is that (allegedly) it is sometimes predetermined and this can be hugely frustrating for those who see themselves as the 'ballast' candidates:

> **Interviewee 18:** We've all been to interviews where you know you're just there to make up the numbers and the selection is as near as dammit already decided.
>
> [Interviewer: But don't you find that frustrating and a waste of time?]
>
> Well, of course. Nothing is worse than realising that the interview panel has already made up its mind and is just going through the motions with you as ballast. On the other hand, that's deeply satisfying when you know that *you* are the preferred candidate and the process glides along smooth as silk. That's happened twice to me now, and I recognise when it's happening.
>
> [Interviewer: How many times have you been the 'ballast'?]

---

[38] Freedom of Information (Act). Principally used by journalists to winkle out information from reluctant public services, the aim of the FOI request is to provide information about processes and budgets.

> Three times to my knowledge. Twice when going for ACC and once when going for a DCC. Never when going for a chief constable's job though.

Appointments are likely to continue to be largely by police authority/ PCC consensus, but the important development noted above is that the chief constable now sits on interview panels as of right, and this has to be an improvement as well as ensuring that the new appointee will be more likely to complement the existing chief officer team:

> **Interviewee 60:** When I sit in these interviews, I'm looking for someone who has a bit of a spark about them.
>
> [Interviewer: could you be more specific?]
>
> Well, it's not just a puppyish eagerness to please – most of the candidates have that, oh and a dog-like acceptance of every fatuity uttered by members of the authority as well. No, the one who I look for is the alert one, the one who challenges politely and who has a real urge to get things done. That's one thing. And the other is how that person will fit my team. I don't want two ex-CIDs or two ex-patrol inspectors together. I ideally want maybe one public order specialist, one detective and one neighbourhood/local policing type, each able to take the appropriate policing portfolio and run with it. And I tell you, I will work that person really hard for a year or two to get the best out of them, before they move on. I've only been wrong once. The police authority has been wrong loads of times.

With confirmation of appointment comes formal membership of ACPO and possibly some interest in national issues in policing.[39] After three or four years, during which the chief officer may have had two posts as an ACC/commander, s/he will begin looking for opportunities to move up to a deputy chief constable/deputy assistant commissioner

---

[39] These are the 'business areas' each of which is owned by a member of the Chief Constables' Council, chaired by the president of ACPO. ACCs and DCCs with a particular interest – say in knife crime, vehicle theft, drugs trafficking or terrorism, will have a portion of their time assigned to 'national work' which often extends the networking that ACCs can do and which brings them into contact with Home Office and other public service officials, politicians, media personalities and academic specialists. Most of those who have a role in the 'business areas' (about a third of all ACPO officers) enjoy the additional interest it brings. The downside of course is that the 'portfolio' adds to the already long working week for the chief officer (see Chapter Two).

post. I note that there appears to be general reluctance to move any great distance to secure the next rank.[40]

An appointment as deputy chief constable follows the same general process as for the ACC appointment, with a greater emphasis on force-specific presentations and usually a larger interview panel, as well as expectation that the successful candidate will be able to take on what are regarded traditionally as DCC's duties, such as force discipline, professional standards and force performance. The DCC is also likely to spend a greater amount of time liaising with the PCC and members of the Crime and Police Panel, which advises the PCC, and with partnerships, including those with the Public Prosecution Service and criminal justice generally.

The DCC usually line-manages the assistant chief officers, reporting to the chief constable, and often deals direct with HMIC and the Home Office in day-to-day matters. In some forces, the DCC is seen as the force 'trouble-shooter'; in others, a kind of *éminence grise* to the chief. The DCC deputises for the chief constable on many public occasions and is likely to have a high profile in the force generally. It follows from all this that the DCC post is pivotal, second in importance only to the chief constable, and experienced, well-rounded individuals are sought. Many DCCs are internal promotions, 'the favoured local candidate', but such expectations can be demolished by external candidates who perform well:

> **Interviewee 33:** Most appointments to senior chief officer [...] are foregone conclusions. A chief may ring you up, or HMIC drop a very broad hint that you are the favoured candidate and that you should apply. There will be a couple to make up the numbers plus one or at most two genuine other contenders. Let's say they are 3:1 on the field and you may be 5:2. You could be the likely favourite, but you could fall on the day, or someone else could put in a better performance and go past you. I've seen it happen.
>
> [Interviewer: you are not suggesting that the process is in any way rigged, are you?]
>
> Absolutely no; if you bomb on the day you don't get the job.

Chief constable posts are not merely titular. The chief constable embodies the force both symbolically and actually, and during his or

---

[40] First noted in the Introduction.

her tenure of five to 10 years, will determine the character and profile of the force. The chief constable articulates the force's vision, sets goals and is the visible leader, has (usually) a high media profile locally and often a national role, such as being the ACPO 'lead' on the Special Constabulary, or roads policing, or gang crime. Most chief constables are appointed from outside the force and many seem prepared to travel greater distances than either their deputies or ACCs to secure the appointments they want:

> **Interviewee 69:** I knew that the [particular post] was coming up for grabs and began to take soundings. There was a general tide of goodwill that I should go for it and, since it was a bigger force, I was prepared to move up in terms both of responsibility and salary. What I hadn't taken into account was [my spouse] who at first simply refused to move from the job [s/he] had and said that if I wanted to go, I'd be on my own. It took ages to persuade [my spouse] to my way of thinking and when finally we reached a compromise, I went for the job and got it.
>
> We had to up sticks and move across half the country, away from relatives, friends and schools to this virtually unknown area and start all over again. The kids found it hard too, going to new secondary schools and having to make new friends. It must have taken us the best part of 18 months to two years to get sorted domestically and for [my spouse] to get a new job [...] and all the time I was fire-fighting crisis after crisis in the job itself. On balance it was worth it, but it was touch and go for my marriage for a while and I had to work really, really hard to keep things together.

I have quoted this interviewee's comments at some length, since they show the extent and nature of the disruption that a chief constable's appointment may cause within a family, and because the attractions of the job itself are put into social context.[41] The same appointment processes are followed for the appointment of chief constables as for DCCs and ACCs, with the difference that there is often a smaller pool of candidates and probably a much stronger input from HMIC. Appointment from outside policing is one solution to a small pool of applicants, which I examine in Chapter Five, but normally, police authorities/PCCs have to deal with what they can get and appoint

---

[41] I apologise for the occasionally clumsy prose here. If the partner is further specified, it could be enough to identify the speaker.

the best of who is available. Not surprisingly, this can sometimes lead to tensions between the chief officer team and the authority/PCC.

Conclusions

Becoming a chief officer in the first place is an arduous and prolonged process. Only the most resilient and single-minded (or what Derek Barham [2010a] calls 'the steadfastly ambitious') achieve the goal of appointment as an ACC in a police force or as a commander in the Metropolitan Police. From being picked out or 'fingered' (an activity I look at in greater detail in Chapter Two) as having potential; latterly, perhaps, going into the High Performance Development Scheme or on a series of Leadership Development courses, the aspirant chief officer has to reach at least superintendent rank to be eligible even to apply to be considered for ACPO rank. At this point, or, more commonly at chief superintendent, the candidate chief officer is encouraged to apply to the Senior Police National Assessment Centre (Senior PNAC) and begins lining him or herself up in front of the many hurdles which intervene between the candidate and the goal of appointment as chief officer.

We have noted in the preceding pages what the Senior PNAC and its companion Strategic Command Course entail for the aspirant chief officer, and there is consensus from those who underwent it that PNAC is exacting and rigorous. However, that is not the same as being equitable and transparent, and some of the processes involved are obscure to the external observer. There is little in the way of independent research to allow dispassionate judgements about PNAC's effectiveness to be made. It is very unlikely that PNAC permits 'cloning' (where selectors deliberately perpetuate their own images in their successors), but there will always be some elements of conformity in any leadership selection system. Few jobs, except perhaps in IT design, entertainment or architecture, deliberately cultivate the iconoclast or the maverick, and police selection is no exception to this general observation.

If the charge of 'cloning' chief officers will not stick, is there any truth in recurrent criticism that chief officers are conformist and conventional (Johnston, 2008; Barham, 2010a)? The structure of the chief officer selection process would suggest that this is not the general rule, and the thrust of the SCC seems very much to be towards helping the candidate chief officer to think for him or herself. Certainly, the personal testimony of those who have been on the SCC suggests that it is a life-changing experience for them and that it is often the first opportunity many have had to examine policing as an entity and from a dispassionate perspective. The majority of chief officers whom

I interviewed showed considerable independence of mind, an ironic detachment about what had happened to them and a refreshingly open way of thinking. No one could fairly call them conventional. Their own words seem to show that conformity is the last thing on their minds, but of course that may be because the remarks were made in private. The PNAC as far as I can ascertain, seems a fair process of selection, but greater *public* transparency might help us arrive at an objective judgement. The SCC appears to work well as a learning experience and most attendees seem to get a lot from it. That much is exemplary, and certainly moving the SCC from residential course to modular programme has met with general approval.

Yet very few of those who come out of the SCC fail to attain, sooner or later, a post as an ACC or commander. I am less convinced (admittedly I have been influenced by the private confidences of chief officers) that the appointments system is either consistent or demonstrably fair. Having the chief constable on any selection panel may help to prevent repetition of some of the really odd appointments of times past, but it is surely bizarre that so few SCC graduates *fail* to get an appointment somewhere in the course of time? Are we rewarding ability or persistence? This whole area needs more research and much greater transparency before I could accept that the chief officer appointments system is above reproach and before I can fully subscribe to Sir Hugh Orde's assertion that

> The quality of people coming through the senior command course is the most convincing argument I have seen for believing the future of the service is in good hands.[42]

As to later selection and promotion, the numbers are such that only about a quarter of all ACCs could reasonably expect to make it to chief constable within five to 10 years. The statistics seem to favour younger appointees who, all other skills being equal, will be promoted: time is on their side. Older ACCs may not make it beyond the rank. Fifteen years is probably the cut-off point after which further promotion is unlikely – indeed renewal of the fixed term appointment is likely to lapse at the same time.

The application done, the research completed, the learning and development consolidated, the interviews and tests and presentations performed, attendance over and stoic endurance of the 'weary round of interviews' having culminated in an appointment, we may conclude

---

[42] 'Character of judgement', article in *Police Review*, 13 August 2010, p 19.

that those people who jumped all the hurdles to become chief officers probably deserve to. They have gone through much to put up the extra silver braid. Where did all that ambition come from? Who spotted that they might make good chief officers? What do they think of each other and their workloads? We need now to look more closely at the person in the post.

TWO

'The golden finger': getting and keeping the top jobs

> **Interviewee 31:** Yes, well, this golden finger tapped me on the shoulder and a voice said 'You could be a chief, you know.' When I stopped laughing I realised that he was serious and that golden finger was 24 carat: it picked me out from the mass of my colleagues and pointed me on my way upwards.

I looked at the candidacy, application and selection procedures to become a chief officer in Chapter One. In this chapter, I examine chief officers' individual and personal experiences of moving up through the ranks and the ways in which they were picked out to apply for promotion. Many of those interviewed commented on how the 'golden finger' touched them to indicate that they were 'chosen' to go further.[1] The strong evidence is that identification of individual potential and the channelling of that potential into candidacy for chief officer is still very much rooted in a personal patronage exercised by senior officers. One chief officer told me how he had to wait three years before he could persuade his chief constable to recommend him for promotion – a delay which cost him some seniority compared with his fellow officers on that SCC intake. Another took his chief constable out for lunch to angle for a job overseas, only to hear his chief unexpectedly confirm recommendation for the assessment process instead.

There are some interesting elements in the individual accounts of aspiration to the ACPO ranks, ranging from those who joined intending from the outset to get to the top, to those to whom the entire process was a series of surprises. The chapter then goes on to explore relationships within the chief officer role, asking about perceptions of security or uneasiness in the various jobs at this level, how chief officers regard their colleagues and what sorts of competition exist,

---

[1] The 'golden' image comes from a series of television and newspaper advertisements in the late 1990s for the (then new) National Lottery, which asked 'Could it be you?' as a gigantic golden finger selected the fortunate winner. There is an additional sense to the 'golden finger': some police officers find the image resonant because it suggests to them something predestined in their appointment to 'top cop' candidacy, almost from before they were conscious that they had been chosen.

or are perceived to exist, around getting and holding on to these 'top team' jobs. This leads me in turn to consider work–life balance and its relevance to chief officers as they cope, or try to cope, with large workloads and a prevalent long hours culture.

First though, I asked the respondents whether becoming a chief officer was deliberate and planned, or accidental:

> **Interviewee 54:** Bit of both – a bit deliberate and a bit by happy accident. I decided from the beginning that I wanted to be more than a constable, because I was sick of thick people pushing me about and treating me as a disposable asset. I wanted to push back and, once launched on the upward path, the thing got its own momentum.

This appears to be a common experience: an apparently reluctant recognition of one's own potential and embarkation on the promotion process. If we compensate for individual modesty and the characteristic disguising of ambition among senior police officers (none of whom openly admits to having any kind of personal strategy)[2], there are plenty of examples of officers wakening to opportunities above them:

> **Interviewee 8:** By default, really. I know who didn't see any potential in me, and that's me! I always had the ambition to be a '30-year cop', but then, through my brother, thought I could do better as a sergeant than the one I had.

For some, the prospect seemed quite alien at first:

> **Interviewee 12:** The idea of joining ACPO was sown when I was on a course at Bramshill. The conversation went like this after a member of the directing staff had suggested that I seek to be selected for ACPO:
> 'I'll never be ACPO.'
> 'Why?'
> 'Because I'm not like them and I don't want to be like them.'
> ACPO then was a clique of self-satisfied, smug, immoveable men who were impervious to new ideas – but my wife pushed me and so did friends, and so I decided I'd take it on, and force change from the inside.

---

[2] Indeed one interviewee commented: 'That certainly is true of the police, because very few would openly say that "I want to be so-and-so" because that's the best way *not* to get it.'

and, in terms of the 'blue glass ceiling', this female officer had to take the issue into her own hands and persist in going for promotion:

> **Interviewee 40:** After about two years in the job, I thought you've got to push your way upwards here because no one is going to do it for you. Then I had a chief officer who took a real interest in pushing opportunities for women and that's how my career took off. I made it to superintendent fairly quickly (11 years) but stalled there for a while because my force seemed to have a policy of promotion and advancement [only] through 'dead men's shoes'. I looked around for openings outside my force but which would not cause too much upheaval for the family, and let it be known that was what I was doing. That was enough to stimulate my force into recommending me for EI[3] and then the SCC for ACPO. After that, it was a matter of picking the interviews I wanted to be short-listed for and choosing the force where I wanted to work.

This last comment is interesting in a number of ways, because it reveals some of the difficulties facing ambitious women in the police service, and the apparent chauvinism of some male chief officers, but also it suggests that personal ambition is a very powerful motivator, which merely needs an external stimulus. Few officers talked openly about formal mentors or mentoring systems, but many of the chief officers interviewed commented how much their promotion was owed to someone spotting their potential. The following is indicative of many similar comments:

> **Interviewee 6:** I was lucky in my old force that the chief constable was a genuine believer in equality and so I got opportunities early in my career to move on to take more responsibility and more challenging jobs. That was the first spur and it was the same chief constable who said I should go for chief officer when I was still an inspector.

Another noted that inspector rank was where a number of officers stalled:

> **Interviewee 79:** I did not set out to be a chief officer, and was a uniformed inspector for more than a decade before my old chief

---

[3] EI (extended interview) was the forerunner of Senior PNAC, the 'gateway process' to selection as a potential chief officer.

told me that I was vegetating and should go for chief inspector. Admittedly, movement after that was rapid; also the service supported me in studying for two degrees whilst all this was going on. It was a bit overwhelming I have to say, because here I was with a young family, studying for a degree whilst being paid as a police officer, and the whole world seemed to be opening up. It was exciting but also a bit scary.

Another looked back on the 'golden finger' with some affection:

Interviewee 11: I was tapped on the shoulder by a chief and it was suggested that I went for chief officer myself. It was a surprise. The police service is less able to do that now, with processes and the HPDS[4] having replaced the older system of selection and patronage. I don't say patronage was all good, but it certainly didn't produce the clones coming through now, via self-selection and self-aggrandising procedures.

This next interviewee indicated that expectations of top rank in certain police occupations were not high, and that being picked out, or at least earmarked as having potential, was often stimulus enough:

Interviewee 23: I became a chief officer because my shoulder was tapped, and without too much arrogance, I thought I could do at least as well as some who were already there. Also, not many CID went on to chief officer rank in those days.

Occasionally, the speed of progression through intermediate ranks could seem breathtaking:

Interviewee 70: It's like the characteristic of success in gambling or on the Lottery: it's a combination of luck, skill and chance. A chief superintendent spotted me because I had the highest arrest rate as a patrol constable and ordered me to put in an application for sergeant. Then the chief constable had a policy of looking at all good sergeants as potential superintendents. Effectively, I went from constable to superintendent in about six years' service, including two at inspector.

---

[4] HPDS (High Potential Development Scheme) is designed to spot and nurture chief officer potential from early in service; see Chapter One.

—

One officer's ambition extended only as far as wanting a foreign posting but things worked out differently:

> **Interviewee 81:** It was a bit of both: both accident and ambition. I was on the HPDS fairly early, and made chief officer after only 14 years' service, so that's quite rapid really. [When I was a superintendent] I took the chief constable out for lunch to try and swing a short foreign posting I particularly wanted, which was at superintendent level. He said 'I know why you've invited me to lunch.'
>
>   'Oh really?' I said.
>
>   'Yes,' he said, 'Don't worry, I'll recommend you for PNAC.'
>
>   And all I wanted was this foreign trip. So you could say I stumbled into it, really.

This is illuminating, both for the endearingly muddled ways in which some officers arrive at chief officer rank without a game plan to do so, and for the ways that patronage (through 'recommendation') still seem to figure largely in getting to the first hurdle of candidacy for chief officer selection, irrespective of either the HPDS (Chapter One) and chief officer competencies (see Chapter Three).

It is often remarked by those on the outside that the police service should be structured more like the Armed Forces, with a two-tier entry system, one at 'private soldier' or equivalent and one at 'officer'. This two-level entry was actually tried by Lord Trenchard[5] when he was Commissioner of the Metropolitan Police in the 1930s but it proved unworkable. Nonetheless, animated discussion of multiple entry is

---

[5] Lord Hugh Trenchard, (1873–1956), created the Royal Air Force from the (Army) Royal Flying Corps in 1918, and was among the first to recognise the strategic role of air warfare. When appointed Commissioner of the Metropolitan Police by Winston Churchill (then Home Secretary) in 1930, Trenchard set up an officer-entry scheme into the police, among other reforms. The scheme was widely criticised as divisive and fell into disuse by the post-war period. However, the emphasis that Trenchard put on training and skills acquisition, and his creation of the Hendon Police College, resulted in a more systematic programme of learning in the police and diminished the 'sit by Nelly' school of unsystematic learning-by-watching. See Boyle, A. (1962, chapters 19 and 20). However, the Dutch Police operate a two-tier system successfully. Their 'first level' equates to community support officer roles with a minimum educational/ experiential level but the 'second level' is entered after attaining a first degree; this latter stage offers the track to full police officer and beyond. The scheme, overseen by the Dutch Police Academy, has the incidental effect of creating very close relations between the police (*politie*) and academic partners in universities.

recurrent, particularly at chief officer level, and we look at this in more detail in Chapter Five.

Many chief officers argue that a prerequisite for high command in the police is operational experience at all ranks and whether or not this observation is valid (also considered further in Chapter Five), it was collectively powerful enough to influence the previous government's Green Paper on the police in late 2008, which affirmed that there was a single entry point system for the police in England and Wales.[6] At best, this gives senior officers a long time span to identify potential in others and to nurture it. It is therefore probable that, in the majority of cases, police candidates at the PNAC have gone through a series of informal selections and 'nurturing' spread perhaps over a number of years and posts, and involving one or more senior 'patrons'.

Not all candidates appear motivated solely by personal ambition. It is worth looking at one chief officer's experience in some detail:

> **Interviewee 27:** With 17 years' service and still an inspector, the world suddenly opened up in front of me. A new chief constable brought a different culture and new opportunities emerged for a different breed of senior manager. I was promoted three times in quick succession.
>
> My chief [constable], who was an excellent mentor, told me that he had never known anyone with 'so little burning ambition achieve so much' within the service. With 21 years' service, I found myself as a divisional commander with nowhere else to go in a relatively small force and the prospect of doing the same job for the next 10 years. By that time, I had become used to moving, making a difference and moving on again and so the potential for stagnation concerned me and I decided to have 'one go' at the Senior Command Course.

---

[6] The Green Paper (a discussion document) was largely derided as tired and derivative when it was published in 2008, but its chapter 3 merits closer examination in terms of what it says about 'defining roles and leadership in the police' and how that bears on chief officers:

> 3.13 While all police officers hold the Office of the Constable, it is also important that all police officers start at the rank of Constable. This enables them to gain a full understanding of frontline operational policing through direct experience. (HMG, 2008)

Some chief officers privately say almost exactly the same thing in Chapter Five of this volume.

—

This is not offered as a typical pattern for a police officer, but its honesty is very telling and it is entirely plausible that the chief officer concerned may not have been driven by a personal will to advance. The mention above of the arrival in a force of a new chief constable with different ideas and priorities acting as a catalyst and picking up on those with potential to lead, is echoed in others' experiences:

> **Interviewee 33:** No, I didn't always want to be a chief. I joined the police when I was nearly 19 and then I was so arrogant I thought I'd become the commissioner! But that was soon knocked out of me and I quickly settled into being a career detective. I was the youngest sergeant by some distance at 24 but then I failed five successive inspector processes. So I got out of [this particular police] force and when I returned from my secondment, there was a different chief [constable] who pointed the golden finger at me. I then went from sergeant to chief superintendent in seven years.
>
> [Interviewer: and when did you start thinking about applying to become a chief officer?]
>
> When I made chief superintendent. I thought 'Bollocks – I can do this!' and just went for it. So it was never planned out, I just grabbed opportunities when they presented themselves.

However, as may be expected, a number of people come into the police with a very different mind-set. These were determined that they would become chief officers as soon as possible:

> **Interviewee 5:** I set out to be a chief officer from the beginning; I did not join thinking that being a sergeant was all I could aspire to.
>
> **Interviewee 48:** I joined to be chief constable, pure and simple. Nothing else would do.
>
> **Interviewee 30:** I thought about it long and hard before I joined. There is no point in being in the police unless you try to get to the top, so I set out from the start with the aim and intention of making chief officer. I'd have quit and done something else if I hadn't got to ACPO rank even if not necessarily chief constable; but when the opportunity is there, you'd be daft not to grab it.

Others seemed to acquire ambition once the initial promotion process began:

> **Interviewee 31:** Once I'd started the promotion process and had passed my sergeant's OSPRE,[7] I had my eye on being a chief officer. There is no point in being the world's best inspector if no one listens to you and you can't change things.

A focused few even gave themselves deliberate and timed programmes to follow:

> **Interviewee 13:** I joined, wanting to rise quickly and I was prepared to put in a lot of effort to do that successfully. I set myself goals: inspector by year five, superintendent by year eight, chief officer by year 10, chief constable by year 15. And it worked, even ahead of time. If I'd missed out on any of the interims to command rank, I would have left policing and done something else

By contrast, another chief officer's experience was much less systematic, and seems to be predicated more on job satisfaction tempered by a low boredom threshold:

> **Interviewee 82:** I never planned anything. I joined the police because it looked like a cool thing to do but I always thought I'd leave after a bit. I was actually on the Strategic Command Course before I finally decided to stay. I'm passionate about policing, but I'm not desperate about it. The thing is that when I'm bored (and I am easily bored), I start to tinker with things and that's fatal – so really that's why I kept moving on, and in my case 'on' was upwards.

---

[7] OSPRE stands for Objective Structured Performance Related Examination for promotion to sergeant and inspector. Each promotion exam is in two parts: the first broadly equating to testing theory and law, and the second concerning decision making based on a series of scenarios. OSPRE is recognised by NPIA, but the examination process has had a highly critical press in recent years with increasing restiveness on the parts of some chief officers who do not see OSPRE as related in any significant way to identifying the leadership potential in prospective sergeants and inspectors. An equal counter-impetus comes from a powerful vested-interest lobby of examination owners and practitioners who campaign for its retention. Some forces have abandoned part two of OSPRE in favour of in-force recommendation, assessment and interview. Neyroud (*Review*, 2011) calls for OSPRE to be replaced.

The Home Office does not provide data for researchers (alas) on the number of people who leave the police service because of frustration at not being promoted to, or selected for, chief officer. That is because the conducting of exit interviews with departing or 'passed over' officers is in its infancy (though normal enough practice outside the police service) and, characteristically of the police service, is not done in all forces. A number of chief officers commented freely that they would have left the service had their upward rise been baulked or made more difficult, but that is not the same as evidence about the motivation of those who do leave. There is a self-selected inevitability, perhaps, about chief officers commenting on how they attained ACPO status and their routes for getting there, which does not always assist in understanding which kinds of officer would fall by the wayside and why.

The same sturdy independence that characterises the way in which police constables take charge in a crisis may be found among those who have risen to chief officer, and some even hark back nostalgically to the days when they were lower ranking:[8]

> **Interviewee 25:** No; the best role I ever had, when I was happiest of all, was inspector. When I was a BCU [Basic Command Unit] commander, I was initially content to remain one, but after four years I became weary of my idiot bosses and decided to join them. I battled for another three years to get a recommendation from my chief [constable], and lost three years' potential seniority as a result.

Another interviewee, newly promoted, was keen to point out to me that being a chief officer is no bed of roses:

> **Interviewee 80:** I really enjoyed being a superintendent and chief superintendent. You were so close to being an expert at that point. I was a detective and in absolute charge of complex investigations and chief officers deferred to me. Now I'm a chief officer, I'm

---

[8] Though we must again note, in this context, how the chief officer's 'recommendation' of a candidate chief officer continues to be a key element of patronage, and how it is unlikely that candidate chief officers could move upwards without it. I recall commiserating with an Army officer colleague who had been horrified at receiving 'only' an Excellent grading in his annual assessment. We all knew that he needed a Top Excellent to be selected to go to staff college (and thus to be eligible for further promotion, perhaps to General). The parallel with chief police officer selection is apt and underlines how subjectivity and personal opinions continue to dominate most selection procedures.

> expected to be master of all trades, but actually I think I'm just
> [a] Jack-in-office.

There is a sense in which nostalgia is a driver in these reflections, but this is so prevalent a comment that the police service generally could well be missing out on opportunities to develop officers laterally as much as they develop them vertically. Some who arrive at the coveted chief officer rank are quite disillusioned by the demands made of them:

> **Interviewee 38:** I'm sent hither and yon and very seldom are my
> opinions listened to. And the job is less secure. If I'd known then
> what I know now, I wouldn't have gone for ACPO, I can tell you.[9]

Others by contrast find the role of chief officer personally satisfying because of what they can get from it and are honest enough (privately) to say so:

> **Interviewee 74:** I'm in this role for the status and power –
> there's very minimal financial reward and nobody who wants to
> be rich would ever go into public service anyway. But the job has
> considerable status and I have lots of power and influence, which
> suits me and suits my ambitions. For all that, I actually think that I
> was promoted too early and climbed the ranks at too fast a pace.
> But I can say that now I have got here.

Some see the attaining of chief officer rank as the only, or the most effective, way to influence change, while others admit to early ambition and a deliberate strategy:

> **Interviewee 14:** I was lucky to be picked out early for high rank
> and so could apply myself to getting the right profile and doing
> the right jobs.
>
> [Interviewer: What were the 'right jobs'?]

---

[9] A report called *Stepping Up: Making the Move to ACPO* (Hay Group, 2010) by Research, Development and Statistics in the Home Office and made the subject of an article in *Police Review* on 26 February 2010, p 31. The subtitle of the report is *A Review of the Demands and Attractions of ACPO Level Roles and the Way the Police Service Manages Talent into those Roles.* One comment in the report is apposite: 'Candidates need particular support in changing their self-image and in "unlearning" some of the things that made them successful earlier in their careers.' This research chimes with the comments made by Interviewees 80 and 38 above, and a number of similar comments from ACCs.

> Oh, things like being on Home Office committees and groups, learning thoroughly things like offender interview techniques or seeing neighbourhood policing coming over the hill, and positioning the force to take advantage of that. Yes, and doing something for a chief officer which obliges him. It's playing the system.

Human resources specialists call this tactical positioning 'managing upwards', but there is a sense here in which the aspirant chief officer ensured that situations and careful manipulation of obligations were deliberately engineered in order to obtain the vital 'recommendation' for ACPO rank.

Another officer was also determined that she would 'play the system', her persistence eventually paying off:

> **Interviewee 11:** I was a teacher in the private sector but decided it was not for me and was looking for other jobs. My husband had joined the police and so I thought OK let's go for it. I loved it once I was in but I always knew I'd never remain a constable. In fact I wasn't the best constable in the world and was infinitely happier doing the supervisory job. I was an acting sergeant before I'd completed probation.
>
> I realised that I could aspire to ACPO – which before had simply not been on my radar – when I had a job as a staff officer and thought I can do this just as well as him![10] No one thought to put me on accelerated promotion.
>
> Yet even when I was put up to try the PNAC it wasn't clear what was wanted. I lacked the necessary experiential learning I suppose, but I must have impressed someone because on the third attempt, I got through the gateway process.[11]

Others, including this female chief officer, had a more purposeful agenda:

> **Interviewee 76:** Not accident. I intended from joining to get as near the top as I could in the course of a shortish police career and I gave myself 20 years from entry to chief officer, and achieved it

---

[10] Chief constables, and occasionally deputy chief constables, have staff officers who organise their working days, meetings, travel, visits, conferences and so on. Sometimes staff officers to chief constables are chief inspectors, but more usually they are superintendents, and in a pivotal position to meet and influence others in the hierarchy.

[11] See Chapter One for an explanation of the gateway process (PNAC).

fairly easily. This was when I actually encountered more chauvinism and prejudice than my time as a constable and sergeant.

She develops this theme by arguing that female officers continue to be disadvantaged once they reach ACPO rank and that some jobs seem closed to them:

Interviewee 76: To the collective judgment of the Chief Constables' Council, a female commissioner of the Met is inconceivable. They might give you CC [chief constable] of some smaller force, but nothing substantial like the West Midlands, Merseyside or the Met. I'm horrified frankly that such attitudes are not more robustly challenged, but the politicians, even people like Jacqui Smith and Harriet Harman,[12] are too busy fighting petty political battles to see that women are held back in the police and the irony is that it is in the top jobs that this happens, not in the lower ranks. I was more 'equal' as an inspector that I am now as a chief constable.

It is not possible to ascertain objectively whether there is a latent prejudice or discrimination against women for the most senior roles in policing or whether or not sufficient candidates of the right calibre have proffered themselves, or even whether this is a perception rather than fact. The recent chief constables of South Wales and of Devon and Cornwall have been women, and neither force can be considered small. It is worth noting too that none of the interviewees, even under the guarantee of anonymity, made *any* remarks to me that could have been construed remotely as gender prejudiced. I certainly did not encounter such sentiments directly in the course of the research for this book, which is not to say they do not exist of course, merely that they may be unspoken.

However, it is hard to prove a negative. The only discrimination case to attain anything like national publicity was that of Alison Halford, the first female chief officer in Britain when appointed as assistant chief constable in 1983 to the command team in Merseyside Police, after a glittering career in the Metropolitan Police. She applied nine times for further promotion at Merseyside and outside, but did not receive

---

[12] Jacqui Smith was Home Secretary from 2006 to 2008. Harriet Harman, a long-serving Labour minister, Attorney General and acting leader of the Labour Party after the May 2010 general election, is a prominent spokesperson for women's rights. No female police officer has commanded the large 'metropolitan' forces of West Midlands, Merseyside, Greater Manchester or London. None has been president of ACPO either.

the crucial recommendation from her Chief Constable, Sir Kenneth Oxford. Eventually she brought a sex discrimination claim against Merseyside Police and won. She retired in 1992. Her case was a *cause célèbre* at the time, as was her account of how she was treated.[13]

A retired chief constable, Della Cannings, speaking at a British Association for Women in Policing (BAWP) Conference in April 2009 wondered if part of the problem of poor representation of women at ACPO level was that, once promoted, '[female] chief officers pull up the ladder after them' and do not spend enough time nurturing and bringing on female officers in the ranks below. BAWP's own newsletters however show considerable activity by the (relatively few) female chief officers in networking, mentoring and publicising the contributions made by female police officers.[14] That there are still, proportionately, too few women among the chief officers is, however, self-evident (Table 2.1).

Table 2.1: Female chief officers in England and Wales in 2010[15]

Chief officer rank (including equivalents)	Number of female officers	Percentage of chief officers
chief constable	5	12% of CCs, 2% of all
deputy chief constable	7	16% of DCCs, 3% of all
assistant chief constable	23	18% of ACCs, 11% of all
Total	**35**	**16% of all chief officer ranks**

Barbara Wilding, retiring in December 2009 as Chief Constable of South Wales Police commented in an interview with *The Daily Telegraph* that

---

[13] See *No Way Up the Greasy Pole*, 1993.

[14] Della Cannings retired as Chief Constable of North Yorkshire in 2007. Her remarks were reported in *Police Review*, 17 April 2009, p 11. BAWP's newsletter is available from its website www.bawp.org. The home page there for BAWP notes that it was 'founded in 1987, and is the only organisation in the UK to draw members from all ranks and grades of the police service, both male and female, and associated organisations. We have representatives not only from most of the 'geographical' forces throughout England, Scotland, Wales and Northern Ireland, but also from many others – including British Transport Police, Guernsey Police, Isle of Man Constabulary, Ministry of Defence Police, and RAF Police.'

[15] Statistics are extrapolated from Hazell's (2010) *Police and Constabulary Almanac*, and confirmed by the Home Office (see Sigurdsson and Mulchandani, 2010).

> We're not representative at all yet. We definitely need
> more women chief constables because we bring a different
> dimension to the debate.[16]

To set this in context, women now constitute a quarter (25%) of all
serving police officers in England and Wales, but this does not find
proportional reflection in the top posts, where the percentage is
16%. These data may change in time. A report by the Home Office
(2010a) entitled *Assessment of Women in the Police Service* noted that
'the recruitment and representation of female officers has improved
significantly in the last decade'. To show the weight of the increase, the
report contrasted 2009 data with that for 1999 and showed that the
35 women currently in ACPO (Table 2.1), compares with 11 in 1999,
while there are 180 women in the superintendent/chief superintendent
ranks compared with 57 in 1999, and 1,393 female inspectors/chief
inspectors compared with 427 in 1999. The data are not simply numeric,
but proportionate too. The likelihood of a woman being promoted to
higher ranks is now higher than for a man, once past sergeant.[17] It is
probable that ACPO candidates have many more hurdles to surmount
before the proportion of female chief officers changes significantly, but
the potential for change is certainly impending. It lends weight to a
remark by a female interviewee:

Interviewee 50: Yes, I was quite ambitious. I looked at those above
and thought 'There's no mystery to this; I could do it,' and besides,
I had colleagues who kept urging me on and pointing to the few
women who had made it to chief officer level.

The employment analyst Tracey Carr carried out research in 2005–06
into reasons why women did not obtain proportionately as many as
men of the very highest jobs in commerce, industry and public service.
Her summary findings make interesting reading:

---

[16] Reported in *The Daily Telegraph* for 26 December 2009, www.telegraph.co.uk/news/
newstopics/politics/lawandorder/6874902/Quarter-of-police-officers-are-women-
figures-show.html; accessed 13 January 2010: 'Almost 35,000 out of the 141,647
police officers in England and Wales are now women – for the first time representing
a quarter of all police.'

[17] Data drawn from *Assessment of Women in the Police Service*, 24 February 2010a, Home
Office, available from http://library.npia.police.uk/docs/homeoffice/assessment-
women-police-service.pdf; accessed 22 June 2010, and reported as *Assessment of
Women In Policing* in www.policeprofessional.com/news.aspx?id=9994; accessed 11
March 2010.

- Women don't network enough – through lack of confidence and know how.
- Women do not put themselves forward for promotion or new projects, unless they are fully confident of doing the job. This means that they are less likely to apply for challenging or high-profile positions.
- Although flexible working arrangements [may be] on offer, women may feel that their career prospects will suffer if they take these up.
- Women do not use their considerable relationship and communication skills enough in influencing and negotiating in the workplace.
- Women praise and sell their teams, each other, their families, but don't talk about the things they have done. They assume other people will notice. (adapted from Carr, 2007)

In other words, women have the skills to succeed but do not push themselves into notice as assertively or as brashly as their male counterparts, and are less likely to draw attention to their own qualities and capabilities. Judging by the comments and demeanour of many of the female chief officers whom I interviewed, there is a clear correlation from Carr's research into the police service.

Perhaps the ultimate test of real equality in the police will be when female chief officers are appointed to the very top jobs, though one aspirant noted that

> **Interviewee 11:** I am under no illusion: I will not get a top policing job this side of Hell freezing over.

But another commented more hopefully that

> **Interviewee 40:** [...] miracles could always happen. Besides, I and my other female colleagues feel that if you're not in, you can't make a difference. I'd probably go further in another profession, such as medicine or academe, but I wouldn't do as much direct good as in this job.

Such philosophical weariness is characteristic of the attitude of many female chief officers in interview; as is their steely determination to stand firm. The relative paucity of female chief officers compared with their male counterparts surely places an onus on the latter and on the

Home Office and HMIC to ensure that their female colleagues receive proportionate representation?[18]

Security of tenure and confidence in the role

I noted briefly above how some chief officers have found that the advancement in rank to membership of the ACPO policing elite is not all that it promised. Disillusionment had set in and their sense of permanence was tenuous. More generally, interviewees were asked whether the role(s) they had performed had made them feel insecure. Was it ever a case of 'uneasy lies the head that wears a crown'?[19]

> **Interviewee 7:** Sometimes very insecure indeed. Being a chief officer can be very exposed and it's really unforgiving out there in the harsh light of day: so many want you to fail, from your rivals to the police authority to the media; all hoping and waiting for you to put a foot wrong.

The sense of exposure and vulnerability in this comment is perhaps extreme, and there are plenty of chief officers who experience only minor twinges of unease rather than thoroughgoing insecurity:

> **Interviewee 21:** Only if I am not master of my brief. I have wobbled once or twice, when my grasp on detail was a little shaky, but not so much since I really applied myself to knowing absolutely all of the spectrum of what we do.

Table 2.2 summarises the preponderance of responses.

Table 2.2: Confidence in the chief officer role

Response	Number	Percentage
Uneasy a lot of the time	39	42%
Uneasy sometimes	26	28%
Not uneasy	18	19%
Secure	10	11%
Totals	**93**	**100%**

It can be seen that 70% of the chief officers surveyed have felt uneasy in their positions, and more than half of these have felt substantially

---

[18] See for example the work done by the American academic, Brian Kingshott (2009).

[19] Pedants' corner: from Shakespeare's *Henry IV*, Part 2 (1597), Act 3, sc. 1, line 31.

uneasy or insecure, while only about a third of all those surveyed felt secure and untroubled. For a police service that prides itself on its robustness and on its confident public face, these private revelations of misgiving may surprise some, yet they are a predictable product of the confidential interview process: if chief officers know that they will not be identified, they may expose, momentarily, vulnerabilities that they normally keep hidden. David Silverman, in his masterly 2000 book on qualitative research, noted potential for a kind of conspiracy of sympathy in this process, generating

> [...] culturally rich methods through which interviewers and interviewees, in concert, generate plausible accounts of the world. (Silverman, 2000, pp 122–3)

which means that you and I must be constantly aware of the potential for manipulation of that 'consensus of reality' by the anonymous interviewee. For the most part, the gain in honesty ('warts and all') outweighs the occasional disingenuous pleading by those I spoke to in confidence.

A constant focus for chief officer uneasiness is in relationships with oversight bodies of various kinds that I analyse in Chapter Four. Here I will focus on the uneasiness that can arise, according to those interviewed, from two discrete areas: role competence and security of tenure in the appointment. On the latter, assistant chief constables used to be (and some still are) granted permanent salaried appointments, and therefore can only be removed from their posts for the same reasons that would entail dismissal in any of the police ranks below them. By contrast, deputy chief constables and chief constables,[20] usually have fixed term appointments (FTAs), which are much disliked:

> **Interviewee 18:** These FTAs are a pain and hold you to ransom if your police authority don't like the way you are running your force. More importantly, FTAs inhibit any long-term planning in the police.

Not one of the chief officers I spoke to was in favour of FTAs. Indeed it seems orthodoxy to decry them. This general disenchantment was made

---

[20] Some appointments vary at chief constable level and beyond (president of ACPO, chief executive officer of the NCA for example), while the Commissioner of the City of London Police and the Deputy Commissioner and Commissioner of the Metropolitan Police are separate appointments again, with different conditions of employment. Here we consider the norm rather than the exception.

explicit by ACPO in its written response to the previous government's 2008 Green Paper:

> Fixed Term Appointments are detrimental to organisational development and strategic partnerships. [...] This reform has a number of unintended and wholly negative impacts which we have raised with the Home Office. ACPO would like to see them removed or adapted in ways which restore equality between Chief Officers and Police Authorities. (ACPO, 2008b, para 7.13.1, p 47)

ACPO notes elsewhere in the same document that:

> The [...] Green Paper fails to acknowledge the impact and influence of [FTAs] of a maximum of five years. FTAs have increased the turnover of chief constables so that there is a constant churn of leadership, which ACPO considers to be detrimental to organisational development and partnership building. FTAs, more than any other factor, put a strain on the pipeline of talent. (ACPO 2008b, para 5.17, p 31)

This official response finds reflection at the individual level. One senior chief officer noted that his FTA made him 'very uneasy':

> **Interviewee 28:** [...] although I have a five-year one with two years still to run on it. It's scary to be subject in this way to an appointment which I cannot influence and which could be terminated without my being able to do a damned thing to stop it. But, this job is not the be-all and end-all of my life and I am confident that, if I leave policing, I am employable elsewhere. This gives me some confidence in these shifting sands of resource constraints, financial pressures and political interference.
>
> [Interviewer: Could you say something more about the political interference you've experienced?]
>
> I've already said too much, and more than I meant to.

Another, equally senior, believed that

> **Interviewee 64:** I'm less secure now, as a chief constable on an FTA, than I was when I was an ACC on a permanent contract. You

can see the teeth being bared in the police authority, as the FTA draws to an end, and they enjoy seeing you squirm: shall we renew? Shall we look for someone else? Shall we tell him? No, let him sweat!

I don't say I have sleepless nights, but I make plans and examine options, lest they chuck me out. The PA [police authority] as a whole becomes more querulous, pickier, less satisfied, when it thinks it has you over a barrel.

One chief officer thought that the FTA was

Interviewee 4: [...] a real bugbear and a nonsense from the commercial world.[21] The police collectively is a public service and there should be a national structure for pay and appointments, not local arrangements.

Others find the job itself inherently insecure because it seems to embrace perpetual flux:

Interviewee 73: The trick is to keep running since a moving target is always harder to hit than one which is static.

[Interviewer: Do you feel that you are a target?]

Well, in the sense that I'm standing in people's way to the top, yes. Would they really go all-out to get me out? Some would, undoubtedly. Others would make supportive public noises but conspire behind the scenes. It's not just the police authority or HMIC or the media which contribute to the precariousness of the job; it's the seismic and continual changes in policing itself and you always have to be ahead of the curve or you'll be cut to pieces. It's hellishly unstable being at the top.

[Interviewer: That sounds to me like a philosophy of despair.]

---

[21] As I remark in the main text, some police authorities have begun to insist on FTAs for all chief officers, rather than permanent contracts for ACCs, so that *any* chief officer incumbent could be dispensed with if need be at the conclusion of the FTA. Police authorities and latterly the PCCs may simply refuse to renew or extend the standard five-year term. At the time of writing (2011), this has not yet been challenged in court but it is probably only a matter of time before a legal ruling on the termination of FTAs is sought. One problem for litigants is that the FTA is not a contract of employment. See also Home Office, 'Fixed Term Appointments for Senior Police Officers', 2002, London: HO Circular 68/2002.

I'm sure you're right; but it's how it is.

It seems that the pressures of the job, together with all kinds of external scrutiny, can make some post holders discomfited as they look at the threats which encompass them:

Interviewee 65: The police appear as a confident, self-reliant bunch – they have to look the part to do the job. If this interview was not anonymous, I'd stop right there but under wraps I'm happy to say that there have been times when I've been very, very uneasy indeed. Have I made the right decision? Will the police authority wear that? Will anyone find out about that? Did that journalist understand me? Will my FTA be extended? Should I look for another job? Even, is policing still for me? But you overcome it: you 'keep calm and carry on'.[22]

One reflective chief officer analysed the nature of the flux and change that affects the police like this:

Interviewee 27: In my view, the police service (like other agencies) is increasingly being asked to provide a five star service on three star funding and the expectations of those who hold us to account for delivery (government, inspectorates, the media, some sections of the public, etc.) are not always realistic. There is an increasing army of bureaucrats developing aspirational standards for policing which are neither pragmatic in the real world nor backed by appropriate resources. I always use the analogy that modern day policing is a bit like a queen-sized quilt on a king-sized bed. It doesn't matter how much you pull it around, it doesn't fit and something ends up being exposed. Against that background, the ultimate responsibility attached to [the] office of chief constable can make it quite a lonely one.

While some critics of the police might regard these comments as 'special pleading', there is no doubt that chief officers *can* feel beleaguered and that what they deliver as 'policing' is too often a matter of damned-if-you-do and damned-if-you-don't – provoking negativity no matter how hard forces and their leaders strive. Some of the more disillusioned of comments reproduced in this chapter are perhaps testament to the

---

[22] This particular chief officer had a coffee mug with 'Keep calm and carry on' printed on it. The mug in which he gave me coffee, read 'Now panic and freak out'.

impossibility of providing 'five star service on three star funding'. Really severe resource constraints in the wake of the economic recession mean it will only get more difficult to deliver that service.

However, the same officer goes on to remark:

> **Interviewee 27:** It would be wrong to allow the threat of losing your job to dictate your actions. There is a great deal of scrutiny and accountability that goes with the job but the greatest motivation to succeed comes from an inbuilt sense of public duty and responsibility.

and indeed, that sense of 'public duty and responsibility' comes across strongly in chief officers' comments about policing itself, which I examine in more detail in Chapter Six.

Other interviewees considered that an intrusive and querulous media pose direct threats to the job:

> **Interviewee 5:** I've felt uneasy a few times; once especially when I was the target of a media campaign. It's hard when the first question a reporter asks is 'Are you going to resign, Chief Constable?'

while some breezily point to the pressures on relationships which can be hard for others to handle:

> **Interviewee 33:** Me? No. Cops are mostly type A personalities:[23] they only feel insecure when their nearest and dearest go off the rails. Otherwise they are so used to sorting other people out that feeling unsure or uneasy never enters the equation.

Others insist that the greatest unease in the job is in the way that it affects marriages and partnerships:

> **Interviewee 57:** At times it can be desperately insecure; this is a fraught organisation for fidelity and it's clear that broken relationships are the commonest cause of what brings people down.

---

[23] 'Type A' personalities are those who are outgoing, confident people, good in a crisis but often reticent about their own feelings and worries; the main research in this area of behavioural psychology has been done by the American behaviourist Meyer Friedman (1996); see also Digman (1990) and O'Neal (2009).

Official data on failed relationships, divorce or separation are not gathered on the police at any level, but there is a great deal of anecdotal evidence and individual testimony that, particularly in the detective ranks, personal relationships are often a casualty of the job. Whether that persists in any wholesale way into chief officer ranks is not clear. Several chief officers remarked that they had 'lost relationships' to the job but numeric or objective evidence is actually pretty sparse. A number of interviewees made the counter point that they are able to survive as chief officers only because a loving partner is loyally shoring up the domestic side of life.

A chief officer who considered that his learning programme on the SCC did not adequately prepare him for the sudden and complete immersion that occurred on joining the chief officer ranks, commented:

> **Interviewee 61:** Oh yes, I was on my very first appointment. I was scared shitless that someone would find out that I hadn't the first idea of what I should be doing. It's different now, I'm quite confident that no one will ever find out! Seriously, though, I didn't think that the Senior Command Course [SCC] prepared me for the reality of the first few months as an ACC. I had not been prepared for the intensity of it, the incessant demands or for the expectations which came with the job. There isn't a honeymoon period to settle in and look around from the new height. It's just join, get your remit, these are your responsibilities and bang: deliver!
>
> Maybe the SCC should be preparing people for the operational pitfalls, the kinds of chief constables you might meet and the wolverines that are your fellow ACPO officers, through 'acting up' or 'shadowing'.[24]

Where this leaves us is that, while many (perhaps even most) chief officers would admit privately to plenty of fears and uneasiness in the job, outwardly and publicly they radiate confidence and self-assurance. Such dissembling, probably inherent in any command role, may actually induce hesitation and over-caution, and may contribute to the frequent observation from the police service itself, that it is becoming risk averse.

---

[24] We should note that candidates for PNAC and the SCC are recommended to do precisely this in preparation for attendance, see PNAC (2010, p 16).

Relations with peers

There are two essential aspects to this: one is the relationship between members of the 'top team' within a single police force and the other is more generally between ACPO members on regional or national bodies or looser groupings of interest. Added to this are relationships forged on the SCC, relationships between adjoining and cooperative forces and also relationships between post holders, such as the Chief Constables' Council or holders of the 'portfolios' of national Business Areas. These networks are wide-ranging and complex.

When questioned about relationships within the chief officer ranks, one interviewee noted that they were

> **Interviewee 27:** Supportive and professional, and courteous. There are huge networks of contacts and influences at work in ACPO and they are forged when you are at the SCC. This was where I made relationships which have endured. I can call on lots of people for support or comment or help across a wide spectrum of things. That's quite comforting.

Another officer also noted the cordiality which characterised some chief officer relationships, but with a strong caveat that suggested considerable distrust:

> **Interviewee 15:** It's actually astonishing how many other chief officers I know. I was in a meeting the other day and realised that I knew everyone in the room – there were about 30 of us – because they'd either been on courses with me, had been on the SCC with me or I had known them from other projects. When you look at it like that, ACPO is actually very small and tight. But would I have them home to dinner and introduce them to my family? A very few. Many of them go out of their way to score points and look good – sometimes at your expense – others simply don't care about anyone else. Not a savoury lot, you know; they carry their knives carefully concealed.

Another chief officer is equally cynical about the superficiality of good relations masking an unspoken threat:

> **Interviewee 69:** I am under no illusion about my peers nor are they about me. We all know each other well, warts and all, and we trust each other as long as we can see both hands above the

table and can hear everything that is said. We are only supportive of each other when there is no rivalry, or no threat posed to the other's advancement.

If the chance to shine is on offer, then you really see naked ambition. I have to say that seeing chief officers toadying to ministers is one of the more nauseating of spectacles.

while this officer evidently believes the worst of his ACPO colleagues:

Interviewee 58: I regard the mass of my peers – the other 200 odd – with disfavour and disdain. They'd fuck me up as soon as look at me: I know that and they know that, and that's why they never get a look in.

[Interviewer: You'll excuse me saying that yours is rather an extreme position, isn't it? Surely they can't all be out to disrupt you?]

Well that shows how little you know, doesn't it? If you've never been on the inside, you can't know what goes on, can you? Some of them would put their own mothers on the streets if they thought it would advance them half a yard.

Very few of those interviewed adopted a position as extreme as this, but plenty of others did not scruple in their judgments of their peers:

Interviewee 22: I'll tell you there are some of my peers who ought to be in Care in the Community, others who need psychiatric counselling and one or two who are clinically insane.

[Interviewer: Can you explain how you know this?]

Oh you won't catch me that way. No names; no libel. Anyway, after all this time of climbing up the slippery pole, which of us are really sane?

and there is, or appears to be, a pervasive undercurrent of distrust and suspicion, among many chief officers. Others try to take a broader perspective when it comes to alliances and enmities:

Interviewee 8: The police service is a big organisation of 140,000 or so. There will be those who hate you, those who love you and those who don't give a toss about you. You know very quickly which is which wherever you are.

while some treat peer group rivalry as a matter for light humour:

> **Interviewee 63:** About half will support you through anything. The other half can't wait to kick away your crutches.

Against this prevailing vein of disparagement and scepticism, only a small number of chief officers seem positive; ranging from the laconic to the contextual:

> **Interviewee 51:** There's no more back-biting or jockeying at this level than at any other rank in the police business. What you mustn't do is let it get to you and put you off your stride.

but those who see their peers as rivals and competitors wear careful masks themselves:

> **Interviewee 40:** I'm always careful that the face my peers see is the face I want them to see. I do wish that police leaders could be more confident of their abilities to lead – they tend to the cloned and suspicious, not amenable to any outside influences.

One sagely observed that chief officers' knowledge of each other could be superficial:

> **Interviewee 3:** What happened with Mike Todd[25] was a surprise to most of us, I guess. But then, what do we really know of each other? You see your colleagues for set times in set meetings each day, or every other day, you don't live in each other's pockets.

Another asked

> **Interviewee 49:** Do you know why police officers have big boots?
>
> [Interviewer: Tell me.]
>
> So that they can stamp on your fingers as you grasp the rungs of the ladder beneath them.

---

[25] Michael Todd was Chief Constable of Greater Manchester Police and met his death in obscure circumstances in Snowdonia on 11 March 2008. Sexual affairs with junior officers and other inappropriate relationships were subsequently alleged. See Scott-Lee (2009). The inquest returned a narrative verdict (ibid.).

Perhaps the most negative comment of all was this, by an experienced chief officer:

> **Interviewee 67:** I don't care what the bastards think.

and this remark from another helps to give the whole opinion-sampling exercise a wry context:

> **Interviewee 72:** Other chief officers always have some conspiracy or other on the go – in fact some don't thrive without a good dose of paranoia. Others are inveterate gossips: who's up, who's down, who's in, who's out – all a bit trivial and pointless, I think. It can be an incestuous world, the upper echelons of policing.

Comment

I don't think I was prepared when I began this sampling of chief officers' opinions, for the depth of suspicion and distrust which characterises many of their private comments about their colleagues. Many of them really do seem to believe that their colleagues in the wider chief officer world would scruple at nothing to advance themselves and there was a strong undercurrent of uneasiness about survival in such a competitive world. While most respondents were men, I met a number of female chief officers who were equally ill-at-ease about what one of them called 'shark-infested ACPO'. This would not be surprising in the world of commodity markets say, or in some pressured senior common rooms, but in a service which prides itself on pulling together (where indeed, *team working* is a specific competence), the sometimes raw savagery which chief officers displayed about each other, was a bit unnerving. No doubt it is a release from being publicly benign and collegiate.

Work–life balance

Chief officers are renowned throughout the police service for their long hours culture, and for the amount of personal stress that results from heavy workloads and the time they spend on the job (Caless, 2005), which, like junior doctors in the National Health Service, gives rise to anxiety that, sometimes, chief officers may be too tired to think straight and may make a wrong decision with literal life or death consequences. Because of their status in having a fixed term appointment, most chief officers can derogate from the European Working Time Directive which applies to other police officers and staff, and which generally limits the average maximum working week to 48 hours.[26] There is therefore no statutory upper limit to the hours that chief officers can work. Some have voiced concern about the example which such workaholics give to their subordinate staff, who may (willingly or unwillingly) embrace 'presenteeism' to get their own work done in support of the driven individuals in the top team. A further concern is about the 'role model message' that excessive time spent at work by chief officers is sending to their workforces at large and what it may suggest to those who aspire to become chief officers themselves (Calvert et al, 2009).

Human resources departments in many parts of working life, not just in policing, deprecate a work-obsessed mentality, pointing to ample evidence that those who do have a work–life balance are adjusted individuals who have their working lives in perspective and who also can make time for families, children, partners, social skills, additional learning, fitness and relaxation. They are less likely to be ill, less likely to die 'in harness', less likely to make errors of judgement or tactical mistakes, less likely to be divorced or estranged and less likely to suffer long-term health problems such as heart attacks, diabetes and dementia. They also have better relationships with their offspring and families. By contrast, those who carry massive work burdens and spend very long periods without respite from them, especially those who work consistently in excess of 65 hours a week, risk directly negative outcomes (O'Driscoll et al, 2008).

Contemporary research has shown that regular overtime may have links with coronary disease. These findings come from a study of 6,000 British civil servants where, after accounting for known heart risk factors such as smoking, doctors found those who worked *three to four hours of overtime a day* ran a 60% higher risk of coronary-related illness. The researchers said there could be a number of explanations for this: people who spend more time at work have less time to exercise, relax and unwind; consequently they may be stressed, more prone to anxiety and to suffer from depression. Career-intensive people, like chief police officers, are often highly driven, aggressive or irritable, and they may also see illness simplistically as weakness; so come into

---

[26] There was correspondence in *The Times* in August 2010 about junior doctors' hours, which gives an interesting comparative side light on the hours worked by chief officers, see: www.thetimes.co.uk/tto/opinion/letters/article2681350.ece; accessed 11 August 2010. The correspondence developed subsequently, with arguments that observance of the European Working Time Directive prevented young doctors from accumulating necessary surgical/clinical experience (see Rose, 2010).

work when they are not fit and thus increase their incidence of stress (and make other people ill).[27]

There is no doubt that the current police culture at many levels involves long periods of the day spent at work; that officers believe that they have to be seen to be at work to be taken seriously; and that workloads are so high that their continual presence is demanded to ensure that a backlog does not build (Caless, 2005). One chief officer noted that he 'nearly always' needed to work on into the evenings after everyone else had gone home, merely to keep up with his 'in-tray'; because so much of his 'normal' working day was spent in chairing or attending meetings.

It is probably necessary to note that constables and sergeants are paid overtime for any extra duty outside their rostered hours, and compensation for loss of 'rest days' is mandatory. The overtime budget for each police force is scrutinised carefully by its police authority/ PCC, which will not hesitate to challenge a rise in costs. HMIC too, will challenge forces whose operational success comes at the cost of a large overtime spend.[28] Police constables and sergeants have come to rely on the permanent prospect of paid overtime to supplement their salaries, and view the reduction in overtime opportunities with dismay (see footnote). However, no overtime is payable at inspector and above, and this is often where the pressures for the long hours culture begin, for police staff as well as for police officers. I recall clearly the insertion into my first employment contract with the police (after it specified that my 'statutory working week was 37.5 hours)[29], the words 'and such additional hours as are necessary for the completion of the work'. The culture of long hours in the workplace seemed then to be part of police 'furniture', and was so familiar that it would have looked perverse had I challenged it: how else could all the job be done except by working longer? At the time (1999), I regarded it as entirely normal that extra hours would be worked voluntarily and I have seen nothing subsequently in contemporary policing to say that it is no longer done. This is particularly exacerbated at senior management level where unpaid overtime is regarded as part of the job.

By the time police officers reach chief officer rank, it is common for them to work a 70–75 hour week and there is almost a 'macho'

---

[27] Summarised from Virtanen, M. et al. (2010). There were contemporary summaries in the main newspapers (see Bosely, 2010) and also the BBC http://news.bbc.co.uk/1/hi/health/8674372.stm

[28] The coalition government quickly targeted police overtime to make savings and has cut the annual £450 million budget for overtime (see Edwards, 2010).

[29] A 40-hour working week less five lunch breaks at 30 minutes each.

culture where officers vie to be longest at work (see comments below and, for example, Brough and Biggs, 2009). One individual noted in interview with me that he had had only four days off *in three years*, and said it in such a way as to invite approbation. These heavy workloads and long periods spent at work are not only for those chief officers in demanding operational jobs, such as overseeing force responses to terrorism or major crime (where occasional sustained bursts of activity can be expected) but also for those overseeing disciplinary matters, volume crimes, logistics, territorial policing, 'informatics' or personnel and training. All seem subject to the same expectation that they will be seen to be present, and for the same enormously long working weeks, irrespective of the actual events on the ground and of the urgency of the task.[30] Either the job of chief officer is a previously unsuspected elixir of life and holds all the pleasures and enjoyment in existence, or these people have some explaining to do. Accordingly chief officers were asked: *What do you do to 'balance' your life outside policing? Does it work – do you feel, therefore, that your life is in balance?*

One individual thought that the key to her survival as a chief officer was a balanced home life and supportive family, and that those who worked obsessively without such balance could be dangerous:

> **Interviewee 55:** I benefit from a safe and secure family life and a circle of supportive friends. I believe that those who do not have this around them are often out of balance, and whilst they may be workaholics, I do not believe this is in the long term of benefit either to the force or the individual. The Home Office and HM Inspectorate of Constabulary should examine this in more detail. Chief officers' working habits quickly become those of the force and have the potential to skew judgment.

But, more prevalently, another was unashamed of his enormous work pattern, finding most of what he needed in the job itself:

> **Interviewee 52:** I don't do a lot [of life balance]; I find the job all-absorbing. I do 80 or more hours a week at this role, though it's not something I think I could sustain for more than five or 10 years.

---

[30] I accept of course that chief officers have duties additional to those of their occupational 'portfolios', such as attending public meetings, standing in for the chief constable and acting as 'Gold' commander on weekday evenings and at weekends, but most of these shared duties are rostered well in advance and can be predicted. Time off *could* therefore be taken as compensation for the additional hours (but probably isn't). Chief constables seldom perform 'Gold' roles routinely.

One chief officer recognised the toll that such a long hours culture was having on his life, but, while chafing at the strain, seemed powerless to change the demands on him. His view was that excessive time spent at work was the product of a risk-averse culture, in which no individual would take responsibility for a decision. As a result, he asserts, meetings drag on and on:

> **Interviewee 16:** I think that working such long hours is entirely counterproductive and it's a macho thing to say 'Oh I've done 18 hours today, aren't I dedicated?', when actually the productive time in that 18 hours was probably only 10 hours. The rest is pointless meetings. If I could change one thing in my work–life balance it would be to go to the gym instead of to meetings. But it never will change as long as people are risk averse and want decisions taken collectively. I'll probably die in harness.
>
> [Interviewer: Seriously? You think the job will kill you?]
>
> Well it might. If you stop in this job, there are four or five who will go 'look at me, I can do it, I can do it!' and before you know it, you are passed over and your FTA is not renewed.

But, as research outside policing confirms, family life and relationships can suffer terminal damage because of persistent presence at work, coping with unending demands (Brough and O'Driscoll, 2005). One chief officer related this to policing, noting the pressures that long absence from home and heavy workloads put on family relationships, as well as on the officer concerned:

> **Interviewee 46:** There's this great story that one chief officer's wife put name labels on each of her children, so that her husband would know who was who when he finally came home. What must he have felt? No doubt they're divorced now. The long hours culture is one of the reasons why the police service has such a record of failed relationships. I can count on one hand the number of long-term relationships and marriages which have survived to retirement in this job.

Some can see the problem in others but will not necessarily change themselves:

> **Interviewee 21:** The chief officer cadre is its own worst enemy because it prides itself on long hours of work and being seen to be at work. I'll bet that most of the officers you have spoken to know to the *nth* degree how many hours they work and they'll tell you that with a sort of stubborn pride. Am I right?
>
> [Interviewer: Many chief officers have acknowledged the immense amount of time they put into the job, yes.]
>
> Well, there you are. They work all the hours God ever sent and then boast about it.
>
> [Interviewer: Are you one to talk? What sort of hours do you work?]
>
> Oh I'm as bad as anyone else on the top corridor: in at 07.00, home by 22.00 six days a week and have to be kidnapped to go on holiday. But I make more noise about work–life balance than others do.

while some individuals clearly resent the burdens put on them from above:

> **Interviewee 30:** Only one person in this fucking force has a work–life balance and that's the chief constable. You know what? Nobody turns a hair: nobody gives a damn, nobody exposes it. It's a bloody scandal.
>
> [Interviewer: what have you done about it?]
>
> Nothing, of course. This is the first time I've felt able to talk about it, other than to my ACC colleagues in the top team. We all feel the same though.

Another chief officer, looking at those above him, remarked:

> **Interviewee 68:** The hours they do are utterly mad: the really high-profile chiefs work 20 hour days; when do they sleep? I don't want that.

One chief constable noted that the time spent at work can only be controlled, or regulated, with difficulty. It is in the nature of the job that long and irregular hours have to be worked. Others become impatient of the whole notion of balancing police work against other things:

Interviewee 15: I'm not big on work–life balance; it's not part of my DNA. The level of commitment goes with being in charge, but yes, it comes at some cost. I'm divorced and don't see enough of my children. There was a time when work came first, second and third in my life but now I try to create downtime for the kids or I'll lose touch with them entirely. I don't have time for relationships other than with them, outside the job.

It is in many ways a reflection on the 'workaholism' of this particular chief officer that his time with his children had to be scheduled into his hectic diary. He acknowledged that otherwise the demands of the job would eat even further into his non-working life. Another chief officer was ready to acknowledge the problems of workload and long hours, but seemed to think too that the problems that resulted were intractable as long as the police service thinks of itself as a thing apart:

Interviewee 81: It's really important to remember what an example you set: if you work excessive hours, your staff will feel that they have to as well, and a culture of 'out-machoing' each other can quickly develop. Then people fall over and get really ill. The police service is utterly opposed to flexibility in things like working from home, flexitime or 'nine-day fortnights'. All these things are seen as HR fads, and not part of 'proper' policing.

One chief constable commented:

Interviewee 37: I heard of some chap in Kent who did a study of chief officers' work–life balance and he concluded that they were all quite mad to work the hours they did, and that it would result in an obsessive, sickness-ridden culture. Do you know about that?

[Interviewer: That was me, in fact. I'm not sure that I showed that chief officers were mad, but my study in 2005 did indicate that chief officers worked excessive hours, and that their workloads seemed to demand that kind of commitment.[31] Kent Police have created another ACC post since – not as a direct result of my study of course, but the work that I and my colleagues did five years ago may have contributed to more rational thinking about chief officers' wellbeing. The sickness outcome is real enough, though, as plenty of research studies have shown.]

---

[31] See Caless (2005, 2006).

> Ah well, come and do the same study here, will you? I've got ACCs who seem to live on the premises and a DCC who never goes home.
>
> [Interviewer: And whose fault is that?]

Some chief officers register concern and understand the consequences of working excessively, but their own actions may not always live up to the ideals they espouse:

> **Interviewee 60:** A colleague of mine had a heart attack brought on by overwork and under-exercise, and this brought home to me how important a genuine work–life balance really is. I go home at a reasonable hour after a reasonable day. It is ridiculous to overwork so excessively, and I will have nothing to do with it. My staff simply love it that I have a home life. You ask them.
>
> [Interviewer: I did.]
>
> And?
>
> [Interviewer: They said you went home two nights out of six in good time.]
>
> Ah, need some more work on that, then.

Others are bluntly honest about why they spend so much of their waking lives at work:

> **Interviewee 36:** I run for exercise, but my kids are with their mother hundreds of miles away. I have no other emotional ties and I don't like soap operas on TV. So I work instead, which is much more interesting.
>
> [Interviewer: Don't you think that you need to balance your work ethic with other forms of socialisation?]
>
> You know me; I never have, so I'm not likely to start now, am I?

a point echoed by a senior chief officer in another force, for whom the job really does seem to function like some elixir of life:

> **Interviewee 19:** The problem is that this job is all-absorbing. If my body and my wife could stand it, I'd do this job 20 hours a day for seven days a week – it's so good and the adrenaline fix is so strong.

Such absolutes are not uncommon among police officers, but a consistent pattern of responses to the interview questions suggests that some chief officers know full well what is wrong with their work–life balance, but they are helpless to break the cycle of workload = long hours = more workload:

> **Interviewee 59:** I work stupidly long hours but so do all my colleagues above and below me, and balancing my life is not an option at the moment. [...] I'd like more time away from the job, but can't see how to get it.

Another chief officer believes that the job demands the effort necessary to complete it:

> **Interviewee 79:** I don't have a balanced life or anything which approximates to it. This job takes up all the time I have.

Some reject the notion of such complete work absorption, but their voices are few and far between:

> **Interviewee 64:** It seems to me wrong that workaholics should impose their regimes on those below. Not all of us dream, eat, breathe, fart and digest policing the entire time, but there are sadly plenty of deeply flawed people who do. You need to be ruthless in your time management and stop people seeing you as a convenient download for the problems they should solve themselves.

while some see a bleak future for those who cannot accept that there is more to life than policing:

> **Interviewee 7:** I don't want to end up on my own at the end of my career in policing; worn out and broken by having given everything to a job that no longer needs you. I work really hard at the intimate relationships in my life. Having a life outside policing is vital – if only to show that you are human.
>
> [Interviewer: and what does your 'life outside policing' consist of?]

If I told you out loud it would too easily identify me, so I'll whisper it.

Other chief officers seem to need their families to give them a context:

> **Interviewee 70:** I had to catch a train the other day, instead of using my driver, and my wife said 'welcome to the real world' – so, yes, the family keeps me grounded.

Some, though a very small number, reveal hidden lives of considerable depth:

> **Interviewee 23:** Well, this will surprise you. I write creatively – poetry and fiction. These are huge relaxations and I enjoy them very much. I can't openly identify stuff I've had published for obvious reasons.
>
> [Interviewer: you mean you'd be teased?]
>
> Teased? I wish! No, my colleagues would never take me seriously again. That's why I publish under a pseudonym but you mustn't say what it is. It's a law of diminishing returns if you become too workaholic, but I try to avoid the 75-hour weeks I used to do when I was an ACC.

A few chief officers privately acknowledge that the risks entailed by long hours and a heavy workload are dangerous:

> **Interviewee 36:** For there to be a real work–life balance, long hours and 'presenteeism' have got to end. That's what's killing: just being there to be seen to be there. Yet as soon as anyone tries to break that cycle, they are seen as skivers or idlers. People break in the end. It's not unusual for ACCs to work 75-hour weeks but one day, someone will die because the person in charge was too tired to think straight.

A poignant closing comment is this from a chief officer who recognises that time lost cannot be recaptured. His observation reminds us that there are other losers when work becomes the only thing that matters:

> **Interviewee 81:** I have a picture on my desk of my two sons in a nativity play. I've got the picture because I couldn't go to that nativity play. There was an important police meeting I absolutely

had to attend. I've forgotten that meeting long since, but I haven't forgotten what I missed.

Conclusions

Patronage, which might be described as the (subjective) capability to identify potential and advance it by granting opportunities and giving recognition to achievement, is still a major factor in the selection of chief officers. Chief officers testify constantly to the 'golden finger' and the 'tap on the shoulder' that identified them as having the wit and will to rise. More claim not to have planned that rise than those who did, but we may have to be cautious about a characteristic police culture of self-deprecation. Many, perhaps particularly women, had to push hard to secure recognition, often in the face of apathy or inertia rather than hostility. Personal ambition is a powerful motivator, needing only a stimulus from outside the self. Sometimes that stimulus is the arrival in force of a new chief constable with new ideas and requiring support to implement his or her ideas. This then becomes a central catalyst for the aspirant chief officer, who embraces the new regime and advances with it. This is not an invariable route, of course, but it is a familiar one.

There is a lack of data about those who do not make the cut and who either stay at the lower rank or leave policing. Knowing who gets a needful recommendation and who does not would put selection and promotion in a more objective context. Some officers advance to chief officer very quickly (in fewer than 20 years), while others take longer (21 to 27 years' service); but there seems to be no template for age profile on selection; nor does there seem to be a template for a career path, though it is still relatively unusual to advance to chief officer entirely through the detective ranks.

Uneasiness or insecurity in the role may develop from several causes, including media scrutiny, poor or hostile relations with either the public or police authorities, or both; and finding that being a chief officer is much more exposed to scrutiny and comment than in the ranks below. Many chief officers point to the inherent insecurity of fixed term appointments (FTAs), which offer tenure only in five-year segments and which can be granted or withheld apparently without appeal. This allows police authorities/PCCs to exert very powerful pressures on deputy and chief constables when renewal of an FTA approaches. There is widespread and unanimous dislike of FTAs among chief officers, including in the assistant chief constable ranks, where increasingly, police authorities/PCCs are introducing FTAs instead of permanent contracts. Privately, chief officers admit to uneasiness and self-doubt, but their public demeanour is invariably confident and self-reliant. This may mean that some chief officers wear a mask much of the time. There is nothing wrong with this – many prominent figures in society adopt the personae which they think are appropriate to their standing – except that reliance on the mask may deny chief officers the chance to make a break with convention – for example by working less frenetically – or it may induce risk aversion.

The mask may also conceal the intense rivalry which appears to exist between some chief officers. Peer competition seems to be thriving, if some of the accounts proffered of attitudes to other chief officers are accurate. There seems to be a distinction between the professional support and cooperation which operates within a chief officer's force and the wider, more competitive world of being an ACPO officer. Some appear mildly (not clinically) paranoid about their peers, while others play a lone hand with some relish. The mass of chief officers is described as 'pretty ruthless and unpleasant at times' which of course is a characteristic not restricted to police officers. It can be found in boardrooms, trusts, committees and senior common rooms across the country. However, it seems clear that the 'blue glass ceiling', where disproportionately small numbers of female police officers make it to the top posts, still exists and that male chief officers do not appear generally disposed to change that, despite female officers now making up a quarter of all police strength. This inequity will continue to cause dismay and concern everywhere but in ACPO itself, it seems.

Work–life balance in senior command policing hardly exists. Those few officers who try to develop additional dimensions to their lives do so in a regretful, half-apologetic way, as though it is something shameful. Indeed, private pronouncements on work–life balance appear to be something of a confessional release, judging from the number of chief officers who asked me for reassurance about their anonymity before discussing the subject at any length. Generally though, chief officers to all appearances are robust workaholics, averaging a 70–75 hour week and taking some pride in describing the long hours culture that they, apparently willingly, espouse. Some believe that the problem is intractable, because the police are resistant to 'HR fads' about balancing life and work, and few embrace the work–life balance concept with any relish. Others seem locked into the workload + long hours cycle of working and frustratedly do not know what they can do to change this predominant culture. A few secretly are creative, or academic, or familial; others are merely wistful.

It seems likely that increased competitiveness, growing resource pressures and a workload that never diminishes will continue to hold chief officer policing in thrall, until or unless serious illnesses, catastrophic errors of judgment or concerted actions (such as with junior hospital doctors in the late 1990s), force a change of culture.

THREE

The challenge of leadership in the police

It was noted in the Introduction that leadership in the police was something of a contested concept: does 'ordinary' leadership theory apply to the police, or is there a definable and distinct kind of leader found only within the police? Robert Adlam remarked that, in studies of leadership in the police:

> No systematic analysis [has been] offered concerning the ways in which police leadership is
> a) like all other manifestations of leadership
> b) like some other types of leadership (e.g. public service) and
> c) like no other form of leadership (in virtue of its specific tasks and functions). (Adlam, 2003, p 40)

We shall see that many in the police think that the last of these, (c), is applicable, and they believe that being a leader in the police is not like any other form of leadership (see Heffernan, 2003), otherwise the single entry to the police (and consequently a single vertical route to leadership) would not have such fierce adherence. Yet, as I show in Chapter Six, there is by no means unanimity among the chief officer ranks about constable-only entry, and some chief officers are amenable to the notion of bringing people in directly at higher ranks.

Currently, the only route to command in the police is by accreted successive experience in the ranks of constable, sergeant, inspector and superintendent.[1] It is possible to 'jump' ranks, say from inspector to superintendent, but, while some superintendents have gone directly to chief officer rank, the majority of ACPO candidates come from chief superintendents. As we saw in Chapter One, the High Potential

---

[1] The additional ranks exist of *chief* inspector and *chief* superintendent, usually as rewards for further experience and command. Under the Sheehy reforms (see Chapter Five) both ranks, together with that of deputy chief constable, were done away with, but later reinstated. 'Detective' is an occupation within policing; the ranks remain the same except for the *Detective* prefix, up to and including detective chief superintendent. No chief officer remains a specialist detective.

Development Scheme affords some fast tracking towards the command ranks, but there is nonetheless little consensus on what police leadership is and how it can be defined. This is not necessarily confined to police leadership; academics have long struggled to agree terms about what leadership constitutes:

> Of all the confounding areas in social psychology, leadership theory undoubtedly contends for top nomination. And, ironically, probably more has been written and less is known about leadership than about any other topic in the behavioural sciences. (Bryman, 1986, p 16)

The police in practice do not divert themselves with such scholarly inhibitions. 'Leaders' are found at all ranks, they say, but those who *command* are at ACPO rank, and that is where strategic planning and direction for a police force are also found. Indeed, the subtitle for Robert Reiner's book on *Chief Constables* (1991) was *Bobbies, Bosses or Bureaucrats?* in an attempt to distinguish between what amounted to leadership styles or typologies in chief officers (see Reiner, 1991, pp 306–8). As we shall see below, the present generation of chief officers was asked in interview whether Reiner's 'types' still applied to them or not. Many took issue with what they saw as simplistic stereotyping, while some clearly saw themselves as incorporating some aspects of each 'type' in the way that they individually showed leadership. More appeared to favour a mix of styles appropriate to the situation (hence, possibly, the popularity of 'situational leadership' across a range of functions – in the public service at large, not just in the police).

As far as the police service is concerned, the leadership issue is one of competency. ACPO believes that if people aspire to be chief officers, there is a suite of competencies which they must attain. Robert Adlam became very exercised by the widespread assertion that leadership was simply a matter of competency, describing competency frameworks as '*banal* [and] *strikingly obvious*' (Adlam and Villiers, 2003, p 40, my italics). Notwithstanding Adlam's reservations, the ACPO/Skills for Justice publication make it clear precisely what competencies are expected of a chief officer. The *Twelve Competencies for a Chief Officer* (ACPO/Skills for Justice, 2003) were first promulgated in 2003, and quickly adopted for use in determining potential for the role, acting as benchmarks for application to the Police National Assessment Centre (PNAC) 'gateway' and for making an annual appraisal (or performance development review [PDR]) of a chief officer's performance. Skills for Justice, the sector skills organisation for criminal justice, expanded the competency categories into 'assessable behaviours'. It is against those assessments that chief officers are judged competent or not.

The 12 competencies are:

- Strategic perspective
- Openness to change
- Negotiation and influencing
- Maximising potential
- Respect for diversity
- Team working
- Community and customer focus
- Effective communication
- Problem solving
- Planning and organising
- Personal responsibility
- Resilience

I should observe at this point that more than half of these competencies are expected of *all* police officers and, indeed, were so prescribed by Skills for Justice in 2003 as basic 'behavioural competencies' for constables starting out in the service. The 'basic seven' are:

- Respect for diversity
- Team working
- Community and customer focus
- Effective communication
- Problem solving
- Personal responsibility
- Resilience[2]

In its 2007 Police Leadership Qualities Framework (PLQF), the National Policing Improvement Agency (NPIA) identified three core leadership qualities: personal integrity, personal awareness and passion for achievement. These may be manifested at any level in the police, but are particularly expected to be highly evident among aspirants to be chief officers (see Chapter One). Such a proliferation of lists of

[2] See, for example, Bryant and Bryant (2009) or Caless (2010), in each of which the behavioural competencies and National Occupational Standards are analysed. At the time of writing, there is much debate about rewriting the behavioural and skills competencies, making fewer but more comprehensive 'occupational standards' for police officers at all levels. Critics of the competency approach are few but vociferous (Adlam, 2003, for example).

desired qualities in leaders is all very well, but the problem persists in ascertaining how one can describe a leader in quantitative or qualitative terms and how one can assess that leader's potential (see, for example, the work of Miller et al, 2009). In the police service of England and Wales, though, the ACPO/Skills for Justice (2003) *Twelve Competencies for a Chief Officer* provides the only available criteria for assessment of police leadership. Consensus has largely been attained that leaders in the police need training and development, but at issue is whether this should be confined to ACPO ranks or whether 'training to lead' should be something that is available across all ranks. The retiring chief executive officer of the NPIA, Chief Constable Peter Neyroud, was asked by the coalition government in September 2010 to undertake a review of police leadership. Neyroud noted that 'four years ago',

> The police service had completely lost faith in what was being delivered [in leadership training] nationally. [...] The queue to attend senior leadership development courses had vanished and delegates simply failed to turn up. (Neyroud, 2010, p 12)

Neyroud reported in December 2010, but his *Review* was not made public until April 2011. Among his recommendations is a proposition that ACPO becomes a 'chartered police institute' that takes over *all* police leadership training. Neyroud's focus is on developing leadership potential, advocating that appointment as a chief officer should *precede* the formal development programmes in leadership, but that the programmes be made more rigorous. His recommendation for the development of strategic leadership in the police is pithy:

> I recommend a new approach to the qualification, assessment and development of the strategic leaders of the service ...The approach is in four steps: obtaining the Senior Management in Policing qualification; a national assessment centre that will focus on the candidates [sic] potential for the most senior roles and the development they may need; application for and appointment to an assistant chief constable role; and in a Strategic Command Programme to develop those appointed once in role. (Neyroud, 2011, p 13)

Before any of Neyroud's cogent recommendations can be realised, there probably needs to be more coherent agreement, probably by ACPO in consultation with academic partners, on what police leadership is, and how it can best be delivered. Competency-based training is still the probable 'best practice' route, whether delivered before or after appointment as a chief officer. Neyroud did not go into particular detail about how his 'strategic development' would be delivered. The current process is governed by assessment against the 'Twelve Competencies' and that is what we shall look at now in the current context of training and developing chief officers. It is worth remarking that while the number and extent of leadership competencies will change, and equally that the mode of delivery may be different, it is nonetheless unlikely that generic development of the capabilities to lead strategically and to command will alter fundamentally. Much, if not all, of what follows will remain, though, as will be seen, I remain unconvinced that many of these standards are 'police specific'.

The police service divides the current 12 chief officer competencies into three groups:

• Leadership
• Working with others
• Achieving results

Perhaps these three groups parallel the three core leadership qualities in the PLQF (see earlier), but if they do, such parallels are neither explicit nor implied. In fact, I have been unable to find in any of the public documentation, evidence of 'joined-up thinking' which makes connections or coherence between different pronouncements on police leadership. Adlam's point is resonant: there is no consensus, despite all this restructuring and reviewing, on what police leadership is. As may be seen below, there is an assumption of shared meanings which are not supported by objective analysis.

Leadership

There are three categories of leadership: strategic perspective, openness to change, and negotiating and influencing others using logic and reason.

Strategic perspective

This category consists of a series of 'desired behaviours' against which the individual chief officer is assessed and where s/he:

• Works towards a future vision

- Links actions to strategic business goals
- Understands complex political issues and how they affect the police service
- Exploits opportunities to achieve longer-term objectives
- Develops ways of working that balance local policing needs and larger police service needs
- Takes a broad view of issues
- Understands external expectations and influences
- Identifies common goals and interests with partners
- Creates a vision of the future and a strategy to realise the vision
- Shares decision making about resources
- Develops policy on operational matters

While these behavioural goals and preferred actions have a policing veneer, they are of course the typical strategic perspectives that one would expect of any board-level executive in any public or private organisation.[3] Few police officers are called on to exercise any kind of strategic grasp below the rank of superintendent. Perhaps the two most fundamental generic issues for the police concern 'understands complex political issues' and 'links actions to [...] business goals', since these do loom large at the strategic level. It is not simply the importance of the Home Office and the law and order interests of the government of the day which chief officers need to appreciate, but the projections, initiatives and suggestions from others such as the proposal for directly elected 'police crime commissioners' (PCCs) as well as direct initiatives from the Home Office or Ministry of Justice (resource constraints or reduction in overtime budgets, for example), national changes championed by HMIC (like the ill-fated and short-lived Policing Pledge) and the increased accountability demanded by many commentators and communities.

In a post-recessional period, the public funding of the police has suffered severe restriction, some forces having undergone as much as 25% reductions in their budgets,[4] with more impending, so that it has become incumbent on every chief officer to try 'to do more with less', or at least stretch the available funds as far as they will go. What this

---

[3] See Rogers (2008) for a good discussion of such generic capabilities.

[4] Following the coalition government's budget of June 2010, it became clear that police forces were expected to take 'a proportion of the pain' of making savings, an assumption confirmed by the Comprehensive Spending Review of public services' finance in October 2010. In some forces, total budget cuts amounted to nearly a quarter, in others a fifth. Averagely, criminal justice took 20%, with a concomitant effect on Magistrates' and Crown Courts too (see Ford et al, 2010).

also means of course is that chief officers will chase those parts of the business which attract supplemental funding; in which case strategic goals may be determined by the money available to support them. It is not helped that 80% or so of all police budgets constitute salaries or pensions, leaving only some 20% or less for operational and equipment expenditure.[5] Additionally, the longer-term needs of the police service are strategic considerations too, such as collaboration between forces,[6] succession planning, changes in the criminal law, oversight mechanisms, human capital and business planning and inter-agency cooperation; many of which topics I touch on in the course of this book.

Openness to change

The behaviours assessed here are:

- Recognises and responds to the need for change
- Identifies ways in which the police need to change
- Personally champions change and encourages managers to make it happen
- Restructures operational units to deliver performance

There is a vagueness about these behaviours that sits oddly with the exhortatory 'responds to the need for change'. It is almost as though the expectation is that police leaders have to be poised to embrace and respond to any change at all, irrespective of the merits and longevity of that change. I presume that such 'wind-affected' policing is not actually what is intended, but rather that change is seen as a catalyst for reconsideration of function (as noted in the opportunity to restructure operational set-ups to make them responsive rather than moribund). Flux and movement are part of any modern management system of course, but there is not much here in the way of *leadership* of change

---

[5] See the Home Office website available from www.direct.gov.uk/en/CrimeJustice AndTheLaw/ThePolice/DG_181750; accessed 26 July 2010. Another useful analysis of how the police spend their budgets is in Loveday and McClory (2008).

[6] Such as the pooling of resources and personnel in 'back office' functions between Essex and Kent Police forces in 2009–11. These include HR, learning and development, IT, finance and administration, but also as 'part of a wider consortium of Forces' for the next generation of crime custody and intelligence systems. Significantly, the two forces have also created a joint Serious Crime Directorate, headed by an ACC, 'which has drawn together officers and staff from both Forces' (quoting from a letter to the author from Jim Barker-McCardle, Chief Constable of Essex, 17 November 2010).

so much as reaction to it, which seems simultaneously simplistic and defeatist.

One wonders how chief officers can be 'scored' objectively for performance in this set of behaviours. Change has to be managed and responses to it carefully planned, but the work of the police service is too often modified or altered at the whim of law makers (3,500 separate pieces of criminal legislation enacted between 1997 and 2010), policy makers (including HMIC) and public events (the G20 protests in London in 2009); any of which could and did skew strategic change management. Too often therefore, strategic change in policing can be merely reactive, brought about as the result of events which the police did not initiate, for which they were largely unprepared and which highlight weaknesses in the undefined behaviours.

Negotiating and influencing others using logic and reason

The behaviours are:

- Stresses the benefit of any proposals and negotiates to find solutions that everyone will accept
- Develops strategies for influencing others at all levels inside and outside the police
- Negotiates satisfactory solutions of broad or complex issues with stakeholders
- Develops operational responses to events through influencing others

Very little of this will be unfamiliar to the police at large, who spend much of their front-line working lives negotiating with people in tense, hostile or potentially fraught situations. The two behavioural skills of *influencing* and *negotiating* are well to the fore in all assessments of competency in police officers. Of course, as chief officer competencies, these are expected to produce dividends at the strategic level, but there is also a central weighting or delineation in terms of process (as though reason and logic were not generally synonymous!). What successful influence would look like and how achievement of competency in negotiating consensus can be evidenced is frankly difficult to evaluate objectively within the compass of annual appraisal, unless as merely 'work in progress'.

Maximises potential (in others)

The behaviours required are:

- Actively encourages and supports the development of people
- Mentors, assesses and develops others
- Motivates others to achieve the force's goal(s)
- Puts systems and strategies in place to develop people at all levels of the service
- Creates an environment where staff are motivated to achieve results

This is about workforce development and will be familiar to the experienced police officer, since s/he will have engaged in most of these behaviours since making sergeant. The difference essentially is that now the activity is at the top end of the organisation and therefore has strategic resonance. The ability to encourage, mentor, develop and motivate staff is fundamental to the successful leader and no one should expect to be a chief officer who does not exhibit this capability in abundance. But there is nothing exclusive to the police in any of this: the competencies apply generically at the strategic level in any responsive organisation wishing to maximise its human capital.[7]

The chief officer is expected to 'create an environment' and put 'systems and strategies in place' precisely to get the best out of people. As any leader will confirm, it is easier to say these things than to do them, but grasping issues such as non-material reward, work variety and challenge, offering staff responsibility and allowing them autonomy, will all help. By the same token, understanding the psychological contract at work[8] whereby loyalty to the organisation is 'traded' for security of employment, is key to any changes in working structures and practices that result from the strategic initiatives of chief officers. These are the skills expected of 'transformational' police leaders, who, as I try to show later in this chapter, often come up against entrenched practice and have to try to go beyond scepticism and a short-term focus.

The second portfolio of behavioural competencies concerns

Working with others

Respect for diversity

There is a range of behaviours in this section; a selection of the most important of which is:

---

[7] See for example work by Baron and Armstrong (2007) and McGuire et al (2009).

[8] A key text on this is Neil Conway and Rob Briner's *Understanding Psychological Contracts at Work: A Critical Evaluation of Theory and Research*, 2005, Oxford: Oxford University Press.

- Actively promotes the police service's standards of behaviour and conduct
- Creates an appropriate environment for discussing difficult issues
- Considers and shows respect for others, whatever their background, status, circumstances or appearance
- Provides emotional and practical support to people who are dealing with difficult issues

It is difficult to understand fully in what ways the third bullet point is specific to the role of chief officer, unless it is simply as an exemplar or role model. This behaviour is expected of *all* police officers and, unlike the other three elements, there appears to be no strategic or command dimension to it. However, the context to this is the responsiveness of the police service to diversity issues in the aftermath of the Macpherson Inquiry (1999) into the death of Stephen Lawrence, in which the chair of the inquiry, Sir William Macpherson of Cluny, famously labelled the Metropolitan Police as 'institutionally racist'.[9] Issues about respect for diversity will always be sensitive in policing and this is reflected in concerns that chief officers should contribute directly by supporting staff engaged in difficult issues, which might include, for example, planning a search for criminal evidence at a gypsy-traveller encampment or justifying the 'stop and search' of people from minority ethnic communities. There are also perceptual concerns, media interest and force 'image' issues to be considered – any of which can lead to strategic caution, or inertia.

Team working

As I indicated earlier, this is a generic competency for police officers, with chief officers having an added strategic and command dimension:

- Develops strong working relationships inside and outside the force
- Breaks down barriers between groups and involves others in decisions

---

[9] Stephen Lawrence was murdered by a gang of white youths in London in 1993 and the Metropolitan Police was heavily criticised in the aftermath for its inept investigation and racial stereotyping. As always, what happened in the Met was taken implicitly as characteristic of the police service as a whole, and seismic changes in the way that officers were taught about respect for difference followed across all forces in England and Wales. Some members of the police service took the accusation of 'institutional racism' personally, mistakenly thinking that it applied to individuals rather than the unthinking built-in prejudices of the service itself (MacPherson 1999).

- Works with external stakeholders and partners to achieve partnership goals
- Develops strategies to encourage people to work together

Chief officers are unlikely to have made it through selection processes without demonstrating advanced skills in networking and influencing, both of which are brought to the fore in these behaviours that promote working together. There are plenty of well-documented tensions within the police service which may require active intervention to promote team working, such as the often invisible prejudices exhibited against non-police staff by the warrant-holding police officers, or hostility exhibited by police officers towards police community support officers and other kinds of community support officers employed by local authorities (Caless, 2007). The age-old division between uniformed and detective branches within the police can be another source of tension, particularly in terms of resources and accountability (see, for example, Kamsteeg et al, 2010). It would indeed be a sure-footed chief officer who could 'develop strategies to encourage' such people to work together in harmony and without friction all the time. Indeed, doing so in some instances may inhibit the stimulus of friendly rivalry, though few would now espouse the more corrosive forms of police elitism.

Community and customer focus

The behaviours here include:

- Focuses on the customer and provides a high-quality service
- Understands the communities that are served by the police
- Maintains a broad understanding of social trends and understands any effect that these will have on policing
- Creates processes that ensure that stakeholders' and customers' views and needs are clearly identified and responded to
- Puts in place strategies for media and community relations

This covers the much-debated importation into public service from the world of commerce: the notion of consumers or share/stakeholders, concepts[10] that continue to meet resistance throughout public service. Yet in policing it has particular resonance, since here the tangible shift from policing being something done *to* people to a service done *with*

---

[10] See, for example, discussions in Charles Hill and Gareth Jones' *Strategic Management Theory* (2010).

people underpins much of the 'engagement strategy' with the public which is current government and police authority policy, as well as being a cornerstone of neighbourhood policing. Denis O'Connor's HMIC 2005 report, *Closing the Gap*, addressed 'engagement' head on, noting the gap between the steady decrease in published crime figures and the rising public fear of crime. He argued that the police needed as a matter of urgency to re-engage with the public both to reassure and to understand. The whole thrust of neighbourhood policing and community focus had vigorous government and police authority support. One chief officer commented:

> **Interviewee 53:** It's all very well that HMIC and the Home Office tell us that we have to treat the public as 'clients' of our 'services', when the truth of the public's attitude to the police is somewhere between undisguised hostility and veiled contempt.
>
> [Interviewer: Do you really believe that? I would have thought there were more shades of grey...]
>
> We still impose acceptable behaviour on people; we still act as the unwelcome guardian[11] when something goes wrong or when motorists for example break the law. Most people want policing to happen to others, and for themselves to be secure and unaffected. Well, the impartial upholding of the law doesn't work like that.

Creating *processes which take account of others' views* are related therefore to the broader strategic aims of the police service. That said, there is considerable disquiet in policing circles, reflected in the views expressed privately to me by many chief officers, that the government, police authorities and HMIC are focused on the local and neighbourhood

---

[11] The reference is to a problem-solving model, called PAT 2 which is familiar to police forces across the country as depicting the absence of a 'guardian' (that is, any responsible adult, not necessarily a police officer, or an inhibitor – like CCTV) when a potential to commit crime exists through the presence of a would-be perpetrator and a victim, in circumstances propitious to crime. So the existence of a CCTV system alone, on this basis, will not always deter crime; the knowledge that it is live monitored *may* do. The basis of these models is that criminals behave logically or predictably, but in the case of violence, particularly alcohol-fuelled violence between young males, there may be no rational process. See Read and Tilley (2000), and www.idea.gov.uk/idk/core/page.do?pageId=12148550, as well as the models' origins in 'routine activity theory' formulated by Cohen and Felson (1979) and developed by Akers and Sellers (2004).

aspects of policing to the detriment of the investigation or prevention of serious and organised crime.

Effective communication

This is another generic skill expected of *all* police officers at all levels but which, at chief officer rank, applies strategically and organisationally:

- Makes sure that important messages are communicated and understood throughout the force
- Explains complex issues, making them easy to understand
- Deals with issues effectively, even when under extreme pressure
- Communicates effectively, both verbally and in writing
- Considers how different audiences will interpret information

There is a lot of tacit assumption here that terms such as 'even when under extreme pressure' are understood. Police officers at all ranks are used to keeping clear priorities in the midst of mayhem and chaos, and the top cop is no exception. However, as we saw in Chapter Two, the workload and long hours culture is taken to extremes among many chief officers, so parts of this competency look like a licence to work excessively rather than decisively. Certainly, any workaholic DCC or chief constable *could* use the caveat of 'under extreme pressure' to mark down those chief officers who do not subscribe to long hours and 'presenteeism', thus perpetuating both; even though the implicit thrust in the competency is about keeping a strong focus on priorities and a cool head.

So, too, there is a vagueness about the adjective 'effective' in communication – is this a process which engages or which clarifies? How is 'effective' measured? If it is measured, by what means is the measurement made objective? What does *ineffective* communication look like? Is it merely inarticulacy, or is it something more profound, involving a lack of understanding or absence of self-awareness? No doubt these issues are teased out at the individual level between the person being reported on and the reporter, but they are not explicit here and therefore consistency between reporters (and between forces) seems unlikely:

> **Interviewee 13:** Give anyone the job of reviewing an organisation or part of it and there will be a key recommendation which is about improving communication. I have never, ever, been involved in any review or assessment where this has not been said. And it's a huge

cliché: of course communication can be improved. It's like saying attitude can be improved, or health can be improved, or poverty can be mitigated. If the system is never going to be perfect then it's a safe bet that you can improve it forever. But for communication to work there has to be a receiver as well as a transmitter, and these roles need to be exchanged frequently. And all too often, they are not.

Achieving results

Each of the four sections in this group has a range of desired behaviours that are generic and fairly predictable.

Problem solving

Some of the behaviours to be assessed are these:

- Takes an intelligence-led approach to complex situations
- Produces imaginative responses to complex problems
- Analyses information to identify problems and makes effective decisions
- Tests widely for possible reactions to controversial decisions
- Makes strategic decisions by analysing relevant factors

The National Intelligence Model (NIM), expressing 'an intelligence-led approach' and introduced service-wide in 2001, is itself based on the European Foundation Quality Management model for business processes. The NIM determines how the police process 'information' (a term used synonymously with 'intelligence') and what operational decisions are made on the basis of assessment of 'knowledge products'. Contemporary criticism of the NIM suggests that it is rigid and compartmentalised, leading to similar rigidity and 'boxing off' in operational policing, so its application to strategic decision making or the solving of complex problems outside crime and criminality is not as straightforward or as resolvable as this behaviour suggests.[12] Indeed, one chief officer interviewee believed that the police service was in danger of applying a template to all problem solving instead of allowing original thinking. This, the chief officer said, was a product of how leadership is being taught:

---

[12] See, for example, Phillips et al (2007). More generally on problem solving see my observations on models earlier, and 'routine activity theory' work by Cohen and Felson (1979) and Akers and Sellers (2004).

Interviewee 47: What the powers-that-be seem to be doing is looking for potential police leaders to fit a model or a template rather than saying that police leadership embraces a wide range of attributes – which must include a refreshingly original approach to problem solving. It's very hard to groom people to fit a rigid template, I think.

This officer's concerns are echoed by several of his colleagues and it would be well for ACPO and others to take note of the disengagement which modelling behaviour and responses can induce. The remainder of the competencies specified here are genuinely at the strategic level, though they are not specifically about policing and have to do with achieving both consensus and direction. Anyone at board level in any organisation should be adept at these behaviours.

Planning and organising

The group of behaviours includes

- Plans, organises and supervises activities to make best use of resources
- Develops structured plans across the force to deal with activities that may be complex
- Monitors progress towards strategic objectives
- Ensures that activities are aligned with efficient and effective policing
- Leads operational planning for major events

Chief officers are expected to lead in planning across the spectrum of police activity and it is a process with which all of them will be familiar, since nearly all policing operations are subject to planning oversight and scrutiny. The strategic end of this activity consists in taking a force-level view of progress, and intervening to align if need be (*monitors progress*), but the precise nature of planning and leading operations will depend on the chief officer's portfolio of responsibilities. Those engaged in 'territorial policing' (usually the oversight of basic command units and areas/divisions of the force geographically) will be different from those who are working in the information/human resources field. That said, strategic planning and organising are emphatically chief officers' skills that need to be demonstrated at the highest level. Sir Ian Blair noted in his short essay 'Leadership that learns', that

> [...] police leaders need to be competent in managing complex and protracted criminal enquiries [...] they need

> to be able to control public disorder [...] and they need to be competent in controlling the scene of major disasters [...] There are certain skills which only the police bring to the party. Police leaders had better be good at doing them. (Blair, 2003, p 170)

Crime, disorder and disaster are three areas where indeed the public expects police to be competent, both in execution and in leadership, but whether one can extrapolate from the effective conduct of police operations the requisite leadership skills and then teach them to aspirant leaders is perhaps not as clear cut as it may appear. Obtaining consensus on what those skills are is often the first hurdle at which many fall.

Personal responsibility

This is another generic behavioural competency, which exists from the moment that a student police officer becomes a warrant holder in the 'office of constable':

- Takes personal responsibility for making things happen and achieving results
- Acts with a high degree of integrity
- Readily accepts responsibility for self and others
- Takes responsibility for managing situations and problems
- Leads by example, showing a commitment and determination to succeed
- Displays motivation, commitment, perseverance and conscientiousness

An individual officer is responsible for his or her decision to use force, to make an arrest, to intervene in order to uphold the law and to exercise discretion whether to act or not. This is because the individual officer is answerable in a court of law for the actions which s/he takes as a police officer. This challenge has always been present and is merely magnified here in terms of the ramifications of getting it wrong at chief officer level. The other behaviours noted here must be subjectively assessed, since they derive from personal motivation and a sense of duty, and do not appear amenable to quantitative measurement. They have, however, a specific public service dimension which resonates powerfully in the police.

Resilience

The final category for chief officer behaviours is categorised in these ways:

- Shows resilience, even in difficult circumstances
- Prepared to make difficult decisions and has confidence to see them through
- Shows reliability
- Remains calm and confident, responding decisively and logically in difficult situations

These behaviours are all about being tough in adversity and sticking with objectives in the face of opposition, and it is again something with which the aspirant chief officer will be very familiar. If police officers were not resilient people who stick to their tasks in the midst of adversity, they would not last for long in the job. By the time police officers reach ACPO level, they are very resilient indeed; often having experienced events and situations of a kind and intensity that most people never encounter. Again, we presume that these behaviours are shown *in extremis* in chief officers, because theirs may be the decisions which spell success or disaster (for example, in authorising an armed response to a siege). While all leaders in all organisations have to show resilience in the face of challenge and change, there is in policing a particularly dogged imperturbability which is a virtue at all levels but especially so at chief officer rank. How you learn that, and how it is developed at a strategic level without becoming merely stubbornness, is not so straightforward.

Summary

There is some truth in Robert Adlam's criticism of the chief officer competencies as both 'banal' and 'blindingly obvious', and the evidence for this is clearly displayed across the 12 competencies shown above. There are some difficult standards to attain, but equally there are also some that are bland and subjective. Few seem specific to the role of chief *police* officer; most of the specified behaviours apply to most of those in command in most organisations. What is more concerning is what the *objective* measurement might be for behaviours that are subjectively displayed and subjectively assessed, such as 'imaginative responses to complex problems' or coping 'even under extreme pressure'. Some of the language is unwarrantably vague ('effective communication') or tends to the coy ('dealing with difficult issues'), or to the meaningless as in apparently indiscriminately embracing all and any *change*.

Appraisal (PDR) of chief officers

The 12 competencies considered above are assessed formally once a year in parallel with agreed 'key personal objectives'. Guidance from the Home Office (2003, p 1) suggests that there should be 'between four and six key personal objectives, and no more than ten' for each chief officer. Indeed, if a chief officer were to be reviewed on all 12 competencies and then on as many as 10 key personal objectives, a PDR might be a prolonged, not to say intractable, business. All the key personal objectives have to be 'SMARTER', which entails the familiar *specific, measurable, achievable, realistic, time-limited, evaluated* and *reviewed* categories, or sententious terms to the same effect. Most ACCs can be first reviewed by the deputy chief constable or equivalent in their force; the appraisal being confirmed by second or 'parent' review by the chief constable or equivalent. Confusingly, in some forces the chief constable reviews the work of all the chief officers as 'first reporting manager'. The DCC is first reviewed by the chief constable, and second reviewed by the police authority/police crime commissioner (PCC) (probably with some HMIC input) and the chief constable is appraised by the police authority/PCC and second reviewed by HMIC. This can be a tense process, fraught with subjective judgements and the opportunity for accusations of bias, but that is inherent in any process of appraisal of performance, unless targets are entirely numeric and lacking in qualitative assessment.[13] Scepticism about dispassion in appraisal strikes a chord with some chief officers, who do not accept that leadership is something that can be learned (and therefore assessed).

> **Interviewee 35:** I watched with amusement the recent, say last three to five years, convulsions over teaching leadership with the Home Office and Bramshill and Centrex[14] and the Police Leadership

---

[13] No appraisal system yet devised is foolproof against bias or subjectivity, though '360 degree appraisal' may come close to a usable standard – but it is not yet in widespread use in the police (see Gillen (2007) and Church and Bracken (1997)).

[14] Centrex was the name for national police training before NPIA (itself now subsumed into the National Crime Agency (NCA). In addition to its initial IPLDP course, NPIA actually ran five programmes on police leadership: the Core Leadership Development Programme (mainly for sergeants and inspectors), the High Potential Development Scheme, the Police Leadership Qualities Framework, the Senior Police Leadership Development Programme, and the Strategic Command Course (SCC). There are other programmes, such

> Programme or whatever it's called because leadership is so elusive of codifying in this way; yet the police as a breed want it codified and delivered in slabs: yes, here's your epaulettes, here's your extra braid, here's your piece of leadership. Pin it on; now lead. It doesn't work like that.

The assumption which underlies the leadership aspect of the 12 ACPO competencies is that the skills needed to function as a chief officer can be taught (or, more strictly, can be learned and developed). Certainly ACPO as a body thinks so, since both the PNAC and the Strategic Command Course (SCC), are predicated on the acquisition of leadership skills. Individual chief officers are not so sure that leadership is so easily acquired. One of those interviewed commented

> **Interviewee 60:** I think that we [chief officers] think now we understand leadership better than in the past and the part that real leadership plays in corporate and strategic planning, but I'll never be convinced that this is something you can teach. You might be able to bring it out, as a kind of latent talent, but if you have no predisposition to lead, no urge to be out in front (the object of derision and admiration alike), you'll not be a leader and not many do have that.

But we must proceed on the assumption that leadership skills *can* be obtained through learning and experience, if only so that we can critically examine what the police service proposes for its candidate chief officers (see Fahy 2008). In advance of the SCC, for example, candidates are expected to

> [...] have the experience of all fields of police operations and strategic management and therefore the period before the course should be used to fill any gaps with participants at least being exposed to some of the key issues involved in

as those specifically designed for underrepresented groups in the police. Interviewee 35 above appears to refer to the SPLDP. ACPO runs the SCC but it is not yet clear which, if any, of the remainder will be retained by the NCA or whether ACPO will run all of them. The issue about ACPO 'ownership' of undercover policing led to a swift decision in January 2011 by the Home Secretary to transfer responsibility to the Metropolitan Police; see Travis, A., Lewis, P and Wainwright, M., 'Clean-up of covert policing ordered after Mark Kennedy revelations', *The Guardian*, 18 January 2011. This episode suggests that ACPO's hold on policing remits, including that for leadership, is not absolute.

these fields. Therefore preparation may include attendance at chief officer and police authority meetings, shadowing of commanders in specialist units, visits to national agencies and time spent with other parts of the public sector leading to a firm grasp of the strategic challenges facing the Service. *Experience shows that some participants particularly lack exposure to strategic financial issues.* (NPIA, Senior PNAC and SCC, 2009 course rubric, my italics)

I have discussed the components of both Senior PNAC and the SCC in Chapter One.

On leadership and theory

Before turning to what chief officers think about their own leadership development in the police, it would be helpful to have, at least broadly, a notion of what leadership is and how its attributes might be acquired. Current thinking about leadership (not just in the police), such as that explored in Bennis and Thomas (2002) or Barling et al (2000), suggests that there are four kinds of leader:

* transactional
* charismatic
* transformational
* situational

The first of these, the *transactional leader,* identifies what his or her 'followers' expect and responds to these wishes, establishing a 'transaction' or trade-off between what the leader can provide (success, advancement, more pay, higher status) and what staff will deliver in return (higher sales, greater spread of sales, more production, market domination). This is a classic instance of effort leading to reward, but it is also characteristic of *leadership by command,* where orders are expected to be obeyed and staff or followers or workforce are not often consulted and seldom deferred to.[15] Transactional leadership dominated British policing up to, say, the mid- to late 1980s, and was predicated on a hierarchical disciplined structure where leadership was usually determined by rank. Some chief officers believe that it still dominates, though in a much more covert way:

---

[15] It is well described by Burns (1978).

Interviewee 55: I believe, with the benefit of hindsight, what I see is a great deal of lip service being paid to the idea of transformational leadership, when in reality many top cops are happier reverting to the old fashioned transactional style. They do so because they see it as expedient, in order to reach short-term targets, however, they often alienate their staff en route. When I first joined, I knew the way top cops behaved and could react accordingly. It is very confusing today when the style says one thing but [the person] does another.

A transactional leader with personality and flair can develop into a *charismatic leader*. People follow because they are roused by the example, rhetoric or achievement of the charismatic leader, and want to share in it. Politicians and military leaders are often charismatic; so too, unfortunately, are tyrants and dictators. All are calculated risk takers, skilled at putting their ideas across simply and in relating to the aspirations of ordinary people, and they are utterly focused on outcomes rather than means. Consultation is rare with such leaders, and they actively encourage sometimes slavish adherence to the cause they espouse, often through adroit manipulation of the media.[16] The police service has had a few of these in the past, but it is now rare for leaders to emerge through the impact of ruthless personality alone.

A *transformational leader*, by contrast, empowers his or her staff, encouraging innovation and experiment and creates a climate in which it is acceptable to fail, (provided always that lessons are learned and that the particular failure is not repeated in the future). Transformational leaders motivate people to make greater efforts, to give more commitment and to reach for higher performance, moving away from a blame culture into one where controls are loosened and 'blue sky thinking' is rewarded. Bass (1985), who was among the first to identify this different kind of 'empowering' leader, suggested that there were clear processes which transformational leaders engaged in. They raised people's awareness about how to get to where they wanted to be; they persuaded people to act more in the interests of the organisation than in their own narrow self-interest and such leaders met their staff's 'higher-level needs' by developing the latter's skills and showing them

---

[16] Max Weber described such leaders as long ago as 1947 in his *The Theory of Social and Economic Organizations*, translated by A. Henderson and T. Parsons, New York: Free Press, also transactional leaders are characterised by Hay-McBer research in David Goleman (2000) as 'coercive and authoritative'.

trust. Transformational leaders 'let go' formal controls and help people to build confidence in themselves by transforming the situation.[17]

Chief officers generally have not been iconoclasts and are not as free as those in the commercial world to break with existing processes and invent new ways of doing things. Some exceptional individuals have been 'transformational' on single issues, such as Sir Ian's 2002 introduction of Police Community Support Officers in the teeth of opposition from traditionalists,[18] or David Phillips' espousal of intelligence-led policing in 1995, or even earlier, when John Alderson proposed community policing in 1979.[19] So it is probably fair to say that the police have produced a few '*semi-transformational*' leaders since the late 1970s. However, the structure and process of policing seems to obstruct or frustrate such would-be transforming individuals in the main. Matt Long, in a perceptive essay, observed that

> Being an inspirational leader is arguably increasingly difficult to achieve [in the police]

and that

> Police leaders are now faced with two competing, and in some ways incompatible, sets of expectations. On the one hand, there are the managerialist pressures of fairly narrow goal achievement [...] On the other hand, there is the increasing emphasis on ethics and human rights, something which sits uneasily with the constraining of professional autonomy [...][20]

There is a continuing assumption, certainly among leadership theorists and to some extent within the police service, that transformational leadership is of itself invariably good, is to be espoused and aspired to. Such belief is not always matched by the response of the individual chief officer:

---

[17] See Bass (1985), but a more up-to-date assessment is in O'Shea et al (2009).

[18] See, for example, Bryn Caless (2007) in which, inter alia, the hostility of the Police Federation towards PCSOs is explored.

[19] Alderson (1979, 1984). Much derided at the time as a 'liberal' police officer, Alderson was Chief Constable of Devon and Cornwall Police from 1974 to 1982. He is now regarded widely as a visionary and highly intelligent chief officer who was decades ahead of his time.

[20] Matt Long was referring to the previous police performance management regime which was replaced by the short-lived Policing Pledge in 2009; nonetheless his point is a fair one (see Long, 2003).

Interviewee 44: We are not good at leadership really. We make the right noises, use the right phrases, tick the right diversity boxes, even put forward the acceptable libertarian front – but, you know, we are just as determined to have our own way and ensure that people do precisely what we want, as in the bad old days of the Copper Barons. It's just that now, we're more subtle about it and better at dressing it up in other clothes. But leadership is still just about getting your own way, isn't it?

This view was echoed by another chief officer who, in response to the question whether leadership in the police had changed, replied:

Interviewee 25: Oh, it's changed immensely. I remember when leadership was interchangeable with command and control. Now, pure control is very rare and we have all learned to parrot the right terms about consultation, empowerment and the 'vision thing' – but lurking beneath every bland ACPO exterior, there's a control freak who lets the mask slip in a crisis.

The fourth category is the *situational leader*, described by Hersey and Blanchard (1969) as the kind of adaptable leader who will suit his or her style of leadership to the prevailing situation. This can lead to a 'chameleon' in command who reacts to different problems by changing colour or ground. To witness, as Interviewee 55 did earlier, a self-proclaimed transformational leader reverting quickly to transaction when opposed or crossed, can breed scepticism on the part of the workforce, who do not know which way the leader will jump next. Others see this 'situational' characteristic rather as adaptable and flexible, often finding favour in a police service which faces many fast-changing situations. One interviewee asserted that such responsiveness is a necessity in a chief officer:

Interviewee 27: My leadership style is predominantly transformational but from time to time it becomes transactional out of necessity. I tend to adapt my leadership style to the prevailing situation. I find it helpful to think about leadership as a toolbox containing a range of tools for different jobs. The skill is in choosing the right tool for the right job. From time to time, it is variously necessary to provide social leadership, entrepreneurial leadership, facilitative leadership, directional leadership and just occasionally heroic leadership.

Other leadership theories

There are many other ways of typifying or describing leaders, from possessors of EI or 'emotional intelligence' (Goleman, 2000; Stein et al, 2009), who can empathise with followers and who have been called 'emotional capitalists' (Newman, 2008), to those who define and achieve tasks while maintaining effective relationships (Adair, 1973), leaders who catalyse change (Senior, 1997) and those who understand and make use of the 'psychological contract' at work (Conway and Briner, 2005). This, however, is not a book about the theories of leadership, or even about leaders in the round; it is about *police* leaders:

> **Interviewee 79:** Leadership is a kind of current flavour with more theories about how to lead than there are people to do the leading. I think it was a great mistake when the police service started to follow this leadership theory line, and got in all sorts of gurus to tell us what we were doing wrong.

This comment is echoed by a number of chief officers who deplore what they see as the over-engineered nature of leadership theory and deprecate its imposition as a template on a reluctant police service. From the point of view of clarity in this chapter, however, it is important to establish a general context of understanding if we are in turn to understand the police service's emphasis on the early identification and development of potential leaders.[21]

In this sense, work by Bennis and Thomas (2002) is perhaps key: they noted that the *competencies of leaders* (their skills, qualities and what they do) are the outcomes of formative experiences. In other words, the competencies of police leaders may have been modelled on either positive or negative role models at a time when the individual leader was especially impressionable. This develops what Bennis and Thomas call 'adaptive capacity': the possession of a strong sense of probity and integrity as well as a determination to engage others in 'shared meanings'. The comments often made by chief officers about the formative impressions which good (and bad) sergeants gave them early in their police careers, may indicate a resonance with what

---

[21] Work that still needs to be developed; see for example the perceptive article by Wright et al (2008). It is worth noting that the preliminary reading list for those attending the SCC includes work by Goleman (2000), Bennis and Thomas (2002) and other leadership theorists.

Bennis and Thomas say. Certainly a number of chief officers pay tribute to those (usually sergeant or inspector) who saw their potential to go far in the police service and encouraged it, often planting, if the chief officers are to be believed, the first seeds of ambition (see Wall, 1994 and Jones, 2009).

The identification of potential leaders tends, at least in part, to be self-elective. In other words, candidates for high office put themselves forward by enrolling on fast track schemes, graduate entry programmes, or by taking advantage of leadership training or learning or circumstances when on offer. Personal ambition cannot be ignored, particularly in the police, where the prevailing culture is one where the display of ambition is often deprecated and which leads to the donning of a sort of mask of modesty behind which the desire to rise is hidden. Whether or not ambition is disguised, there is a sense in which every leader has sufficient egotism to believe that s/he can do a good job once given the chance to shine (see O'Shea et al, 2009). I noted above how role models play a part in helping to mould 'formative experiences' in potential leaders, but the modern police leader

> [...] requires more subtle skills than in the past, and a different emphasis, as organisational cultures change. The movement is from a 'comfortable' command-and-control approach to an 'uncomfortable' requirement to be an empowerer, a coach, a facilitator and an educator. (Hooper and Potter, pp 68–9)

Some of the discomfort described here can be discerned in the chief officers' comments which follow.

I began by asking each interviewee 'Would you describe your role as 'Baron', 'Boss', 'Bobby', 'Bureaucrat' [Reiner, 1991] or as something else?' and then went on to ask 'How would you describe your leadership style? Is it, for example, transactional, or transformational, or facilitative, or situational, or a blend depending on circumstances, or something else entirely?'

There were 94 respondents (Table 3.1). Given that the majority of answers were in free text, preponderances in the replies have been taken to indicate preference for a state or position.

Table 3.1: Preferred leadership style

Type	Number	Percentage
'Baron'	0	0
'Bobby'	12	13%
'Boss'	6	6%
'Bureaucrat'	4	4%
Mixture of styles	48	51%
Reject the typology	24	26%
Totals	**94**	**100%**

One chief officer had no doubts about what he ought to be, but felt constrained by the circumstances of the role and by the general structure of policing:

> **Interviewee 33:** I want to be a bobby, a cop's copper, but I am forced by circumstances to be a bureaucrat – this is because life as a chief officer is dominated by a performance culture. To succeed and make sense of the performance culture, you have to engage almost exclusively in processes which can get in the way of more useful and productive (and leadership) things in policing, such as mapping/understanding the future and developing good people.

Another acknowledged that fitting into any of the modes was a struggle:

> **Interviewee 21:** I really struggled with these four names: I'm part of a team but I also exercise independent command. It's not my job to be a Bobby any more and I do my best not to be a bureaucrat, but I am forced to [be] by circumstances. You can't work on a whim in policing but on the other hand the procedures and processes create great complexity. It means that we can't respond quickly to change, so we're all part of the bureaucratic machine, even if we would rather not be.

This chief officer thought that being a Bobby was simply a form of practical leadership:

> **Interviewee 34:** I'm a Bobby. I have never lost that mindset of sceptical enquiry, despite moving up in the hierarchy. I guess the best description of me would be '*transformactional*'.

but while there was a distinct and emotional response to the notion of being a Bobby which has much to do with previous experience as a police officer, other chief officers uncompromisingly located themselves in different Reiner typologies:

> **Interviewee 13:** I can understand where Reiner is coming from. I'm a Boss. The Baron has all but disappeared now except in small shire forces; the Bureaucrat is still prominent and some police leaders hide behind the need for bureaucracy and process. But being a leader is about leading an organisation and empowering the front line, oh and holding your nerve.

and:

> **Interviewee 83:** I am emphatically a Bureaucrat because the performance culture, however 'pledged', is dominant and all-pervasive in policing. I'm also a change-agent and therefore my style tends to be persuasive, wheedling and 'big sell' rather than command. I think the days of 'do this because I say so' are pretty much gone; which is not to say that I do not give orders when I have to.

However, a majority of chief officers (more than 50%) said that for them no single style of leadership particularly predominated and many noted that they moved across a spectrum of responses:

> **Interviewee 40:** We all do lip-service to the 'transformational' thing, but the truth is that we are more across a command continuum dipping into the appropriate leadership style and stance. I'm none of Reiner's stereotypes all the time, and I don't know anyone who is.

One deputy chief constable observed that the role that he was required to play made it imperative that he could move through a spectrum of leadership styles, that had to do with expectations rather than personal preference:

> **Interviewee 41:** My role is multiple: I am responsible for performance, discipline and standards in the force as well as leading on public reassurance and I do duty as 'Gold' commander, as well as standing in for the chief when she is away – so I move right across the roles in many ways. In disciplinary matters I can be a Boss or

a Bureaucrat, in reassurance I am the Bobby (which is what the public responds to) and in relations with those who drive the police service I am a loyal Number Two, which I suppose is also the Bobby. I don't think I'm ever a Baron – that sort of autocrat went out of the police 10 years ago.

There is a sense then, in which leadership is role playing. It is acting out the part that is required by the event or the circumstances or the demands of the situation (see Shafer, 2009). One chief officer went on to note that selecting the particular leadership mode to suit the situation was akin to a mechanical process, but a significant number (more than a quarter) of chief officers expressed impatience with the whole notion of labelling what kind of leader a chief officer is:

> **Interviewee 67:** None of these stereotypes. I doubt they were ever true of policing, even back in the Dark Ages when Reiner did his research of the 43 robber barons who ruled then. I am a chief constable who has interim command of a police force for about five years or so. I'm the one who gives the lead, sets the tone and embodies the character of that force for the time I'm in charge, But others will come after me with very different styles and tones, as remote from me as I am from the old-style chiefs who reigned when I joined. The four [Reiner] stereotypes are actually gross generalisations of what police leadership really is: we are all of these things in different concentrations, different strengths. No one should predominate; none should be absent.

Research by Marisa Silvestri in 2007 suggested that women police leaders incline to the transformational, but seem forced by circumstances to be transactional, like some of their male colleagues (see also Kingshott, 2009). Silvestri's sample was too small to be definitive but her findings certainly are echoed by this chief officer's comment:

> **Interviewee 76:** I'm impatient of these labels which have hung about police top leadership for 20 years or more. I'm a chief officer who happens to be a woman. Yes I try to be transformational but the 'gender thing' – which still persists by the way – means I often have to be dictatorial and order something to be done.

Another officer believed strongly that 'Reiner's journalistic clichés' did not aid understanding of the complexity of leadership. The nature of decision making was not expressed by labels, he said, but by difficult judgements:

> **Interviewee 15:** None of these outmoded notions. The new formulation of police leadership does not lend itself to quaint one-word labels to typify an enormously complex process. My role is to understand how a big organisation like a police force works and to know what I can change and what I leave alone

A colleague agreed, adding:

> **Interviewee 5:** I am an innovator, a seminal thinker, who leads. I'm not a stereotype or a label, especially as I spend a huge amount of time teaching people to think for themselves and showing them how to construct their own paths within a broadly agreed landscape.

One interviewee was emphatic that chief officers should not accept simplistic solutions:

> **Interviewee 32:** You're the sum of all that you have been influenced by and your accretion of experience makes you very individual. I can't stereotype others, so why should I stereotype myself?

but other chief officers want to redefine the nature of what they do and how they do it and thus want to give the process a different descriptive label:

> **Interviewee 89:** I prefer the term 'senior executive leader' to describe my role.
>
> [Interviewer: Do you really? It's a bit of a mouthful, isn't it?]
>
> Well, it is the appropriate style in most circumstances and I am not a one-trick pony: the entrenched style limits your responses, even though you have to be transactional in command and transformational in planning. Policing from the top means that you have to be able to run a complex organisation and dictators don't do that very well, because they simply are not right every time. Using persuasion and consensus means that you are probably more often right than wrong, or that you can flex if things don't go according to plan.

It is interesting to reflect on this comment that the interviewee feels more comfortable with being able to change from one stance to another if circumstances demand flexibility, than in having what he called 'an entrenched style' which would not allow him such manoeuvre. Taking people with you and agreeing a way forward enables this chief officer to attain preponderance in 'right' decisions, though it is not clear at what cost to time and how widespread and extensive the consultation is.

Others saw the whole process as a piece of theatre:

> **Interviewee 49:** Boss by default if nothing else, because that's the role I have as a chief constable. Do you want to persuade, cajole, insist, override, determine or evaluate? Depending on what you want, you'll adapt your command/lead profile appropriately. All an act, really.

One sceptical chief officer thought that the dominant characteristic of police leaders was more destructively about self:

> **Interviewee 82:** What is self-evident is that all leaders in the police service have huge egos; that must be so or none of us would have persisted in getting to the top. The important thing is to manage those egos. Among Nolan's seven principles for probity in public office[22] is selflessness and this is where police leaders fail again and again, because there is often no more room once the ego is accommodated.

There is, then, little consensus now on whether a 'type' of police leader predominates, let alone whether it is one of the labels that Reiner came up with a generation ago. Today's chief officers decisively reject 'simple labelling' by some margin. Although 23% can live with some form of single designation, 77% cannot. Of the latter majority, more than a quarter rejected what they saw as the misleading nature of leadership labels and stereotypes, whether they came from Robert Reiner or from leadership theorists. Just over half of all those questioned believed that the most practical response was to suit the style to the occasion, and that therefore they embraced a pragmatic mix of leadership styles according to the demands of the situation they faced.

---

[22] Lord Nolan, who had a reputation as a difficult and anti-establishment Law Lord, was asked to chair a Committee which would examine and determine Standards in Public Life. The Committee first sat in 1994 and reported in 1995 offering seven principles to guide public conduct (Nolan, 1995).

Leading from the front?

Chief officers were also asked *How do you get people to follow you?* (see Table 3.2).

Table 3.2: Getting people to follow your lead

	Number	Percentage
Consult/persuade	40	44%
Order/command	25	28%
Mix of styles	6	7%
'Vision'	19	21%
Totals	**90**	**100%**

One chief officer saw the answer in terms of proportions of the workforce:

> **Interviewee 79:** A third of your force will follow you unquestioningly because that's what they do. Slightly less than a third will follow you because, like you, they believe that where you want to go is the right direction. The remaining third, or perhaps a little more, will dig in their heels like mules and budge only with much swearing and resistance.
>
> I don't think that that is peculiar to coppers alone but it's certainly characteristic of every single innovation I have tried in policing.

Another agreed, identifying one hard-to-convince layer of management as being particularly intransigent:

> **Interviewee 67:** The hardest bunch to get to follow you are the inspector ranks – what would be middle management in private organisations. Those near the top [of the force] will follow you because you have persuaded them and they have listened and discussed with you. The bottom ranks don't give a stuff as long as the overtime continues. But the inspectors – I've had session after session with them, explaining something quite uncontroversial, like shift systems or media strategy, and I've been stone-walled all the way. They listen with blank faces, say nothing, ask no questions and then do bugger-all to help. So most initiatives founder on this rock of indifference and obstinacy. And I'm not alone. Most of my colleagues will tell you the same.

Others though, saw the problem of 'conversion' as located among their chief officer colleagues rather than with the rank-and-file:

> **Interviewee 11:** I have no problem with lower ranks: they mostly are signed up to the same changes as I am, and I've been blessed with excellent chief superintendents […] who have been brilliant. It is among my peers and higher up that I have problems in selling new ideas or approaches. Getting them to agree to a new idea (which in a sense is 'following' in the way you mean it) is difficult because all the battery of assumptions and accumulated wariness come into play, plus I'm a woman and that makes some of my male colleagues nervous – not just of the change but of the origin of the change. They find it threatening.

Another saw resistance to change as a natural feature of people management:[23]

> **Interviewee 5:** Resistance to change is endemic. If I want to introduce change (and leading change is integral to the leadership job), then I need to identify who the opinion formers are. There are about 15 to 20 of them in any group of 100 officers, right across the ranks. Find out who they are and what makes them tick. Then work out ways to get them to follow your lead, and the others will follow them. […] It's necessary too to identify how factions work in a force. There are alliances which are built up over a long time (for example, there are a dozen chief constables who were on the sergeants course with me 20 years ago), and these can permeate whole structures to protect people.

One chief officer noted that success as a leader depends on acknowledging that a leader has to deserve respect. It is not something that can be commanded, and the police service accepts only those who deliver, not those who posture. He went on to observe that

> **Interviewee 27:** My bottom line is a belief that you can't choose to be somebody's leader. They will give you a chance by virtue of your rank or status but at the end of the day they will decide whether [or not] they want to follow you.

---

[23] See Maccoby (2007) for an intelligent essay on this aspect of leadership.

Others believed in an honest, no-nonsense approach to staff, noting that not telling the truth, or even delaying the release of information was actually misleading and patronising:

> **Interviewee 70:** It's important to focus on the positives in any change of direction or emphasis, and to 'get ugly early'.
>
> [Interviewer: What does that mean?]
>
> If it's bad news on Monday, it will still be bad news on Friday. People don't want you to dance about; they'd rather know the truth early. Too many leaders make the mistake of trying to let people down gently: at best, you'll confuse them, at worst it will seem to them that you are evasive and dishonest.

but some showed impatience for engagement:

> **Interviewee 67:** I do it by showing them what benefits are in it for them. Ultimately, if they don't come on board they have to walk the fucking plank.

Others rely on persuasion, but it has its limits. One officer thought that the changes which came from politicians or from the government 'machine' were the most difficult to implement, because people could be sceptical about them. However, even apparently minor matters, like uniform, could rouse antagonism:

> **Interviewee 53:** Sweet reason usually works, plus the fact that most changes are painfully obvious and necessary. Changes as the result of a political decision, such as Best Value or neighbourhood policing, are always the hardest to sell. That said, black polo-neck shirts proved sticky[24] – memories of the fascists and Mosley, I suppose.[25] Nothing causes more upset and furore among police officers at every rank than suggestions to change uniform or

---

[24] From about 2007, changes to the police 'standard' uniform of white shirt, tie and tunic were discussed and black polo-neck shirts were a popular option, with blouson style jackets. Not all forces adopted the proposals and many continue with the shirt, tie and tunic conventions. Others have embraced the new uniform with enthusiasm.
[25] A reference to the 'black shirts' worn by the British Union of Fascists (BUF), admirers of Adolf Hitler and the Nazis in Germany, who were founded by Sir Oswald Mosley (1896–1980) in 1932.

equipment. I've seen grown men almost come to blows about what is displayed on epaulettes.

and the notion of success is key:

Interviewee 50: Bringing people with you and convincing them that you mean business, is all about 'propaganda of the deed'.

[Interviewer: Can you explain what you mean?]

It is not what you say that convinces people to support you and to implement your ideas; it is what you do. We all arrive at command with baggage and people know all about us. Some will follow you because of that baggage, some will follow you because they want a piece of what you are going to do. The rest fall into place behind without having thought much at all. But you'll be swiftly abandoned as just another flash in the pan unless you deliver by doing.

This goes to the heart of an issue in leadership in general which is that leaders have to be successful. There appears not to be much open recognition of the 'success factor' in leadership competencies, but the inescapable and obvious fact remains that few people will want to follow someone who has missed the target, and none at all will want to be associated with a leader who is a persistent failure. Success on the other hand attracts numerous adherents, most of whom want to share in the spoils or the spotlight which comes with a track record of achievement. The police leaders who are talked about as exemplars by other police officers are those who have stunning and evident successes to their names.

Changes in police leadership

Finally, I asked chief officers (Table 3.3): *Has leadership in the police changed since you joined? How? What has stayed the same?*

Table 3.3: Leadership in the police now

	Number	Percentage
Better than it was	50	53%
Worse than it was	34	36%
Same or not sure	10	11%
Totals	**94**	**100%**

The following may be taken as typical of the responses from those who think that leadership has improved markedly in the last few years, with apparently a greater emphasis now on skills than on networking opportunities. This respondent believes that the police service is indeed better than it was, but there is still a tendency for chief officers to revert to command strategies when threatened:

> **Interviewee 15:** Leadership has changed enormously. When I first joined in the 1980s, policing was still very heavily transactional; nearly all chiefs had done National Service and were influenced by military thinking. It was incestuous, inward-looking and chiefs then did not see that change was part of management. Now, it is much more to do with the quality of service and there is a much more professional ethos. Sadly, when threatened by external change, the police service reverts to transactional leadership and consultation or consensus go out the window.

Another chief officer speaks for many when he says that the police are not good at making a coherent case either for leadership or for value:

> **Interviewee 70:** Leadership is in crisis in the police; I mean that. There is incoherence about what leadership means; indeed [the service's] strategy on leadership is meaningless. [...] The police can't evidence that they are value for money or rebut the Treasury criticism that we waste money, and the effect is that the government mistrusts the police. Leadership of and through change is vital, but we'll get it only when we have a proper police staff college and it's run by ACPO not by NPIA.

This chief officer presciently saw that ACPO would take control of the police leadership agenda once NPIA was abolished (in 2010). The upshot of the police not being able to 'evidence that they are value for money' is that public sector finance cuts lie heavily on them and many forces have suspended recruiting. It is often an easy default to suppose that the police are best able to judge themselves what they need (Neville, 2003), but others, including HM Chief Inspector of Constabulary (see Chapter Four), disagree strongly.

This next interviewee believes that management change in policing is in response to changes in society generally, producing leaders with a different way of doing things, but the essence has changed only on the surface:

> **Interviewee 27:** In my view, police management has changed immeasurably in response to changes in society and general business trends. It has had to. I suspect that many of my old bosses wouldn't have survived long in today's performance-driven, litigious, over-regulated, wired for sound (and vision) world. Senior police managers [now] shout less and negotiate more. Police leadership, on the other hand, has changed far less. Leadership styles may have changed generally to become softer, more communicative, more transformational but the same qualities and characteristics which caused me to follow my sergeant into a pub fight, knowing that I was likely to get hurt in the process, are still as relevant today as they were 30 years ago.

The final comment for which there is space, is from someone who clearly believes that the police manage, but do not lead:

> **Interviewee 36:** It has changed on the surface, I think, with greater media savvy and more evident skills in handling the public appearance of policing, but I don't think that leadership has changed fundamentally. It is still absolutely bloody awful, basically, and most people who get to the top, including me, get there because they can manage, not because they can lead. I think leadership in the police is still in its infancy and it has got to develop if it is ever to be taken seriously. At the moment it is all froth and bubbles.

If this is true, then the outlook for policing is not promising. If the emphasis really is still on management rather than leadership, and if it is true that 'at the moment it is all froth and bubbles', then the onus on ACPO, and on the Police National Leadership College *and* on the current generation of emerging chief officers, is heavy indeed. It is they who will have to strike out a new way and develop a fresh direction in which police leadership can thrive and properly define or describe itself. The alternative is dependency on the policy makers, law givers and stakeholders to define what a police leader is or should be. At the very least therefore, ACPO should have ownership of the process by which chief officers are made, whether or not 'chartered institute' status is a precursor.

Peter Neyroud's recommendations in his *Review* (2011), if implemented, will have profound impact on how the police themselves conceive leadership and whether or not they 'own' it professionally.

Conclusions

There seems to be considerable pessimism among chief officers about the nature of leadership in the police and about what its constituents should be. Some of that pessimism, or scepticism, stems from bad personal experiences; some from strong leaders who were nonetheless eventually defeated by the inertia of the policing 'system'. Yet more seem daunted by the size of the task and the contradictions inherent in leadership styles to do more than muddle along.

Chief officers generally reject the typologies suggested by Reiner 20 years ago, and a substantial majority thinks that leadership styles should suit the occasion in which the most appropriate is selected and followed. Some reject the labelling tendency out of hand, and believe that policing needs to mature and move away from the shackles imposed by such received wisdom or typologies. Many think that the lead which they give is about 'selling' ideas to the uninvolved rank-and-file of the police, who view their efforts with amusement but little toleration. Others believe that they are followed for as long as they are successful. Remarkably, there is little unity on what constitutes a successful police leader and even less on whether such attributes can be taught (Schafer 2009). The notion of chief officer competencies indicating, by their attainment, leadership qualities, is regarded with scorn by some and as over-generalised by others.

Much more in the way of objective scholarly research is needed into whether or not there is a specifically *police* leader, or whether leaders from any sphere would translate successfully into the upper echelons of the police. Most of the police themselves, as we shall see in later chapters, regard policing experience and consequent credibility with the rank-and-file as more important than leadership skills and aptitudes. It is difficult to see how these insistently experiential and accretive approaches can modify the leadership skills sets, simply because the ranges of competencies from the 12 categories espoused by ACPO and Skills for Justice, are mostly generic to any leader in any occupation. It remains to be seen whether the government will implement the recommendations in the Neyroud Review (2011), but they seem cogent, largely pragmatic and may help to systematise chief officer development ('after the fact' of appointment as a chief officer may be less sensible). The competencies will almost certainly change in number and range; it is to be hoped that they can be more specific to police leadership than they are currently.

If 'any leader' can command those competencies from any other walk of life, it would seem to follow logically that those in possession of such skills would be able to lead police forces (see Chapter Five). Yet there is some instinctive rejection inside the police of such a notion and a widespread insistence that there must be some sort of quantifiable policing leadership skills which have not yet been properly identified, except as banal descriptions of behaviours. Clearly there is more to be done, more to be understood, and more research to be undertaken in longitudinal studies if the conundrum of defining police leadership is to be properly resolved.

FOUR

Oversight and chief officers' relationships with police authorities, directly elected police crime commissioners, HMIC and the Home Office

Relations between chief officers and police authorities

Responding to the initiatives, requirements and oversight of the police authority, both as a corporate body and in individual interactions, is one of the clear divides between the largely operational command role of a chief superintendent and the strategic command role of the chief officer.[1] This interrelationship is unlikely to change substantially when the police authority as a body is replaced in mid-2012 by the directly elected police crime commissioner (PCC) and his or her supporting police and crime panel. The 15% or so of an average chief officer's time which is devoted to police authority matters (local oversight) does not always produce or encourage mutual cooperation or understanding. Occasionally, the contrast between private and public demeanour can be startling:

> **Interviewee 26:** I was once fronting at a public meeting – you know, one of these dreary 'meet the people' affairs in a cold and draughty village hall where you speak to four malcontents, two ne'er-do-wells, a trio of worthies and the local idiot. The chair of the police authority was with me and she and I had never got on. I couldn't do anything right for her. Anyway, someone got up and

[1] There are exceptions to this, of course: there are chief superintendents who play a markedly strategic role just as there are chief officers who have active operational tasks that seldom reach the strategic dimension. The difference generally between the highest 'executive' rank and the lowest 'board' rank is in the application of strategic considerations across the spectrum of work. In policing that inevitably incurs contact with oversight mechanisms, and locally, that means the police authority, or the PCC.

started slagging off the police and me in particular and the chair pitched straight in and really did this man's legs. She fairly ripped into him, saying about what a fantastic job the police were doing and what a marvellous chief constable I was, and how he wouldn't recognise the value of his freedoms if he fell over them and the audience cheered her to the echo. Exhilarating stuff. But there she was next day at headquarters back to having a bloody good go at me as though nothing had changed. If I hadn't been there to see it, I'd never have believed it.

The bemusement of this chief officer at the unpredictable actions of the chair of his police authority, the scarcely veiled antagonism between the police and their local oversight mechanism, and the ubiquity of the political games that seem to be played out both in private and public between chief officers and those appointed or elected to the police authority, are nicely captured in this rueful anecdote. I propose to explore in greater depth the tensions that appear to exist between some chief officers and their police authorities (collectively and as individuals), the ways in which those tensions are sometimes expressed; the origins of the unease which the police feel about 'supervision by amateurs' and the ways in which some wily police officers manipulate their sometimes naïve or gullible police authority members. The viewpoint I give is almost entirely that of the chief officer rather than the police authority member, partly because this is a book about chief officers, and partly because the opportunity to respond on behalf of police authorities, though extended several times to the Association of Police Authorities (APA), was not taken up.

The responses which I now examine are derived from a single question posed to chief officers: *How would you describe your relationship with your police authority or other oversight body?* There were 89 respondents to the question (Table 4.1), more or less starkly in two camps:

Table 4.1: Relationships with police authorities[2]

	Number	Percentage
Negative about police authorities	62	70%
Positive about police authorities	27	30%
Neutral or no comment	0	0%
Totals	**89**	**100%**

[2] Or an equivalent oversight body composed of lay or criminal justice members.

To understand the tensions that might exist between some chief police officers and members of their police authority, it is necessary first to have a brief foray into history. From before Tudor times, the function of maintaining law and order in a local community was overseen by the 'watch committee', a group of respectable residents in a town or district with a vested interest in maintaining the peace. Following the establishment of uniformed civilian police forces across England and Wales during the 19th century (counties and cities having taken their lead from the establishment of the New Police by Robert Peel in London in 1830), the watch committees needed reformation and re-evaluation. In 1889, 'standing joint committees' were created, which were composed of local and county councillors and magistrates. This formal oversight mechanism for the police remained until the Police Act 1964, when police authorities were established.[3] This new body consisted of two thirds local and county councillors and one third magistrates. Power in policing was effectively shared on a tripartite basis between the Home Secretary, the police authority and the chief constable, where none had an absolute monopoly of power, but where all three were supposed to work in balance.

Under subsequent legislation (Police and Magistrates' Courts Act 1994), most police authorities were defined as consisting of 17 people in a mix of elected councillors, independent appointees and the magistracy.[4] The remit of the police authority was laid out in schedule 4.1 of the 1994 Act as follows:

> It shall be the duty of every police authority [...] to secure
> the maintenance of an efficient and effective police force
> for its area.

The composition of police authorities changed again with the Police and Justice Act 2006, when magistrate members no longer formed a separate category, but at least five (though normally eight) police authority members – one of whom must be from 'lay justice' – are formally appointed as *independent* of any political party (appointments are, however, approved by the Home Secretary which may allow political patronage to show its nose from time to time).

---

[3] APA, the national body, was not formed until 1997.

[4] London's Metropolitan police authority has 23 members, and there are 19 in each of Greater Manchester, South Wales, Thames Valley and Devon and Cornwall police authorities (mostly because of police authority amalgamations), each comprising of 10 elected councillors, three lay justice members and six independent members.

All this is of a piece with contemporary political platforms about empowerment of local communities and the realigning of relationships between neighbourhoods and the police within a 'Big Society'. Police authorities are representatives, collectively, of the public. They are, or should be, responsive to the public's sense of security, its fear of crime and its satisfaction with the police. The Home Secretary acts on behalf of the government (and, theoretically, expresses the will of the whole electorate) by delivering central policy direction to the police service of England and Wales, and to police authorities. The police, for their part, are the 'gateway' to the criminal justice system: investigating crime without fear or favour, keeping the peace, preventing lawlessness and acting independently of any political agendas, local or national.

Day-to-day contact between police authority/PCC, Home Office and the police tends to be at the chief officer level, strategically geared and oriented in terms of police performance. It is here, among chief officers anyway, that we find the private frustrations, the hidden anger and resentment and the relative intensity of feelings about being held to account. Most chief officers understand that they must be held to account; it seems to be the ways in which this happens, including degrees of relish or venom within the processes, that they object to.

However, a couple of significant changes have been made, more or less quietly, to the tripartite 'balance of power' described in the preceding paragraph. The Home Secretary has taken powers, under the Police and Justice Act 2006, effectively to be able to remove, or require a police authority to remove, a chief constable. This was in the wake of a highly public and rather unedifying battle of wills in 2004–05 between the Chief Constable of Humberside and the then Home Secretary, David Blunkett, following Sir Michael Bichard's report into the police investigation of the Soham murders in 2003.[5] At the same time and through the medium of the same Act, the powers and remit

---

[5] The chief constable, David Westwood, refused to step down when his force was accused of mishandling the intelligence which might have prevented Ian Huntley being appointed as a primary school's caretaker in Soham, Cambridgeshire in 2003. Huntley used his appointment to obtain access to Holly Wells and Jessica Chapman whom he subsequently murdered. Sir Michael Bichard in his 2004 report on the murders noted that 'There were very serious failings in the senior management of Humberside Police and [...] the current Chief Constable Mr Westwood must take personal as well as corporate responsibility for not identifying and dealing with these earlier, once he became Chief Constable in 1999' (see Bichard, 2004). The then Home Secretary, David Blunkett, was frustrated by his inability to demand the chief constable's departure and by the refusal of the Humberside police authority to sack him. Mr Westwood eventually reached a compromise with both the other sides of the

of police authorities were extended. To understand the significance of these changes and the uneasiness with which they are regarded by some chief officers, we must look in greater detail at how police authorities function.

The primary remit for police authorities is, as noted under Schedule 4.1 of the 1994 Act, to ensure on behalf of the public, that their police forces are 'efficient and effective'; this usually entails scrutinising the work of the force and holding the chief constable to account. In practice, the principal contacts that police authority members have with their police force are the range of chief officers, whom they meet regularly. For their part, chief officers tend to modulate or control the individual police authority member's access to other policing ranks and the general workforce below the board level. The police authority is formally responsible for consulting with local people about the kinds of service the public expects from its police; it publishes an annual plan setting out targets for and required services from the force and it holds the purse-strings. Because the police authority also sets the 'precept' (the amount by which local council tax rises annually or sometimes triennially to pay for policing), it has a powerful voice in how much money there is and where it goes.

Scrutiny of the force budget and the detail of expenditure is one of the primary means by which a police authority holds a chief constable to account. The non-elected (local civil servant) role of police authority finance director or treasurer — there are a number of designations — is a very powerful one, second only to the elected chair/PCC and the appointed chief executive or clerk. There are various other factors for which the police authority has responsibility, such as ensuring proportionate ethnic and gender mixes in the police force, quality assuring the nature of learning and development and overseeing 'comprehensive performance improvement' (which used to be called Best Value) (Raine, 2008).

But there are two remaining areas of considerable power. First, the police authority/PCC is the designated employer of all police staff (that is, all employees of the force other than warrant-holding police officers) and it can hire and fire the chief officers themselves. Second, since early 2009, the police authority has conducted the annual appraisal of the chief constable and has an input into the performance development reviews (PDRs) of the other chief officers. This combination of the

'triangle': he remained as chief constable to put Bichard's proposed reforms in place and then quietly retired.

employer role and the assessor role makes police authorities increasingly powerful, and has led to many chief police officers feeling uneasy.

With such augmented powers, police authorities can often be accused by chief officers of interfering with the operational independence of the police, a point made clearly by Sir Paul Stephenson (former Commissioner of the Metropolitan Police and successor to Sir Ian Blair), when he remarked, during his keynote speech at the annual Conference of the Superintendents' Association in 2009, that:

> There must be appropriate space between policing and politics. The principle of the operational independence of the police was set in stone and must not be compromised. (O'Neill, 2009a, 2009b)

This seems to have been provoked by a comment by the Deputy Mayor of London, Kit Malthouse,[6] that he and the Mayor now 'had their hands on the tiller' of the Metropolitan Police. Sir Paul's comments caused a minor political storm at the time (September 2009), and provoked an idiosyncratic letter to *The Times*, part of which read:

> Independence in policing means to apply the law fairly and impartially, free from any influence other than the decisions of the courts. The founders of modern policing were as much concerned to protect the public from the tyranny of government as they were to save the citizen from the partiality of local politics.[7]

'The partiality of local politics' indeed concerns some chief officers, who see the steady encroachment of the police authority into police operational matters as the beginning of the end of police independence. One chief officer laconically noted:

Interviewee 54: Sadly, my relations with my police authority have become frosty and correct rather than warm and informal,

---

[6] From February 2010, Deputy Mayor Kit Malthouse took over from Boris Johnson as the chair of the Metropolitan police authority.

[7] Letter from Lawrence T. Roach (Deputy Assistant Commissioner, Metropolitan Police Service, 1990–96), published on *The Times* Letters to the Editor page on 19 September 2009. The late Mr Roach (he died in 2010) was an inveterate but delightful correspondent on policing matters. For his part, Sir Paul Stephenson took issue with a press report that he resented *all* MPA interference, noting that a police authority's job was to hold the police to account (letter to *The Times* on 17 September 2009).

and that's down to them. They flexed their muscles after the Boris Johnson/Ian Blair business and encroached significantly on my command boundaries. So I had to drive them off and that has set back relations somewhat.

Another was sure that the police were disadvantaged by processes owned by the police authority and that the 'partnership' was inequitable:

> **Interviewee 89:** Well, their [police authority] role is not just to challenge, but to be supportive and helpful. They'd soon bleat if we weren't here, yet nearly everything we try is challenged, criticised, dismissed or patronised. It should not be an adult–child relationship, but a serious partnership between equals. Sometimes I think my team and I are the only ones playing by the rules.

One chief officer thought that it was not simply the police who needed oversight: the whole monitoring system was at fault:

> **Interviewee 30:** Police authorities may want to throw their weight about in the wake of Boris Johnson's sacking of Sir Ian Blair, and the sad thing about all that, is that no one has the responsibility for keeping the balance between politics, public and police.

However, some forces have tried to create precisely that 'responsibility for keeping the balance' by signing up to protocols with their police authorities to make the boundaries between operational policing and the exercise of oversight clearer and less ambiguous. The following is adapted from the protocol in Gwent:

> *It is the chief constable's job:*
> - to lead the police service
> - to formulate policy
> - to manage operational policing
> - to make the best use of financial and other resources made available by the police authority
> - to deliver efficient and effective policing. (Gwent Police Authority, 2009, p 1)

We may observe here that *what the police force actually does* remains, or should remain, under the 'direction and control' of the chief constable (and therefore with the chief officers in the force).[8] This is what is meant by the shorthand term 'operational policing'. Note too that ancillary actions, such as showing leadership, and presumably example, and formulating policy, are also 'pure' functions of the police. It is only when we reach the final pair of bullet points that we encounter qualitative performance measures: the chief is to spend wisely the money that s/he gets from the police authority, and will 'deliver efficient and effective policing'.

The police authority is joined in judgement whether or not the force's expenditure is wise and its policing 'efficient and effective' by HMIC (Her Majesty's Inspectorate of Constabulary) and the Home Office in the wake of force or thematic inspections. The HMIC inspection reports are provided to the police authority, of course, but these triangular oversight mechanisms are those that make *qualitative* judgements of the force, and therefore of the chief officers, and they are reinforced at both local and national levels. Nonetheless, the phrases used above to describe what a chief constable may do, look simple enough, but in fact they mask a world of complexity and multiple assessments, where power struggles are often implicit or disguised.

What is the police authority's responsibility? The Gwent protocol tells us that

> *It is the police authority's job:*
> * to promote, support and uphold the police service
> * to ensure through consultation that the demands and aspirations for policing of local people are reflected in policing policy
> * to determine an affordable budget
> * to approve policing strategies and organisation
> * to monitor and review policing performance and to hold the Chief Constable to account for it
> * to account to Gwent people for policing performance. (Gwent Police Authority, 2009, p 1)

The members of this police authority stand *in locus* for the people and they are guardians of fiscal responsibility. Active verbs such as 'ensure', 'determine' and 'approve' are all testament to the deliberative proactivity of the police authority role, though it is probably more accurate to

---

[8] Section 2 of the Police Reform and Social Responsibility Bill (2011) provides, in a time-honoured phrase, that 'a police force and the civilian staff of a police force, are under the direction and control of the Chief Constable of the force'.

say that the elected and appointed members of the police authority symbolically represent the public, rather than that they are genuinely representative of the people. Only some 30% of the electorate votes for local councillors across England and Wales, so the mandate that provides nine of the authority's 17-strong membership is hardly overwhelming. The other eight appointees represent only independence of *politics*; they can make few claims to representativeness of the population at large.[9] We may presume that, from 2012, the PCC will have a remit similar to that of the police authority – and presumably may attract precisely the same opprobrium from chief officers for precisely the same reasons. It is not clear yet whether the police and crime panel which supports the PCC will be elected or appointed.[10]

But look too at what this typical police authority has described as its remit: it can 'monitor and review' policing performance, so a failure to attain a target such as reduction in anti-social behaviour, can be used currently to bring the chief constable to account, while at the same time ensuring that further measures against anti-social behaviour will appear prominently in any subsequent policing plan. The HMIC report *Closing the Gap* (O'Connor, 2005) noted *en passant* that anti-social behaviour hardly registered with the Home Office or with the police service, but it had enormous resonance for local people who were subject to it.

Elevating such (often non-criminal) matters to the level of strategic priorities for policing is within the scope of a police authority. It is then, hardly surprising that the police can privately resent the power and influence that an authority has over how policing is conducted. These reservations can be interpreted as the pangs of slow adjustment from policing as something about which 'the police know best', to something where the public knows full well what its worries are and wants to determine the appropriate police response. Police authorities seem to be very willing midwives to this new birth, ensuring that 'the demands and aspirations for policing of local people' indeed find

---

[9] See Mortimore (2002) and IPSOS/MORI psephological studies which found in 2000 that turnout in local election was '36% in the shire districts, 31% in the unitary authorities and 26% in the metropolitan boroughs'. Electoral Commission findings in 2001 and local election results in May 2010 tell much the same story.

[10] See Home Office (July 2010) and the *Draft Protocol* (Home Office, 2011b). The police and crime panel will probably consist of 'elected councillors' but it is not clear whether they are elected precisely on a police platform or whether they are appointed once elected. Former Chief Constable Dr Tim Brain wrote a thoughtful piece in which he asked some thoroughgoing questions about the PCC vis-à-vis the chief constable which need to be resolved (see Brain, 2010).

reflection in local policing priorities. In their turn, the police authority is technically *accountable* to the local populace *for policing performance*, so it is again not surprising that the mechanisms for evaluating policing performance should loom so large in the police authority's planning, discussions, meetings and assessments.

But let's unpick this for a moment. In what precise sense is a police authority 'accountable' and to whom? How does it show its accountability to local people and what are the sanctions for failure? It seems highly unlikely that police authority members will be hurled from office by a vengeful electorate if they do not deliver promptly on policing performance. Indeed, amid its many other concerns, it is not really credible that a local electorate would take specific account of people from the police authority, some of whom will be up for re-election every three or four years. What voter, worried about mortgages or jobs, loans or credit, would be bothered that 17 low-profile or unknown people missed their avowed targets? How could a bruising media campaign develop on such slight foundations? And even in the event that nine councillors are dismissed by the voters successively over three years, what happens to the other unelected eight? Do they step down in solidarity with their colleagues or tough it out with a new crowd of nine elected representatives? The same questions may be asked of the PCC who will serve up to two four-year terms. Will the citizens respond to any intransigence or lack of responsiveness to local issues on the PCC's part through mass disobedience in paying the increased police precept? Will the local community embark on a media campaign to demand the PCC's resignation? Can the panel which advises the PCC respond to public concerns and thereby influence the PCC? Will even fewer of the electorate bother to vote?[11]

I do not know the answers to any of these questions because no police authority or PCC has ever been subject to such detailed public accountability, nor is one ever likely to be so at the hands of a bemused or distracted electorate. So 'accountability to the people' appears to exist in name only as far as most police authorities are concerned. It remains to be seen whether the PCC, elected precisely on a 'crime ticket', will exercise more control over chief officers than police authorities have done, or whether the relationship will be marred (as some believe) by unseemly squabbling and political positioning (Brain, 2010). Indeed, a Lords' amendment to the Police Reform and Social Responsibility

---

[11] See for example, IPSOS MORI, 2000.

Bill on 11 May 2011 required appointment rather than election of the PCC.[12]

But police authorities *are* now subject to an examination or assessment of sorts. In late 2009, the Audit Commission and HMIC together took on the inspection role first mooted in the Policing Green Paper of 2008 (Audit Commission/HMIC, 2009). Twenty-two of the 43 police authorities were inspected between September 2009 and July 2010, and a report on the findings was published in October 2010 (HMIC, 2010), in which it was noted that only one in four of the police authorities performed well in securing 'value for money'. Zoë Bellingham, HM Inspector, noted that

> Police authorities are ill-equipped to deal with the financial crisis. (Bellingham, 2010, p 22)

before concluding that

> [...] authorities were better at meeting short-term challenges than developing long-term strategy. (Bellingham, 2010, p 23)

It is perhaps no accident that reports critical of police authorities' functions have started to appear in advance of their demise and replacement by the PCC. In the absence of details, I presume that some sort of inspection regime will persist to cover the PCCs when they take office from May 2012. I further presume that the police and crime panels that support the PCCs will also be inspected and that HMIC will do the inspecting (the Audit Commission quango having been abolished), but both the consultative document and the government spokespeople have so far been unwarrantably vague about how the assessment mechanics will be done and who will do them (Brain, 2010; Home Office, 2011b).

None of this gives us guarantees that police authorities (or what replaces them) will be subject to the same monitoring rigour and challenge to which they subject police forces, and it will be interesting to see how high the barrier is raised in evaluating police authorities'/ PCCs' actions in 'setting the strategic direction and priorities of the police force' (Home Office, 2011b, p 2). There is nothing here, of

---

[12] That is, appointment of the PCC by the Police and Crime Panel (Amendment 1). The Lords then defeated the Bill by 186 votes to 177, so the Bill returned to the Commons, (*Hansard*, Lords, 11 May 2011, cols 895–932).

course, about accountability to the people and what the penalty is or should be if that accountability is found wanting. Indeed, there is nothing said about what happens if police authorities are found wanting by the inspection process itself. There is certainly no suggestion of government's usual sinister threat of 'special measures'[13] being applied to police authorities. At the same time, both the need for joint inspections and the nature of the distinctions made in the Gwent protocol, actually serve to remind us how powerful police authorities are and how many chief officers increasingly regard them with a mixture of disdain and unease. It is only right, surely, that police authorities, and subsequently the PCC, should also be subject to inspection and made accountable? They may not cost us as much as the police, but police authorities/ PCCs are certainly not free.[14] As citizens, we have as much right to expect that members of a police authority/PCC deliver 'efficiently and effectively' as we have to expect it of the police.

It is notable that none of the examples of protocols or explanations of respective responsibilities actually define what is meant by 'operational policing'. As a result, some chief officers argue, the encroachment is both stealthy and deliberate:

Interviewee 8: They are very slow to decide things and there is 'role creep' as well.

[Interviewer: Role creep?]

---

[13] As, for instance, were imposed on Nottinghamshire Constabulary in February 2010, when chief officers, police authority members and private company executives (all from outside the force) were brought in to review perceived failures: sourced from BBC report dated 30 January 2010: http://news.bbc.co.uk/1/hi/england/ nottinghamshire/8471697.stm; accessed 22 February 2010, and a report to HMIC from the review team on 8 March 2010, reported in *Police Review*, 12 March 2010, p 6, which noted additionally that the DCC had resigned and two of three ACC posts were being advertised. The report concluded that leadership in Nottinghamshire Constabulary and in its police authority was 'weak overall'. See also *Personnel Today* article online: www. personneltoday.com/articles/2010/01/21/53760/nottinghamshire-police-failures- result-in-team-being-sent-in-to-turn-it.html; accessed 5 May 2010.

[14] Some estimates are that the PCC will cost £54 million to install and run; see 'Authorities Query Cost of Commissioners', *Police Review*, 22 October 2010, p 8. The amount of a PCC's salary disproportionately occupies some chief officers as they deplore the possibility that the PCC might earn more than the chief constable. Police authority members are paid expenses only.

> It means that slowly the authority tries to take over the police operational and command structure and starts giving orders, telling us how to do policing. They are deliberately letting their role as an authority develop into something it was never designed to be. I'm not comfortable with my police authority at all.

Gwent police authority is aware that guidelines and boundaries can be crossed and that, ultimately, the success or otherwise of such agreements comes down to the spirit in which they are observed:

> The police authority and the Chief Constable will be successful in carrying out these roles only if they do so in a spirit of partnership. The [...] guidelines flesh out the mutual expectations and responsibilities that are more likely to make this happen. (Gwent Police Authority, 2009, p 1)

But ambiguities remain. Consider this:

> The Chief Constable [of Gwent] will manage all policing operations but will involve the police authority in decisions about the organisational structure of the Force. (Gwent Police Authority, 2009, p 2)

The very existence of protocols which attempt to define boundaries, or make distinctions between respective activities, bespeaks the essential ambiguity which exists between the overseen and the overseer, between chief officer and police authority/PCC.

However carefully they seem to walk around each other publicly, and show overt respect for each other's territory, there is frequently a distinct sense of hackles being raised between some chief officers and their police authorities:

> **Interviewee 11:** I've known three, no four, police authorities now. The recent trend is for them to become more than they were intended to be, and they are demonstrably interfering in how policing is being done. That can't be right, because they are making pronouncements on things that they cannot possibly understand; the consequences of which they cannot possibly appreciate.

It is hardly surprising then, that chief officers regard their police authorities with some reservations. What is at issue is that those reservations can be very negative indeed. This chief officer pulled no punches in describing his antagonism:

> **Interviewee 67:** Fraught, suspicious and mutually antagonistic. The police authority thinks it knows all about policing (actually, of course, it knows fuck-all).

and another was bitterly dismissive of the claims of a police authority chair to be helpful and supportive:

> **Interviewee 48:** They made the most awful pig's ear of the precept here to raise money to pay for the police and it's no surprise that the public is pissed off with the cost of policing; then the chair has the nerve to tell me that he did his best for me. Most disappointing all round, really.

One chief officer, who said that she had tried very hard to engage her police authority members, found that there was sometimes a culture of indifference which translated into stasis:

> **Interviewee 9:** I have worked with three police authorities and they are all different. One authority had no passion for policing at all, just went through the motions: for example, [only] eight out of 17 attended their own annual planning away-day.

while some chief officers were reduced to risky tactics to retain control (as they saw it) and prevent further encroachment on operational policing:

> **Interviewee 60:** I have a hands-off relationship at the moment. They tried to interfere with my operational decision-making, so I froze them out for a while. Now they're really keen to look helpful and supportive.
>
> [Interviewer: Isn't that a bit dangerous as a tactic?]
>
> No, not dangerous. A calculated risk I'd say. They have to know that there are limits beyond which I will not tolerate their interference, however supportive and well-meaning they try to be.

but for many the threat of that 'interference' [15] is real and present:

> **Interviewee 89:** They are lay people seeking to direct and control things that they don't understand. Potentially, this could be explosive. There has been a noticeable swing over the last two years to the PA [police authority] being more directive and really trying to get involved in how we handle crime.

Individual members of the authority can provoke strong reactions from some chief officers, especially when challenge seems a form of posing:

> **Interviewee 56:** Challenge is OK but it has to be proportionate to what the problem is, and too many of them are making political points or strutting their stuff, saying 'Look at me: I ask tough questions, and I'm so clever!' There's one on the authority we call 'Figjam'.
>
> [Interviewer: OK, I'll buy it. What does it mean?]
>
> It means Fuck I'm Good; Just Ask Me.

One chief officer had no doubt about the privileged 'golf-club' exclusivity of the police authority, which stood at odds with the equality and diversity that it officially espoused:

> **Interviewee 32:** The police authority is the last major bastion of white, male, middle-aged, middle-class, conventional do-gooders who have finally made it beyond Neighbourhood Watch.

The published statistics challenge this view. According to HMIC and Audit Commission figures for 2008–09, there were 785 people serving as members of police authorities across England and Wales, of whom 65 (amounting to 8%) were currently drawn from minority ethnic backgrounds, and 224 (amounting to 28.5%) were female.[16] These

---

[15] It is well to remember that antipathy between chief police officers and police authorities is nothing new. Alison Halford's restrained account of the gender-ridden and highly prejudicial treatment she received (1989–92) at the hands of the Merseyside police authority is sobering reading. See Halford, 1993, chapter 7, pp 131–63.

[16] See for example: www.westmerciapoliceauthority.gov.uk/uploads/ 1160140953IndMemberPAs-facts-and-figures%5B1%5D.pdf; accessed 16 February 2010. Other data are presented by the APA itself in publications such as its *Police Authorities: A Quick Guide*, 2010 (or on its website www.apa.police.uk).

data bear comparison with diversity statistics in the best-performing police forces. That said, the majority of authority members *are* male, white and middle class, so there may be some preponderant basis for this chief officer's belief that appointed members bear some affinity with those in Neighbourhood Watch.

For some police officers, a really acidulated few, the question is not the ethnic or social origin of police authority members, but their mental capacity:

> **Interviewee 36:** [...] by and large, the people who go into local politics, let alone into police authorities, have the mental capacity of an egg. They are almost all very stupid, prejudiced and egoistic people who do not have the remotest notion about policing. I know that my police officers have a much closer relationship with the community they police than any local councillor or police authority member has, and as long as that persists, police authorities, whether magistrate or local councillor, will always be seen as peripheral or irrelevant.

This sense of aggrieved defensiveness, which has characterised many of the chief officers' views expressed to this point, is by no means universal. Some chief officers say that they get on well with their police authorities and see relations as:

> **Interviewee 27:** A healthy blend of support and challenge built on mutual respect. We have a shared ambition to provide an effective local policing service which by and large keeps us pointing in the same direction. There are occasional tussles over control and accountability but they are [usually] resolved amicably.

a point echoed by another chief officer:

> **Interviewee 81:** Intrinsically, the PA members are good people who you can get on really well with if you are prepared to meet them halfway. They are key stakeholders and we are daft to try to control them. What we must do is channel them. I've heard of spiteful agendas and character assassination in other authorities, but the three I've had have been excellent, and hugely, hugely supportive of the hard bits of the job.

It could be that something as simple as taking time to explain issues properly yields dividends for the attentive chief officer:

> **Interviewee 16:** It's OK and I work hard at it: relationships forged in the fire together are enduring and I am quite close to some of my PA members. Certainly they support me and are very positive once they understand the issues fully.

Other chief officers, less well supported perhaps, have a variety of tactics which they use in dealing with the police authorities. One, whose contempt is searing, prefers to treat the authority members like children:

> **Interviewee 58:** They spend most of their time looking bemused, but I work really hard on them. You know, speaking slowly, lots of pictures, that sort of thing. It isn't my fault that they're a bit thick

while another has an oblique, carefully calculated approach:

> **Interviewee 47:** It's well worth wooing the police authority with lots of attention and giving them small 'victories' which don't really matter but which make them feel good about themselves. I always give them choices – carefully constructed so that it is a win-win for me – and they feel so happy at making a decision, that they're easy to manage.

Another has a more manipulative tactic:

> **Interviewee 70:** I've learned that the way to get them to do what you want is to lay on some sort of demonstration of something like a Taser or dog and handler, something practical and 'policey' and they love that. Then you can hit them with a difficult paper or a tough decision – like increasing the precept – and they'll play along. It always works.

A similar practice is followed by this officer, who mobilises the 'active' elements of policing to sell the brand:

> **Interviewee 19:** It's OK. They're pretty malleable and respond to basic manipulation.
>
> [Interviewer: What sort of manipulation?]
>
> Oh, you know, sob story followed by success-against-all-the-odds story, and they love it when lower-ranking cops come and talk to

them, calling them sir and ma'am. Prime the speakers first and it's kids' play, really.

Other chief officers seem to see the police authority as an obstruction which comes with the strategic territory and which has illusions about its own capability:

> **Interviewee 82:** My police authority is well-meaning but slow to learn and weak in understanding. Its best role is in budget challenge; its worst role is in thinking it understands policing.

One chief officer was dismissive of the majority of police authority members she had encountered, but she admired one exceptional individual for his business skills (which incidentally assisted her in delivering efficiencies):

> **Interviewee 55:** I have little regard for the majority of the members of the police authority as they do not have the skills or knowledge to properly oversee what the force is doing. The one exception that springs to mind was a retired chief executive of a building firm who was really on the ball and helped to bring in a custody suite rebuild on time and on budget – the only capital project to do so in the history of the force!

Admiration of individuals is not unusual, even if chief officers find the authority en masse a source of head-shaking resignation. But this chief officer believes that things are getting better and a more efficient business person is joining the police authority than in the past:

> **Interviewee 13:** Times are changing: police authorities are more intrusive than ever before and the type of authority member is changing too. There are fewer of the old guard political time-servers and more of people with a better business background, which is challenging but often vastly more efficient.

But some police authority members appear to be no match for wily chief constables who keep their private agendas well hidden and who will not scruple to manipulate the authority for their own ends:

> **Interviewee 89:** It seem to vary according to how strongly individual members feel (or have been primed to feel) about particular issues. It got very fraught over amalgamation and tense

over neighbourhood policing: suddenly every authority member was an expert on communities and how to police them. Fortunately, that particular theme happened to chime with my own views and so it went ahead. The police authority now thinks it knows how to influence me, but they're a long way from the truth. To be really honest; very, very few of the police authority earn their place at the table.

A further cause for chief officer concern lies in the political decision in late 2008 to make police authorities responsible for the performance development review (PDR)[17] for chief constables. As I noted in Chapter Three, the police authority also has an input into the PDRs for other chief officers too, either as 'second reviewer' (deputy chief constable) or as a route for appeal (assistant chief constable). Some chief officers are relaxed about the prospects of being reviewed by non-police officers:

Interviewee 64: I am entirely comfortable with the police authority doing my annual PDR, but it means that political control of the police will grow. The need for chief officers to work closely with the police authority has never been more important, and that means working at a range of relationships.

Other are far less comfortable with the prospect:

Interviewee 98: I dread the first PDR with the chair to be honest. I don't know what HMIC has said about me, but I know very well that there are undercurrents and briefings against me. The force record is a good one and we have performed exceptionally well in the last two years, but I really do not know how much credit I will get for that. The police authority thinks, wrongly I believe, that it got these excellent results in spite of me.

The other role of the police authority as the 'hirer and firer' of chief officers and the increasing use of fixed term appointments at all ACPO ranks, means that the antagonism felt so strongly in some police quarters may only get worse:

---

[17] The Policing Green Paper in 2008 suggested that primary responsibility for assessing a chief constable's performance would fall first to the police authority, with career development, promotion and posting continuing with HMIC. I assume that the PCC will take on this role comprehensively from late 2012, but detail is lacking.

Interviewee 72: I've no problem at all with oversight: it's a necessary and healthy part of democracy at work, but the police authority has long exceeded its democratic remit and now sees itself as some sort of 'OffCop', a watchdog investigating the corruptly incompetent. The police may not always get it right but we are by no means the power-mad, repressive and sinister organisation which police authorities all over the country are making us out to be.

The relationship between chief officers and HMIC is examined in detail later in this chapter, but it is worth noting here that some chief officers not only did not want police authorities to assess them for PDR, but did not want to perpetuate the old system where HMIC did it, either. Instead, they thought that ACPO should assess chief officers, arguing that fellow police officers at least understood what their colleagues had to do and what their resources were, which police authorities did not; while HMIC could not both inspect and appraise in the same body.

The Chief HMIC, asked about this proposal, thought that chief officers needed to think more carefully how what amounted to 'self-assessment' might look to the public. Sir Denis O'Connor went on to remark that:

> If chief officers can sell the concept that they self-assess to the 'police market', then fine, but I am sceptical. It would look great on paper, but we're talking about understanding risk. Chief officers cannot be their own judges and juries; there must be external assessment of some kind. If not HMIC or police authorities, then who?[18]

The matter rests with police authorities to make the assessments for PDR of chief officers at the moment, but only an optimist could believe that it will stay there unchallenged. It may be that some compromise is reached eventually where the lay members of the police authority share with an independent professional body (such as the Chartered Institute for Personnel and Development or the Chartered Management Institute or an independent human resources company), the process of PDR assessment. The alternative may be a proliferation of employment tribunals. Certainly, from 2012, the PCC will have the power to hire

---

[18] On-the-record conversation with me, 4 December 2009. Presumably, the coalition government's answer to Sir Denis' rhetorical question might be the PCC?

and fire chief constables[19] (as well as other chief officers) and therefore there will be an employer–employee relationship between them from the outset. That will extend to evidencing competency or otherwise. It is likely too that dismissed chief constables will challenge the PCC's competence in turn, and perhaps seeking the office of PCC for themselves.

Another frustrated chief officer had argued earlier that the police authority seems to believe in some mythology whereby they challenge for challenge's sake, but could not themselves survive in the climate they create for others. The whole process was thereby hypocritical:

> **Interviewee 21:** Sometimes they do not take a sufficiently corporate view of the problem, working in a narrower sector than the police could do – over diversity for example – and they take pleasure in constantly challenging everything I do. I don't object to the challenge but to having to defend my actions and decisions repeatedly, often weeks apart on the same things. I find it particularly disappointing to be challenged on the Force budget when I am doing more with less than they could ever manage.[20] Some of the PA who are ex-business have confided to me privately that their businesses would not have survived on what I have to play with.

One chief officer found that the effort she put into understanding her police authority and its concerns was wasted, simply because members did not understand the quality or nature of improvements in policing when presented to them:

> **Interviewee 76:** When I got here the police authority was part of the failure of the failing police force. I've instituted proper away-days with them because they normally have very little time together and they don't know much about policing, or even about managing and leadership. When we improved our citizen satisfaction with the police by 10% – which by any measure is a staggeringly huge move

---

[19] This was highlighted in late 2010, when the Head of the Chief Police Officers' Staff Association criticised the Home Secretary in these rather convoluted terms: 'There are real concerns among chief officers about what any legislation might bring forwards with regards to checks and balances to ensure that short-termism in the minds of Commissioners does not lead to a Chief being unilaterally dismissed (see 'Commissioners' power to fire is attacked', *Police Review*, 26 November 2010, p 7).

[20] An objective report on police expenditure from which an assessment of chief officers' effectiveness in managing budgets may be made, is Mills et al (2010).

forwards – the PA took it all in its stride and asked me to do the
same thing again the following year!

One fiscally aware chief officer explained that the police authority had
its own responsibilities, which were increased by engagement in Crime
and Disorder Reduction Partnerships (now called Community Safety
Partnerships) and which he, the chief constable, could not help them
with. The relish in his voice is apparent:

> **Interviewee 95:** I enjoy a cracking relationship with my PA, but
> I have had to point out to them that they too have vulnerabilities:
> if they are engaged in things like Crime Reduction Partnerships
> at a local level and things go wrong, they can't then hold me to
> account for their failings. One or two members understood what
> I was saying. Fortunately, we have not yet had to put it to the test.
> IT systems espoused by them look to be going off the rails – the
> line of accountability will stop with them, not me.

The resistible rise of the police crime commissioner

Dissatisfaction with the structure of police authorities and the capacity
of their membership is not confined to chief police officers. Consider
this comment by Michael Gove:

> The level of democratic accountability to which the police
> are subject in Britain today is woeful. The police authorities
> who exercise nominal responsibility for holding the police
> accountable are staffed by well-meaning and in many cases
> capable individuals. But they have limited powers and
> operate without a direct mandate.[21]

Gove was evidently influenced by examples from the US of elected
individuals holding police leaders to account. He suggested that

> The route out of this unhappy impasse is simple, but it
> needs political courage. It requires politicians in Whitehall

---

[21] See Michael Gove, 'If Crime's on the Up, Your Chief Constable Must Explain why
or be Sacked', *The Times*, 15 March 2005, available from www.thetimes.co.uk/tto/
law/columnists/article2042724.ece; accessed 21 June 2010. Mr Gove subsequently was
elected to Parliament and was appointed (2010) as Secretary of State for Education
in the coalition government.

to let go, and allow policing priorities to be set by local people through the direct election of individuals who bear responsibility for crime fighting in their locality. Incompetent chief constables, and we should not be shy of acknowledging they exist, should be forced to fear the wrath of local voters instead of hiding — as so many can — behind [the Home Secretary].[22]

Gove's enthusiasm for this idea made it a reform proposal for the Conservative Party. In opposition, the party appeared resolutely unimpressed with the character and capability of police authorities and supported Gove's idea of replacing them with directly elected crime commissioners. The police immediately registered objection to this notion when it was published in the party manifesto. Sir Hugh Orde, President of ACPO, spoke for many when he averred that some chief constables would resign rather than be subjected to such a regime. However, the Conservative Party manifesto pledge survived the general election in May 2010 and was expressed like this in the coalition government's Queen's Speech to the new parliament on 25 May 2010:

Police Reform and Social Responsibility Bill
Creation of a border police force and overhaul of the 24-hour Licensing Act. *Make the police more accountable through 'directly elected individuals'.* Make sure health and safety doesn't get in the way of 'common sense policing'.[23] (my italics)

Chief officer opposition continued unabated however, and the Prime Minister summoned all 43 chief constables to Downing Street on 21 June 2010, to explain the proposal (in the context of talks about resource constraints). His approach was generally consistent with the view first advanced by Michael Gove, when the latter made his opinion of 'failing' chief officers quite plain:

There is no adequate mechanism in Britain for holding a failing chief constable satisfactorily to account. Like bishops they are nominally accountable to a higher authority, but in truth enjoy near-total job security. Making chief constables

---

[22] Ibid.
[23] Queen's Speech, available from: www.thetimes.co.uk/tto/news/politics/article2525411.ece; accessed 21 June 2010.

directly accountable to a single individual elected to oversee their efforts would not be welcomed by all. Real accountability never is. But our weakest chief constables, like our feeblest bishops, desperately need someone to put the fear of God into them.[24] (Gove, 2005)

It is not entirely clear how a chief constable's perceived 'failure' will be mitigated by terror of the divine, but Gove's views have since become political orthodoxy and may gain greater sway still as police resourcing is increasingly squeezed and force budgets reduced. The coalition government determined quickly that PCCs will replace police authorities from May 2012 (Home Office, 2010b). The prospect seems to make the police as a whole quite nervous. In this context, it is worth noting a comment by a senior official in the Police Federation about the PCC:

> This does not seem to be a recipe for Chief Constables having operational independence. Rather it has all the ingredients for political interference and an irresistible pressure to get quick headline-grabbing results for the sake of political expedience. (Pointon, 2010, pp 18–19)

Sir Hugh Orde, President of ACPO, echoed this concern in his own comments about a single police watchdog':

> Chief Officers understand the need to be accountable to local communities – policing's relationship with the public we serve is the source of its legitimacy and consequently its effectiveness. We now need to examine in detail the government's proposals for maintaining operational independence against the practical reality of directly-elected Police and Crime Commissioners. (Quoted in Caswell, 2010)

The upshot of that 'examination' has been, in the rather bitter words of the departing APA, that ACPO has dropped opposition to the notion of the PCC in favour of increased police powers, but no evidence has been forthcoming in public to support this view.[25] What is clear is that

---

[24] Ibid.

[25] Indeed, the original report of a split between the APA and ACPO over the PCC, in *Police Review*, 22 October 2010, p 5, was qualified the following week as having

the so-far untested areas of accountability to a PCC will preoccupy chief officers increasingly over the next few years. No doubt each will jostle and elbow for room and for power in the interim. What is equally probable is that no single chief officer will resign merely on the principle of the PCC replacing the police authority, no matter what sabre rattling has occurred. In May 2011, the Home Office published a *Draft Protocol* for the police crime commissioner, setting out the role expected of the PCC like this:

> [The PCC] will reconnect the public and the police, and allow us to replace bureaucratic accountability to Whitehall with democratic accountability to local communities. As a result the police will have greater freedom and discretion to fight crime as they see fit within a rebalanced and strengthened tripartite structure. (Home Office, 2011b, 'Introduction')

The *Draft Protocol* goes on to note that the PCC is charged 'with responsibility for the totality of policing within [the force area]' but that 'the will of Parliament and Government is that the Office of Constable shall not be open to political interference' (ibid., p 2). It is too early to say, of course, whether these will become reality or remain aspirations, but it does signal at least that the government is aware of the *potential* for political interference. The inclusion of this sentence may be designed to mollify those chief officers who drew attention to the potential for political interference in the election of single individual. The PCC will hold and control all funding 'related to policing and crime reduction' and will 'set the strategic direction and objectives of the force', as well as 'appoint and where necessary, remove the Chief Constable', while holding the chief constable to account for force performance and function (ibid., p 2). It is perhaps worth remarking that none of these functions varies from those of the police authority other than that they are invested in a single individual rather than a group of 17 or more. However, in the same month (May 2011), the House of Lords defeated the passage of the government Bill which will create the PCC, by 188 votes to 176, endorsing an amendment by Liberal

been 'remarks made in discussion', not as APA public policy (*Police Review*, 29 October 2010, p 12). Nonetheless, as one chief officer (Interviewee 34) told me, 'The APA has thrown its teddy bears out of the cot because it sees the ACPO accommodation of the "crime commissioner" as the beginning of the end for police authorities.' And so it is, despite some convulsions on the issue in newspapers and magazines, and a hiccup in progress through the Lords.

Democrat peers, and signalling that the change from police authorities to police crime commissioners was by no means as automatic as the government had supposed. This does not mean that the Bill will not eventually become law, but the process will be delayed, perhaps delaying in turn the implementation of the PCC in May 2012, and there may be modifications to the post itself, such as appointment rather than election and an increased role embracing oversight, for the crime and police panels designed to support the PCC's work.[26]

Certainly, the transition will not be the simple process that the government evidently hoped for, and police authorities do not intend to go quietly. It is conceivable that the eventual crime and police panels may contain many of those who were in the police authority, which would be a relishable irony, given the entrenched positions that all sides seemed to adopt, once the notion of the PCC started to become more concrete during 2011–12. In terms of operational independence, the *Protocol* notes carefully that the chief constable 'remains free to exercise the powers and duties of a constable without fear or favour' (p 3). Additionally, the PCC is expected to have 'a wider responsibility for the delivery of community safety' and 'the ability to enter into collaboration agreements' (p 3), which opens up a whole field of further speculation as PCCs seek to control or influence local Community Safety Partnerships (CSPs), which are currently under the auspices of local authorities.

The important thing from the point of view of the strategic police leader is that an accommodation with the new PCC will be a priority. Each will treat the other fastidiously to begin with, but no-one can rule out the likelihood of conflict in the future. Perhaps the least debated, but potentially most interesting aspect of the whole process has been the deliberate distancing of Whitehall from the police, expressed by the *Protocol* as 'the establishment of PCCs will allow the Home Office to withdraw from day-to-day policing matters' (Home Office, 2011b, p 5). Whether this distance will persist over time is anyone's guess, particularly given politicians' penchant for interference with policing, but for the present it seems clear that the Home Office (see later) will be more 'hands off' than in the past.

---

[26] See 'Ministers Defeated in Lords over Police Reforms Plan', available at www.bbc.co.uk/news/uk-13368514; accessed 12 May 2011 and Savage, M. Watson, R. and Sherman, J. 'Lib Dem Rebellion Scuppers Tory Policing Plans', *The Times*, 11 May 2011, available at www.thetimes.co.uk/tto/news/politics/article3016317.ece?CMP=EMCeb2; accessed 12 May 2011. The *Protocol* is referenced in the Bibliography under Home Office 2011b.

Relations between chief officers and Her Majesty's Inspectorate of Constabulary

> **Interviewee 57:** Relations with HMIC are mostly cordial on the surface, but you have to remember that these people are poachers turned gamekeepers and that they are not there for you. They're creatures of the Home Office, not chief officers any more.

There have probably always been tensions between the five HMICs and the chief officer ranks from which they are drawn. In a sense, HM Inspectors are easy targets for police scorn: all have long experience of policing having come up through the single-entry system to the chief officer ranks, all of them have been chief constables[27] but are now charged to look on the work of their erstwhile colleagues and estimate its worth. The charge by the chief officer quoted above of HMIC being 'poachers turned gamekeepers' is harsh perhaps, but it is how many chief officers see the inspectorate:

> **Interviewee 12:** People who struggled with their own resources a few months ago are now telling you that you should use yours more wisely. It's hypocrisy in some respects, gratuitously insulting in others.

Indeed, some chief officers see the role of HMIC in the same terms as they see the role of highly paid consultants, and about as much use:

> **Interviewee 64:** Like consultants, [they] would borrow your watch and then tell you the time.

For their part, HM Inspectors do not expect to be popular. They are invited to become Inspectors by the Home Secretary and their concern is to be 'fierce guardians' of the public interest, which at times, will bring them into conflict with their former colleagues. Sir Denis O'Connor, Chief HMIC, remarked

---

[27] One Chief Inspector of Constabulary and four inspectors, normally all former chief constables. The appointment in 1999 of Col. Robin Field-Smith, late Army Education Corps, as HM Inspector of Training was a departure from the norm. Mr Field-Smith later took human resources and diversity into his portfolio, to oversee almost the full spectrum of what police officers call 'soft skills'. Assistant inspectors are usually ACC or equivalent grades who move from forces on temporary promotion to deputy chief constable.

> I would not expect chief officers to be happy with the public inspector who holds them to account: I am moving HMIC from the old comfortable position of 'critical friend' to 'public interest regulator' and we are more willing as a result to tell it how it is. Of course that brings tensions into the relationship. HMIC's mission is to acknowledge the difficulties which chief officers face, but also to shine a light into dark corners on behalf of the public.[28]

It is probable that few chief officers would recognise Sir Denis O'Connor's description of the (previous) 'critical friend' stance of HMIC as a 'comfortable position', and they are likely to be even more uneasy about the mission of shining 'a light into dark corners'. Yet HMIC's determination to act in the public interest is unmistakeable and is of a piece with the government's resolution to put the citizen at the centre of public service delivery. It is no accident that Sir Denis' major report when he was an HMI, was titled *Closing the Gap*.[29] He identified that there was a gap between what the public wanted of its police service and the provision that the police themselves were willing to make.

In a published interview, Sir Denis expanded on this gap:

> It is well documented that, at the moment, the public feels that they are not well informed about the police service when compared with other sectors such as health and education, and they disbelieve crime statistics, so I think we have to put decent information out there so they can assess the police for themselves. I hope that in doing this, this will enhance the public's confidence.[30]

This uncompromising stance by a former chief constable (of Surrey) who is known colloquially in the service as 'Denis the Menace',[31] points up the philosophical and practitioner gulfs which now appear to exist between HMIC and the body of chief officers.

Before we enter the 'rich detail' of chief officers' opinions about HMIC, it is worth spending a little time in understanding where the

---

[28] On-the-record conversation with me on 4 December 2009.

[29] Published in 2005.

[30] *Police Review*, 3 July 2009, p 18.

[31] Well known enough to be used as the title of a profile of Sir Denis by *Police Review* in July 2009.

Inspectorate has come from. When the Victorians decided in the 1850s that they should regulate manufacturing and services in their expanding industrialised society, they found that they needed inspectors to survey conditions across the UK on a regular basis and to make reports on their findings. This applied to factories, hygiene and health as much as it did to policing, and a number of inspectorates were created in the mid-Victorian period. A history of the Home Office notes the proliferation like this:

> [...] inspectors in the mid-nineteenth century were the new aid to central government in its attempt to solve problems caused by comparatively rapidly changing social, economic and scientific conditions [...] the variety of new subjects which were attached to the Home Office [...] was bewildering. (Pellew, 1982, p 122)

The Inspectorate of Constabulary was established by Act of Parliament and an extract from Section 15 of the Police Act 1856 reads:

> It shall be lawful for Her Majesty, by Warrant under Her Royal Sign Manual, to appoint during Her Majesty's Pleasure Three Persons as Inspectors under this Act, to visit and inquire into the State and the Efficiency of the Police appointed for every County and Borough, and whether the Provisions of the Acts under which such Police are appointed are duly observed and carried into effect, and also into the State of the Police Stations, Charge Rooms, Cells, or Lockups, or other Premises occupied for the Use of such Police...

At the outset of the creation of a police inspectorate, the inspectors themselves were drawn from the ranks of the police service, but it was not until 1869 that all 'Three Persons' were former chief constables (Cowley and Todd 2007). The 1856 Act had four provisions in terms of the Police Inspectorate:

- Every county and borough must maintain a police force.
- This police force must be 'efficient'.
- To ensure this efficiency, every force will be inspected annually by a newly created Inspectorate of Constabulary.
- If found efficient by the inspectors, central government will pay one-quarter of the annual cost of the force, the

> other three quarters coming from the local rates. (Cowley and Todd, 2007, p 11, col 2)[32]

It may be seen at once that the primary sanction which inspectors had to apply to 'failing' forces was financial; and while that single sanction may have mutated in the interim to include unwelcome publicity and comparison with other forces in an unofficial 'league table' of police forces, it was the withholding of the government's grant to the police which originally gave the Inspectorate considerable power and influence over forces, both of which it has retained ever since. The other point to make about the 1856 Act is that the word 'efficient' is used in respect of a desirable standard for policing and the word continues to be applied today, bracketed with 'effective' in terms of outputs. 'Public satisfaction', introduced in 2009 as the new 'single confidence measure' of a police force did not exclude these concepts from HMIC's estimation of a force, and in some ways, the short-lived Policing Pledge returned to the spirit of the 1856 Police Act. Indeed, HMIC was strongly in favour of the pledge when it was current, but moved quickly away when it became clear that the incoming coalition government intended to abandon the pledge and the 'single confidence measure' in June 2010.

My purpose is not to describe in detail the vicissitudes and fluctuating influence of HMIC during the nineteenth century (which is paradoxically a record of more or less failed attempts to interest successive Home Secretaries in the police), but some sense of the historical development of HMIC would not be complete without reference, following a damaging post-war national police strike, to Lord Desborough's Committee of 1919. The 'Desborough Report' noted that the number of HM Inspectors should be increased to three (having fallen to two for much of the preceding half century) and proposed that some of the administrative functions previously the province of the Inspectorate (such as pay and pensions) would in future be handled by the Home Office itself. Accordingly, the Inspectorate should ensure:

- sufficient manpower;
- maintenance of discipline;
- efficient management of the force; and
- full and proper administration of the police service as a whole. (Cowley and Todd, 2007, p 48)

---

[32] The 1856 Act did not apply to the Metropolitan Police or to the City of London Police, each of which had their own inspectorates.

---

and this was how things remained until, towards the end of the Second World War, a committee met under Home Secretary Herbert Morrison which changed the nature of HMIC's reporting and structure:

> The Police (His Majesty's Inspectors of Constabulary) Act was passed in 1945. [...] In effect, the Act gave the Home Secretary power to have as many inspectors as he thought fit, and not to be tied to the three stipulated by the County and Borough Police Act 1856. Also, under section 1, the Act specified that one of the inspectors could be appointed as His Majesty's Chief Inspector of Constabulary. (Cowley and Todd, 2007, p 57)

HM's Chief Inspector role did not actually come into being until 1962, but it has since become a position of increasing influence, both in policing and in Whitehall, because, as Sir Ronnie Flanagan, the Chief HMI in 2005, observed:

> HMIC works alongside the Home Office. I report directly to the Home Secretary. Therefore, what is in the minds of Home Office Ministers has a strong influence on the work of HMIC. The present Home Secretary[33] made it quite clear when he assumed his responsibilities that he saw HMIC at the heart of improvements in policing. (Flanagan, 2005, p 42)

But Sir Ronnie went on to acknowledge that, in his words, 'HMIC inhabits an odd place', by which he meant

> the essential conundrum that is HMIC: working alongside the Service; drawing many of its staff directly from that Service; yet adopting the position of critical friend of that Service. (Flanagan, 2005, p 42)

It seems an unresolved ambiguity at the heart of policing that a body (HMIC) so clearly influenced by government, should report on an organisation (the police service) which the government wishes heavily to influence and direct. Sir Ronnie explains that the link between government and HMIC is both clear and very powerful:

---

[33] Charles Clarke, who succeeded David Blunkett, was Home Secretary from December 2004 until May 2006.

> HMIC sets out to be the impartial voice of policing at the very heart of Government, and in doing so adding [sic] value to Government understanding of the policing landscape and environment. (Flanagan, 2005, p 42)

The essential question must be how impartial that 'voice of policing' is. Some chief officers think that HMIC is not at all impartial; indeed they think quite the opposite. But Sir Ronnie's successor as Chief HMI, Sir Denis O'Connor, associated inextricably in chief officers' minds with the mantra of being 'a fierce advocate of public interest', appears content that HMIC has moved substantially away from Sir Ronnie's notion of the 'critical friend' into something altogether more partisan. However, Sir Denis commented to me that

> Actually, the phrase ['fierce advocates, or guardians, of public interest'] is not mine. Someone commented on the HMIC strap-line, which is 'Inspecting policing in the public interest', and put in that bit about 'fierce advocates', which of course is what is reported. The [strap] line says it all. I want to share with chief officers the task of winning public confidence, but police officers cannot be the judges of what gains public confidence.[34]

But presumably, HMIC can, or thinks it can, be judge 'of what gains public confidence', if it is wholly devoted to the public interest. Richard Cowley and Peter Todd,[35] agree with the Chief HMI, claiming that

> Throughout its history, the Inspectorate has in many ways mirrored the police service; sometimes it has lagged behind developments but often it has led the way to significant evolutionary, even revolutionary, change. (Cowley and Todd, 2007, p 8)

'Revolutionary change' may be right. There are strong internal commitments in the Inspectorate about how HMIC will assess police forces 'in the interests of the public', let alone whatever modulation is added in from 'the minds of Home Office Ministers' exercising 'a strong influence on […] HMIC' (Flanagan, 2005, p 43). The 'interests

---

[34] On-the-record conversation with me, 4 December 2009.

[35] Richard Cowley is a former police officer and Peter Todd was, until 2007, a serving Assistant HMI.

of the public' were enhanced in early 2010 by a website, MyPolice, which was run by HMIC and allowed members of the public an online instant access to a 'report card' about its local police force.[36] Sir Denis O'Connor noted that this would make 'uncomfortable reading' for some chief officers and would 'highlight forces that underperformed'. It is quite clear from MyPolice (now renamed Police)[37] that the Inspectorate is determined to make local police accountability a public and open matter, presumably in default of the police authority doing so. Such views may be contrasted with equally strong opinions on the part of many chief officers:

> **Interviewee 36:** Talk about power without responsibility – look at HMIC and the way it jumps whenever the Home Office barks orders.

which expresses a view common among chief officers that HMIC has no voice of its own, only one provided by the Home Office. Indeed, one officer believed that the function of the HMIC is merely to reassure the Home Office that deviance would be dealt with:

> **Interviewee 32:** They are really just a kind of comfort blanket for the Home Office, but of themselves they are quite inefficient and the quality of their work is very variable.

while another officer, echoing some of the earlier criticism of 'poachers turned gamekeepers', considered that the contradiction lay within HMIC itself because

---

[36] HMIC notes that the original website www.mypolice.org.uk/ was set up in response to the results of a public consultation exercise in 2009 in which the Inspectorate asked the public what it wanted to know about its police force. See www.hmic.gov.uk/AboutUs/Pages/home.aspx; accessed 11 May 2010, and *Police Review*, 12 March 2010, p 5, where an HMI, Bernard Hogan-Howe (former Chief Constable of Merseyside), said of the report card that 'I think [chief constables] being held to account is a good thing,' which produced a counter-response from Chief Constable Peter Fahy of Greater Manchester Police who observed that '[this report card] does not give enough recognition to the challenges that a large metropolitan area faces', *Police Review*, 12 March, p 5.

[37] Though HMIC did score something of an own goal in March 2010 when it found it was using another's already allocated domain name: www.mypolice.org (see a press statement at www.hmic.gov.uk/news/press/releases-2010/release-010-2010/; accessed 22 July 2011). HMIC had to change its web-title to www.police.uk instead.

> **Interviewee 11:** They turn up and lambast shortcomings they themselves were never able to do much about. There is the rich reek of hypocrisy about HMIC's pronouncements.

Another chief officer criticised HMIC at some length before revealing that there was a very personal reason for distrusting HMIC's capability:

> **Interviewee 89:** [...] I deplore this 'fierce guardians' nonsense,[38] which unfortunately the HMIs themselves will believe. Anyone can criticise – it takes greater vision and more depth, as well as more intelligence, to be constructive. Constructive is something HMIC doesn't do.
>
> [Interviewer: You seem very hostile. Can you tell me why you feel like this?]
>
> In the fairly recent past I sometimes met with [an HMI] to discuss a really delicate issue, which revolved round my deep concerns about one of my top team, only to discover later that [the HMI] had passed on my comments to [the chair of the police authority]. This was completely out of order and betrayed the trust that should exist between us, as well as running the risk of getting back to the individual. If the HMI does that for such really confidential issues, why should I believe that they have any interest in my continued effectiveness as a leader? Why should I ever trust one of them again?

This chief officer's experience appears to have been traumatic and it has evidently soured the individual's attitude towards HMIC, but such hostility is by no means shared by all. Some (though in a minority) expressed a qualified approval of what HMIC does, and the following example suggests that opinions of HMIC might well be moderated by the relative intensity of contact:

> **Interviewee 27:** HMIC is helpful and supportive, [...] there on the end of a telephone if I need to speak, but the relationship is generally a remote one. The relationship in respect of inspection activity is currently reasonably productive. [...] It remains to be seen

---

[38] See comments by HMCIC above. The phrase has taken time to gain currency. Those chief officers who spoke about it, unanimously deplored this new aggression or 'adversarial' relationship which impended, but some of my interviews had been completed before the phrase gained familiarity, so it is difficult to establish if the criticism of it is a consensus view. Throughout 2009–10, when the bulk of interviews was conducted, it was rare to find approbation of this phrase, or of the Policing Pledge.

how the recent announcement of a change to a more adversarial approach will affect that relationship.

The advocacy of public interest has struck a chord with chief officers, many of whom seem to believe that this is not within HMIC's 'proper' remit, and that it is an unwelcome development that will drive a wedge between the police and those who pass judgement on them. Indeed, one officer believed that part of the problem was a characteristically 'mechanistic' approach by HMIC to 'guarding standards'. The officer went on to draw distinctions between policing and other professions and noted how HMIC seems ill suited even to undertake its primary inspection function:

> **Interviewee 35:** I cannot believe that any other profession would put up with such weak, mechanistic [ways of doing] its important job of guarding standards. If these people were in medicine, they would have been put out to grass years ago. If in engineering, they would have been quickly replaced. I grant you that if they were in law, no one would have noticed. But this is policing: up front, hands-on policing and we have the Society of Antiquaries doing our inspections and standards-guarding. It's like having The Sealed Knot[39] doing health and safety.

The questioning of HMIC's role is a common theme, returned to again and again by chief officers who do not appear to accept that HMIC has the interests of policing at its heart. One chief officer, qualified as a career adviser before joining the police, suggested that there is an inherent contradiction in HMIC's simultaneous attempts both to assess the police force and develop the chief officer team in that force:

> **Interviewee 30:** I think the job that HMIC does is schizophrenic:[40] they are supposed to inspect your force to see if it is doing what the Home Office wants, but at the same time HMIC is supposed to act as your 'guide, philosopher and friend' in counselling you for your own career in ACPO and looking to offer you opportunities for advancement. I really don't like the idea of them doing both things.

---

[39] The Sealed Knot is a band of enthusiastic history amateurs who re-enact past military battles, principally from the English Civil War.

[40] From the Greek for 'split mind': the speaker means that HMIC does two almost contradictory things at once; but the medical term (often misused, as here) properly describes a breakdown in a person's thoughts and feelings, often accompanied by delusions and a retreat from social life.

and another officer argued that it did not make sense for an organisation largely concerned with punitive sanctions for failure, to have a supportive career guidance role for individual chief officers at the same time. The two things might collide because of circumstances over which the individual chief officer has no control:

> **Interviewee 53:** Tell me what other organisation would use an inspectorate function to look at police effectiveness and efficiency and at the same time use the senior inspectors (the former chief constables) as career managers and mentors? It's potty; completely bonkers. We need two separate functions, because HMIC cannot divorce what it thinks of your force from what it thinks of you.

One experienced chief officer was uncompromising in his insistence that HMIC has had its day:

> **Interviewee 26:** I think the present structure is pernicious and HMIC has far too much power to enforce the Home Office's bidding. I'd dismantle the structure tomorrow, if I could.
>
> [Interviewer: replacing HMIC with what?]
>
> With [...] a completely new body of professional careers' assessors and advisers, appointed by and answerable to ACPO itself. That would keep the Home Office out of the loop too, and there would be no danger of appointing a government lapdog instead of a mastiff.

But in essence this takes us back to Sir Denis O'Connor's pithy comment that 'the police cannot be judge and jury of themselves'. The argument seems unassailable that there ought to be an independent assessment of the functions of a police force. Equally, the development, selection, promotion and appraisal of chief officers require professional and dispassionate assessments. There is no cogent resource argument which says that HMIC has to do both, nor that chief officers themselves should 'own' the process, which indeed would tend to the incestuous. The *Draft Protocol* for the police crime commissioner notes that the 'Police and Crime Panel' will have the power 'to ask HMIC for a professional view when the PCC intends to dismiss a Chief Constable'(Home Office 2011b, p 4). This no doubt accords with what already happens in practice, if out of sight, but making it a formal duty for HMIC is not likely further to endear the Inspectorate to the run of chief officers.

One senior chief officer who enjoys cordial relations with HMIC wondered whether the critical comments about it might originate from those chief officers who have most to fear from a critical appraisal (either of themselves or of their forces):

> **Interviewee 82:** I actually get on with the HMIs and C[hief]/HMI rather well and enjoy the challenge they pose. It's not easy being the upholders of standards and of course they will incur the dislike of poorly performing forces and weak or back-sliding chief officers.

This suggestion, that the negative views of HMIC might derive directly from malice or fear expressed by chief officers who do not perform well, is not actually supported by the statistics of the survey. Of 89 respondents who answered the question *Can you describe your relationship with HMIC?* (Table 4.2), the preponderance of opinion of HMIC looked like this:

Table 4.2: Opinions of HMIC

	Number	Percentage
Negative opinions of HMIC	71	80%
Positive opinions of HMIC	17	19%
Neutral or no opinion of HMIC	1	1%
Totals	**89**	**100%**

These data strongly suggest that highly able and very senior police officers shared disquiet about HMIC as much as any who needed to look to their laurels. We cannot take this sample of opinion as overwhelmingly definitive, but its statistical validity is such that it is highly representative and therefore we can conclude that negative opinions of HMIC are widely held, at least in private. The preponderance in chief officer ranks of hostile and negative opinions about the Inspectorate cannot be gainsaid by anyone, however well disposed s/he may be to HMIC. The hostility is there; it is more constructive to ask what can be done about it.

Even here, the same officer who showed above some approbation of HMIC wanted to see the personal assessment of chief officers separated from HMIC's force assessment:

> **Interviewee 82:** For the most part, I think they do a difficult job well, but I'd personally want to separate their assessment of forces

from their assessment of chief officers, even though some of that
has gone to the police authority as a result of the Green Paper.

The Green Paper of 2008, noted earlier, passed responsibility for the
annual appraisal of chief constables, from HMIC to individual police
authorities and has given them a role in the assessment of their whole
chief officer team. That does not mean that HMIC no longer has any
part to play in the assessment of the potential of chief officers. The
Inspectorate will continue to assess 'readiness' for key chief officer roles,
and will continue, I presume, to influence the Home Office in making
key appointments. Some of the secrecy surrounding these appointments
has been the subject of criticism (for example, by Savage et al, 2000,
p 113; Bebbington, 2010b).

It is probably too early to assess how HMIC's role will be affected by
the creation of the PCC from 2012, but the chances are that HMIC
will have greater power still and, in exercising (I presume) an inspection
function over the PCC and the crime and police panel which supports
the PCC, will sustain authority and influence over individual forces
as well as those who hold those forces to account. HMIC, for the
foreseeable future, will do the Home Office's bidding.[41]

This link between the Home Office and the Inspectorate seems to
be indissoluble however chief officers may deplore it and it may be
apposite at this point to turn to consider the role of the Home Office
itself and how is has come to play such a prominent (some would say
intrusive) role in the direction of the police.

The Home Office

The Home Office itself was created in 1782, when the former
'Southern Department', previously concerned with foreign affairs
was instead made responsible for internal (home department) matters,
while the 'Northern Department' became the Foreign Office. The
Earl of Shelburne was appointed as the first Secretary of State with
responsibility for domestic and colonial affairs.[42] The division was
initially very simple, all things to do with Britain's internal organisation
were located with the 'Home Department' and all things to do with

---

[41] An example surfaced at the end of July 2010, in which HMCIC said that there will
be 'absolutely relentless exposure' of police forces and police authorities which make
poor spending decisions (*Police Review*, 23 July 2010, p 5); see also HMIC (2010b).

[42] See *The History of Home Office* from The National Archives website (www.ndad.
nationalarchives.gov.uk/AH/2/detail.html; accessed 23 February 2010).

'abroad' were with the Foreign Office. Each of the two departments of state was led by a Secretary. Over time, the simplicity of internal security changed as responsibilities were added and the Home Office in particular became the repository of some arcane political remits, among which were yeomanries and militias, highways and turnpikes, mining, poisons, 'policy in regard to pet shops, dog breeding establishments and boarding kennels',[43] slaughterhouses, lunacy and reservoirs. A large number of such arcana was transferred as recently as 2001 to other government departments and in 2007 major responsibilities for criminal justice, probation and prisons were moved to the newly created Ministry of Justice. This rationalisation of the Home Office[44] did not exclude the inward transfer, in 2007, of counter-terrorist strategy from the Cabinet Office to the Home Office. Currently, the Home Secretary is responsible for the police, the UK Border Agency (UKBA) and the Security Service (MI5), but some anomalies remain: for example, s/he still regulates British Summer Time.

Since the creation of the police by a Home Secretary, Sir Robert Peel, in 1829, it is not surprising that the 'Home Department' (as it is still officially known) retains its policy-making remit for policing and that the Home Secretary answers to parliament for the police. However, imposing some sort of central control of policing was not properly formalised until at least 1874. This suggestion was first raised in a Home Office memorandum sent to the Home Secretary, Richard Asheton Cross, on 27 April 1874. Advice to Mr Cross included this:

---

[43] A further list of Home Office responsibilities, which make amusing reading, are on the same website (www.ndad.nationalarchives.gov.uk/AH/2/detail.html).

[44] The Home Office has had various 'public safety' functions too, including 'control of explosives (since 1875), firearms (since 1920); and policy on dangerous drugs. In 2001 the Home Office absorbed the Cabinet Office's UK Anti-Drugs Co-ordination Unit, while at the same time the Home Office's former responsibilities for liquor and public entertainment licensing, gambling, horse racing, and film and video licensing (though not matters relating to the law on obscenity), were transferred to the Department for Culture, Media and Sport. The Lord Chancellor's Department took over the Home Office's duties in the areas of human rights, open government, freedom of information and data protection; plus royal issues and matters relating to the Church, hereditary peers and Lords Lieutenant; however, the Home Office continued to be responsible for race equality and race relations' (adapted from *The History of Home Office* from the National Archives website, ibid., p 5). It seems, from this history, that the Home Office became a default option for every regulation and concern which did not have an already defined home.

> The very considerable addition about to be made to the contribution from Imperial funds in aid of local police expenditure affords the government an opportunity, of which it may be well to take advantage, of endeavouring to secure for the Secretary of State a greater amount of supervision and control over the police forces of Great Britain than he now possesses. (Cowley and Todd, 2007, pp 32–3)

The memorandum also commented on how limited the Home Secretary's powers were over county and shire police forces and borough (town and city) police forces, which by 1870 had proliferated:

> [...] he has no power whatever beyond that of withholding a certificate of efficiency; and it is therefore clear that the supervision exercised by him, in counties as well as in boroughs, is very limited both in character and amount. [...] [T]he conferring of additional powers of supervision upon the Secretary of State would be [...] entirely warranted, if not absolutely called for, by the appropriation of so large a sum of public money towards its maintenance. (Ibid.; see also Pellew, 1982)

Thus the equation was firmly established that those who funded the police expected to exercise control in return. Initially this was entirely the Home Office, but now the budget for the police is split between the Home Office and the police authority which exercises local oversight of expenditure (and therefore can demand 'value for money') and latterly, the PCC. Further, it may be noted that back in 1874 it is the civil servants who urge the Home Secretary to take greater powers to control the police, not the electorate or even parliament. Many chief officers would assert that little has changed. It was the Desborough Committee Report of 1919 (which we have already glanced at above in terms of its impact on HMIC), that formalised a 'Police Department' within the Home Office which would be responsible for central police budgets, policing policy and oversight. Power was given to the Home Secretary to regulate police pay and conditions of service in 1919 (Cowley and Todd, 2007, p 47). Inevitably, this entailed a close interest (and often involvement) in senior appointments and the eventual creation of a chief officer cadre, as well as the selection of candidates for promotion.

I have already noted above that the bulk of chief officers strenuously oppose any external interference from police authority, government or public in what they regard as necessary police operational independence. So too, in the second part of this chapter, I noted the majority opinion which viewed HMIC in a negative light. When a critical view of political opportunism is combined with their dislike of interference with operational independence, chief officers' views of the Home Office become very negative indeed:

Ninety-one chief officers responded to the interview question *Can you describe your relationship with the Home Office?* (Table 4.3).

Table 4.3: Preponderance of attitudes to the Home Office

	Number	Percentage
Negative	78	86%
Positive	13	14%
Totals	**91**	**100%**

This records the highest negativity of all chief officer responses in the interview subjects and near unanimity of this kind seemed to me something to which the Home Office might wish to respond in turn. Accordingly, I approached the then Home Secretary (Alan Milburn), suggesting that he might care to discuss with me what the chief officers had been saying but I was referred instead to Andrew Wren, Head of the Police Productivity Unit of the Home Office, responsible for setting the chief officer policy.[45] I began by asking Mr Wren what he thought of the expression of hostility from the bulk of chief officers interviewed. He replied, that such negative feelings were

> **AW:** [...] characteristic of the relationship between any great department of state and the public service. It's important to realise that this happens in many of the departments (health for example) and is to do with being partisan.

In essence, this official response from the Home Office is that there is no expectation of approval because 'great department[s] of state' invite critical or hostile responses merely by existing. I commented that it would not be helpful to either side if matters rested there and asked

---

[45] Mr Wren arranged to see me on 19 October 2009 at Marsham Street in London, the new(ish) HQ of the Home Office. The interview that ensued was held entirely on the record and I supplied Mr Wren with some extracts from chief officers' anonymous views so that he could gauge the depth of their negativity, but he was not privy to all the comments they have made. What follows in the main text is drawn from my contemporaneous notes of the meeting.

what the Home Office would do to engage more closely with chief officers. Mr Wren's response was

> **AW:** We already have a dialogue with ACPO and chief officers individually. The Policing Minister and the president of ACPO have frequent bilaterals[46] and groups of Home Office officials also meet ACPO members, perhaps the heads of business areas, or those involved in particular issues, and there are workshops and tabled agendas. A more formal mechanism is the National Policing Board which meets every six weeks or two months and which has a whole spectrum of discussions.[47] Lastly, there are frequent visits to forces to discuss subject areas.

I noted that this described mechanisms to meet; it did not suggest any concerted attempt to turn officers' opinions around. I then asked whether the undertone of hostility and dislike in chief officers' comments was disturbing, and if so, what might the Home Office do about it? Mr Wren declined to comment. It would seem from this that the Home Office is used to and probably expects to be the target for criticism but that this hostility does not fundamentally affect or modify its need, on the surface at least, to get on with the chief officers of police. For its part, the Home Office clearly believes that it is doing enough to satisfy its remit, if not its police critics, and it would seem to have no plans to seek a more constructive relationship than it already has. Nonetheless, in the detailed comments from chief officers that follow, it is quite clear that the Home Office is found wanting. How does chief officer negativity about the Home Office show itself?

The question I asked at the confidential interviews was *Can you describe your relationship with the Home Office?* The following may be taken as typical of the chief officers' comments about the senior staff at the Home Office:

---

[46] That is, one-to-one meetings.

[47] Membership of the National Policing Board (NPB), first formed in 2006, is made up from the Home Secretary (chair) and representatives of the Home Office including the Minister for Security, Counter-Terrorism, Crime and Policing and senior officials, ACPO (including the president), the Metropolitan Police Commissioner, the Association of Police Authorities represented by its chair, vice-chair and the chief executive, HM Chief Inspector of Constabulary, and the chair and chief executive of the NPIA. See for example http://police.homeoffice.gov.uk/publications/police-reform/npb-summary-minutes-15-10-2009; accessed 10 May 2010. See also http://police.homeoffice.gov.uk/police-reform/nat-policing-board/; accessed 10 May 2010, for details of the Board's structure and remit.

Interviewee 64: They have to be taken gently by the hand, and some of them are really grateful when you explain why some bright notion won't actually work on the ground. But at the back of all of it is this notion that they know best and that, in policy and strategy, the police are pretty useless. We think that it's actually the other way around.

The theme that 'the mandarins don't know what they are talking about' is a dominant one, and it is a posture that chief officers often adopt if they anticipate or experience criticism. This time though, the chief officers themselves seem to believe that the Home Office's impact on them is more profound than those of either the police authorities/ PCC or HMIC, because policies and laws can be directly applied across England and Wales. This makes the police reservations about some Home Office policy initiatives quite intense:

Interviewee 49: They forget that policy isn't policing. They're all very well in their remote ivory tower, handing down writ to us but they don't have to get fucked trying to make it work. Too many of them wake up with an idea and fly down to us from the Planet Loony the same day, without testing it, thinking about it or knowing whether or not it'll work.

The 'credibility gap' between chief officers and Home Office officials often leads to a weary resignation, as this comment shows:

Interviewee 8: I recall one visit to the Dream Factory [the Home Office building in Marsham Street, London] where I tried to talk to this highly regarded mandarin and all he was interested in were clauses of 'his' forthcoming Bill. What hacked me off was that the Bill was about policing, and he had a live chief in front of him and couldn't engage at all.

Not all the comments are wholly negative. Some chief officers present a balanced view, but inevitably the distance between law makers and law enforcers brings tensions to the surface:

Interviewee 79: Elements of [the Home Office] are pretty good and a very few people are knowledgeable and supportive, but the whole idea of it seems flawed. We don't have a Ministry of Policing like we have a Ministry of Defence; which means that there is no involvement of police officers in the political process as there is

> with senior military officers. Consequently, many of us are ignorant of political protocols and procedures and sometimes even where real power lies. We have to run fast to keep up.

There is a distinction between the reservations expressed by chief officers about the knowledge and understanding of Home Office officials on one hand and about the actions of the politicians who lead the department on the other. The Conservative Party in opposition claimed that too many chief police officers were too close to the Labour government during the early years of the century, which provoked furious responses from chief officers deprecating such suggestions.[48] The majority of the chief officers whom I interviewed considered that the Home Office, whether in the person of official or politician, needs to listen much more intently and more systematically to those who have to implement the policies. Too often, officials and politicians are too remote from the people and the situations on which they pronounce:

> **Interviewee 70:** The Home Office arrogates to itself the pronouncement upon two things: what 'the people' want and what 'policing' needs. The sad thing is that they haven't the first idea about either. And we, who think hard about policing and who talk to people on the street, have to give to the Home Office's half-baked stupid bloody notions the seriousness we'd deny a drunk-and-disorderly on the street.

Another chief officer, who has had dealings with both Home Office ministers and senior officials on a consistent basis over a number of years was sorrowful but implacable in suggesting that too often the Home Office ignored advice and rode roughshod over counter-arguments,

---

[48] See, for example, the article by Sean O'Neill in *The Times* for 8 March 2010 entitled 'Leading Tories View Senior Police as Little More than New Labour Stooges'. The article included a photograph showing a chief officer talking to the Home Secretary to suggest that ACPO itself was 'too close to Labour'. The article is available from www.timesonline.co.uk/tol/news/politics/article7053384.ece; accessed 22 April 2010.

This then provoked a strong letter from Chief Constable Peter Fahy (the officer pictured) to *The Times* on 12 March, deploring the suggestion that he supported a political party. He went on to say that 'There is inevitably a close working relationship between the Home Office and chief constables but political neutrality is crucial and must remain one of the fundamentals of policing.' See www.timesonline.co.uk/tol/comment/letters/article7058657.ece; also accessed on 22 April 2010. There is an element of political ping-pong in all this; during the miners' strike of 1984, the police were criticised for too tamely doing the (Conservative) government's bidding.

almost as though it had decided what it would do irrespective of nominal consultations:

> **Interviewee 15:** The Home Office knows nothing of policing and never listens. I've attended endless meetings with senior Home Office officials, where unanimously chief officers have pleaded with them not to take a particular route and explaining in detail why it was inadvisable. Next thing you know – sometimes before you'd even got back [to the] force – there'd be a splash on the TV news or in the papers saying exactly what you'd so strongly advised against.
>
> [Interviewer: can you give me an example?]
>
> Not without blowing my anonymity. But my colleagues will recognise the symptoms: Home Office officials do what they want; whatever the advice or the police view and that's neither democratic, nor sensible, nor appropriate. We very occasionally and collectively tell the Home Office where to get off,[49] but not often enough.

The police attitude to politicians, as this comment suggests, is coloured by a belief that ministers follow a populist, expedient line, itself based on short term considerations or what police officers term a 'knee-jerk':

> **Interviewee 89:** The Home Office is in a mess: it's undergoing great changes – not just the periodic changes of ministers, but of the permanent officials who seem ruthlessly career-minded at the top. This produces inconsistency. I presented on one issue to the Home Office on an almost weekly basis for practically a year and yet directions were changed on a media whim or because of a political knee-jerk.

One officer thought that the dismay which she and her colleagues felt was in part owing to the divisions which existed within the Home Office itself, which the creation of the Ministry of Justice in 2007 to take over criminal justice and other matters, has not mitigated:

---

[49] One outstanding example occurred in 2008 when the Home Secretary told chief constables to transfer police constables to the newly formed UK Border Agency (UKBA). The Chief Constables' Council refused and the project to transfer the officers was quietly shelved. Relations were icy for several months afterwards, I'm told.

Interviewee 36: It's still an astonishingly broken organisation and is still not fit for purpose.[50] It tries to do too much across too many specialist subjects, without a scintilla of understanding or knowledge about what is actually involved. I had had high hopes when some of its function was hived off to the justice ministry, but what is left behind still stubbornly refuses to act in the public good. They have lost their way; they've lost the sense of delivering the public good by a public servant.

I put some of the criticisms on this and preceding pages directly to Andrew Wren, asking first if the Home Office was too dysfunctional for purpose, which was what many chief officers were suggesting. He replied:

AW: It is difficult to respond meaningfully to non-specific criticism of this kind. Do police officers understand the Home Office? Some of our most senior people spend a lot of time talking to chief constables.

I noted that a perennial criticism is that Home Office officials seem to know very little about policing and chief officers have suggested that such officials make little effort to find out anything. Mr Wren commented:

AW: The Home Office does try to improve its knowledge about policing, and interestingly, this is also what street cops say about their chief officers [that they are out of touch and don't know what's going on], but there is a new induction process for incoming civil servants to explain police work, and we are urged to understand, and if we do not, to ask for explanations. You have to remember that the HO [Home Office] isn't just about the police: there's immigration and border controls too. Just because half of the work was hived off to the justice ministry does not mean that only policing was left.

But chief officers return again and again to the charge that the Home Office pursues the 'new and shiny' for its own sake, so that its political

---

[50] This echoes a comment by the then Home Secretary, John Reid, in 2006, when he said that the Home Office was 'not fit for purpose' and divisions of responsibility occurred shortly afterwards. Many police officers believe that political responsibility for policing should have been transferred into the new Ministry of Justice rather than being 'bracketed with UKBA and the spooks'.

masters have something to proffer party and Parliament. One chief officer believes that this pursuit of the new is at the expense of what actually needs to be done:

> **Interviewee 93:** I hate the heavy-handed politicisation of policing which always means you have to chase after something new and shiny whilst what you really ought to be doing is lying dull and rusted from lack of use. Remember them chasing 'zero tolerance' or 'problem-oriented policing'? The lesson is never learned that what works in the streets of New York will not necessarily work in the streets of [British cities]. Yet the Home Office slavishly follows the American lead every time, fearful to think for itself, fearful to search for a home-grown solution to a home-grown problem.

Mr Wren was adamant that there was no inclination in the Home Office to follow leads from the US but would not comment on chief officers' suggestions that the appointment of Paul Evans from the Boston Police Department to the Home Office Policing Standards Unit in 2006 was indicative evidence of an Americanisation of British law enforcement.[51] He noted that the tripartite structure was one that had been tested and had worked (see below).

One chief officer noted the central importance of the Home Office at the same time as drawing attention to its perceived weakness:

> **Interviewee 13:** It is a key part of the triangular relationship and that cannot be denied. The sad thing is that there is no corporate memory in the Home Office; it becomes increasingly difficult to find anyone there who has the remotest notion about the police.

When I raised this point with Mr Wren, he noted that the relationships between the Home Office, ACPO and the Association of Police Authorities (APA) gave the lie to suggestions that there was 'no corporate memory' in the Home Office:

> **AW:** The tripartite relationship is the dominant paradigm and defines much of the Home Office's landscape. It is unique in Whitehall. The Home Office is a single entity headed by Sir David Normington [Permanent Under Secretary]; ACPO and the APA are representative bodies. How effective the tripartite relationship is

---

[51] See www.dailymail.co.uk/news/article-195386/Ex-marine-heads-police-standards-unit.html; accessed 10 May 2010.

> depends on how tractable the issues are, and how well participants mesh and cooperate is also a factor. A good example of how it works is the Policing Pledge in the 'new public management' framework.[52] It is not true that there is 'no corporate memory' and unfair [of chief officers] to characterise the Home Office as transient. (See also, Wall, 1994)

The Policing Pledge was something of a sore point with a number of chief officers, who felt that it had assumed an undue prominence simply because of the emphasis by the then Home Secretary and the Whitehall machine on 'citizen focus' and the political capital to be had from police engagement with local communities. Its abrupt cancellation in June 2010 is believed by them to be of a piece with the short-lived nature of political initiatives. In the same vein, an HM Inspector of Constabulary openly criticised the tripartite system because

> [...] it tends to encourage delays in decision-making and a culture of making slow progress on big issues. (Bellingham, 2010, p 25)

Many chief officers in conversation with me drew attention to the way in which different political administrations developed different policing priorities, so that

> **Interviewee 49:** [...] one week 'X' is the predominant flavour; next week it will be 'Y', and 'Z' is on the horizon, like this commissioner business,[53] and meanwhile we are trying to do policing – a serious and complex job – in a consistent and thoroughgoing way. Politicians often describe us as entrenched and resistant to change. We're bloody not – only resistant to the latest fad until it has stood some kind of test of time. But none of these initiatives are there long enough to do that.

---

[52] NPM was first introduced under the John Major government in 1994 but was taken up enthusiastically by the Labour administrations from 1997 as a means to ensure that those who provide public services and those who spend public money are made accountable for what they do and what they spend. The advent of the Policing Pledge in 2008, as a 'single confidence measure' of public satisfaction with the police *was* a qualitative measure, but of course it applied only to community policing and not to the police provision of 'protective services'.

[53] The 'police crime commissioner'.

Equally serious matters such as homicide and fraud are, chief officers believe, actually subordinated in importance, simply to satisfy an electorate. One chief officer's explosive response may be taken as characteristic of many others:

> **Interviewee 67:** They [the political ministers in the Home Office] sacrifice quality and integrity for expediency whenever it suits them. They specialise in stampeding the police into premature action to satisfy some political imperative and we're too feeble to say 'No – not now Minister! Wait!' We never do. An example is the Policing Pledge – delivered far too early and before all the research had been completed and then taken away by the Home Office from the people who were busy trying to put it together and just imposing it to meet some arbitrary deadline. Half-baked or what?

Mr Wren's response was

> **AW:** Public confidence must increase in policing.

There was some confusion among chief officers in June 2010 when the incoming Home Secretary, Theresa May, spoke to the ACPO Spring Conference in Manchester and announced the abolition of both the Policing Pledge and the 'single confidence target'. She went on:

> I know that some officers like the policing pledge, and some, I'm sure, like the comfort of knowing they've ticked boxes. But targets don't fight crime. In scrapping the confidence target and the policing pledge, I couldn't be any clearer about your mission: it isn't a 30-point plan; it is to cut crime. (Fresco, 2010)

However, the same chief officers are perfectly well aware that some form of assessment of police performance will be imposed: if it isn't a 'confidence' measure, it may well be a requirement to '*be ruthless in cutting out waste, streamlining structures and improving efficiency*' which was the Home Secretary's declared mission in the Home Office (Fresco, 2010). It is also noteworthy that what the Home Secretary says is the police mission is only a partial truth. There is much more to 'public policing' than cutting crime (Reiner, 2010, pp 239–54).

Another officer in a different context raised the charge that Home Office officials spend too long chasing the chimeras of change, and noted that there is a perception among ACPO ranks that criticism of the Home Office carries with it concomitant risks to officers' careers:

> **Interviewee 74:** Policing in the last 10 years has been bedevilled by rank amateurs in the Home Office who think they know best, but who change tack every few months, trade in old fads for new, pursue the [Will o' the] wisps of legal fashion and who seem surprised when they meet chief officers who are weary of change for its own sake. Oppose the Home Office and you kiss goodbye to advancement, interesting jobs and any recognition – but it has to be done. These people can be reckless and dangerous in their sublime carelessness of others.

Other chief officers also argued that any public pronouncement by a chief police officer which was critical of Home Office policies or action would result in the critic being refused advancement or being 'shuffled off into a policing backwater' (Interviewee 11), 'using HMIC to do the dirty work' (Interviewee 46). However, when I asked Mr Wren whether it was true that opposition to or criticism of the Home Office would debar chief officers from further promotion, his response was unequivocal:

> **AW:** This is not reflective of Home Office policy. A constructive discussion is a key part of any public service and the Home Office has no mechanism to be intolerant.

Perhaps the key to this lies in Mr Wren's phrase 'a constructive discussion' because many of the descriptions used by chief officers of the Home Office tend to the immoderate. This could genuinely be the result of years of frustration (which is how many chief officers have prefaced their criticisms). Alternatively, it may be the product of anonymity in interviews with me, at least in part, since officers can say what they think and feel without being identified and therefore without suffering any repercussion. This comment is characteristic:

> **Interviewee 24:** There is breathtaking effrontery there in this posse of people who think that they understand policing and can write policy, as though delivering policing is like weighing out 250 grammes of cheese.

There are instances however when individual chief officers will make public their opposition to the Home Office. In 2009, a chief constable sought a judicial review of a decision by Home Office ministers to impose 'irrational and unreasonable' budget cuts on his force. Mark Rowley, Chief Constable of Surrey Police, made his on-the-record comments[54] in criticism of the 'Home Office culture of targets in policing' which meant that Mr Rowley had had to cut 144 posts in a year. The chief constable was supported by the chair of his police authority who noted that

> Over the past year, we have repeatedly asked to meet the Government to discuss the rationale behind [budget] capping decisions. We have been refused on every occasion. (Ibid., p 8, col 5)

The budget reductions have continued however, and most police forces in England and Wales have introduced a recruitment moratorium to hold places vacant and therefore reduce numbers. This is a constraint likely to continue beyond 2013, partly as a result of the continuing economic recession, partly as a consequence of the coalition government's policy to cut departmental and public service budgets.

Nonetheless, the paradigm of the 'Surrey response' does seem to support the general thesis which chief officers advance: the Home Office does not engage meaningfully with police practitioners who oppose policy changes. Indeed, one chief officer pointed to specific initiatives that the Home Office had got wrong despite specialist police advice:

> **Interviewee 62:** Politicians are here today, gone tomorrow and they can't see, though we're fairly polite to them, that the majority of ACPO has no time at all for the Home Secretary or the Policing Minister. The same applies to Home Office officials: other than one or two of the directors at the very top, the civil servants are a sorry bunch: see what a pig's ear they made of amalgamation and then of leadership selection when they ran PNAC and HPDS.[55] These systems only started to work at all when we grabbed them back. In HPDS, the [individual] force was not allowed a say in the selection of a candidate. How fatuous that was!

---

[54] Sean O'Neill, reporting in *The Times*, 28 May 2009, in an article entitled 'Police Chief takes Home Office to Court over Secret Culture of "Irrational" Cuts' (p 8). A compromise of sorts was reached in 2010, with Mr Rowley heading a task force looking into funding and budgets for the police.

[55] PNAC (Police National Assessment Centre), the 'gateway' to the Strategic Command Course). HPDS is the (revised) High Potential Development Scheme, see Chapter One.

The amalgamation of forces' proposal (brainchild of Home Secretary Charles Clarke, based on an HMIC report) which was floated in 2006, led to considerable amounts of work by forces to develop a means by which adjacent forces could combine.[56] The stated aim was to produce amalgamated police forces of 6,000 officers or more 'critical mass' who had the capability to respond to major incidents without invoking mutual aid from other forces. It would have had the incidental effect of reducing police forces from the current 43 'home' forces in England and Wales to something like 12 or 15 much larger regional forces. Opposition was considerable while there were many in favour, but it was not until July the following year (2007) that a new Home Secretary, John Reid, abandoned the whole scheme abruptly. It is estimated that planning and research for the amalgamation cost the taxpayer something like £6 million but that does not take into account the hours of discussion (and acrimony) that chief officers had to devote to the project. It has left a bitter legacy which may inform some chief officers' attitudes towards the Home Office (exemplified by the extracts quoted above). Noises about amalgamation and the reduction of the police forces of England and Wales to 'about 20' were heard again in July 2010.[57]

The three instances cited above by the chief officer as indications of poor Home Office management continue to resonate: amalgamation, chief officers feel, is merely suspended, not abandoned, while there is disquiet at what looks to chief officers to be renewed Home Office efforts to influence PNAC and HPDS. Indeed, the Metropolitan Police appears sufficiently unpersuaded of HPDS' merits that it developed its own scheme in 2009 to identify and develop potential chief officers.[58]

---

[56] The plan was based on an HMIC report asking if 43 forces were 'fit for purpose'. See http://news.bbc.co.uk/1/hi/uk_politics/4771812.stm; accessed 23 April 2010; and www.telegraph.co.uk/news/1526849/Abandoned-police-force-merger-plans-cost-11m.html; accessed 23 April 2010.

[57] Townsend, M. and Helm, T. 'Halve number of police forces, says spending tsar', *The Observer*, 4 July 2010, available from www.guardian.co.uk/uk/2010/jul/04/police-force-cuts; accessed 5 July 2010. The 'tsar' in question is former chief inspector Jan Berry, ex-chair of the Police Federation who was appointed in 2007 by the then Home Secretary Jacqui Smith to investigate bureaucracy in the police service. Mrs Berry's term came to an end in September 2010. The current Home Secretary is reported as having 'set the ground for the extent of the transformation', warning that 'cuts to police budgets over the next few years would be 'big and tough to achieve' (ibid.).

[58] See an article by Sarah Bebbington entitled 'Fast Track' in *Police Review*, 5 February 2010b, pp 18–19, in which the Metropolitan Police is reported as saying that their

One chief officer, who has had experience of working in other parts of government on attachment, offered a more detached view of how police officers almost perversely seem to want to challenge policy and political direction:

> **Interviewee 21:** It's this business about being politicised. Chief officers are the only Crown servants I've ever come across who offer commentary on policies. You can't whinge about being politicised if you then comment publicly on policy, off the cuff often, and implicitly criticise the government. No other Crown servants, in the home ministries, or in the Foreign Office, would dream of such actions: policies are for ministers, actions for the agencies. The police have a lot to learn about dealing with central government.

This observation was echoed by Rob Adlam in his 2003 essay on police leadership, when he noted that the police have [an] antipathy towards 'government' and the wider 'administration', within which 'the peculiar and 'sacred' doctrine of constabulary independence [...] seems to help sustain a generalised negative attitude towards the institutions and processes of government' (Adlam, 2003, p 40). Against this observation, many chief officers argue to the contrary that policing is unique and that no other government department expects its 'executive arm' to implement policies and to embark on initiatives that have not been tested.

It is probable that there has always been a tension of some degree between those who formulate policy and those who have to carry that policy out, but in the case of relations between the police and the Home Office, antagonism seems now to have advanced to a stage where it might become corrosive. Many officers point to the sheer weight of criminal legislation which was enacted by the four Labour administrations between 1997 and 2010 (amounting to more than 3,000 separate items of new criminal law according to a criminal barrister, Charles Foster, and a study by King's College in London)[59], and the burden that new statutes and practices put on the forces who have to police them. It is of course of point that chief police officers are sometimes involved in framing or outlining new laws, but, as Andrew

---

candidates on HPDS 'end up in middle management posts' rather than as chief officers. This is discussed in more detail in Chapter One.

[59] He claims that 'In [Prime Minister] Blair's ten year rule well over 3000 new criminal offences were created. Nearly two-thirds of those were created by way of secondary legislation.' See www.charlesfoster.co.uk/worddocs/blairlawcrpdf.pdf; accessed 23 April 2010; also CCJS (2007).

Wren noted to me, the initiative for new laws more often comes from the minister or the political party in power:

> **AW:** ACPO is consulted and is involved in the making of legislation; which results either from pressure on the minister from his/her party or from the minister individually.

However, when I asked Mr Wren to comment on police unease about the amount of criminal legislation brought in since 1997, he refused. There is no absolute right or wrong in this tension between law makers and law enforcers, but the tension itself seems not to be creative so much as destructive. One chief officer made the point strongly that manipulation of the police by the Home Office was not the prerogative of any one political party, commenting *before* the general election in 2010 that

> **Interviewee 40:** I very much doubt if the present crowd [...] in the Home Office will survive an election but the incoming government, if Tory, has little love for the police and all politicians have an inbuilt tendency to meddle – especially in matters they know nothing about and about which they are resistant to learning; so I see very little on the horizon to be hopeful about. The permanent civil service people in the Home Office will jump about in response to whoever tugs their strings; [...] [t]hey can craft an elegant policy, I'm sure, but they wouldn't understand what makes an effective counter-drugs operation.

This has brought us back to the perennial police complaint that policing is not properly understood by those outside policing who oversee it.[60] This applies, in the view of chief officers, very emphatically to the Home Office. Chief officers deplore the tendency on the part of those charged with oversight of the police to experiment with social engineering, arguing that the Home Office does this in ways that would not be tolerated in other government departments such as health or education. Evidence of such interference abounds, they say, from HPDS to 'amalgamation' (see p 170) and in much of it chief officers see HMIC as complicit. On the face of it, the coalition government is not regarded any differently, especially as the strong emphasis on

---

[60] And, as we have seen, the judgements of HMIC are accepted grudgingly and with reluctance, even though HM Inspectors are drawn almost entirely from the ranks of the police.

reducing costs and streamlining budgets has hit hard at chief officers' strategic planning. Subsequent contact with chief officers in the wake of the ACPO Conference of 2010, indicated pretty clearly that the Home Office was seen as 'the same old bumbling bureaucracy'. The announcement, in the *Draft Protocol* for the police crime commissioner, that the Home Office will 'withdraw from day-to-day policing matters' (Home Office, 2011b, p 5) may be greeted with relief by some chief officers, but withdrawal does not mean absence. The Home Office will continue to influence the strategic direction of policing, and will no doubt exercise some sort of control of police forces, and especially their chief officers, at arm's length through the PCCs and HMIC.

Summary and conclusions

Police authorities are the current local oversight mechanisms which hold police forces to account for 'efficiency and effectiveness'. There continue to be ambiguities where police authority interests end and those of chief officers of police begin; nowhere more controversially than in 'operational policing'. Police officers themselves can be defensive about or hostile towards what they see as encroachment on their preserves. Unsurprisingly, the general run of chief officer opinions about police authorities and their members is negative, but deeper analysis shows that some chief officers can be adept at manipulation and 'mind games' with police authority members, individually and collectively. The increasing involvement of police authorities in the day-to-day management and activity of the police, extended now to hiring, reporting on and firing chief officers, is likely to intensify chief officer distrust of what many see as interference by amateurs. I see no likely change in this distrust when the PCC replaces the police authority in 2012, since the anxieties and frustrations currently felt by chief officers about the 17 strong police authority may simply be more narrowly focused on a single individual. However, as noted earlier, the passage from police authority to police crime commissioner may not be as frictionless as the government had hoped, and it is even possible that the PCC may be overseen or constrained by the crime police panel (Savage, M. et al, 2011; Hansard May 11 2011).

There is no consensus among chief officers whether police authorities are malign or supportive: many authorities stress the support they offer to the police, but chief officers are apt to stress the negative to the exclusion of all else, and for that we should perhaps allow for that expression of partiality a little. The preponderance of views expressed to me suggests that tensions are increasing proportionally and in line with police authorities' greater powers, and that sooner or later, those tensions, irrespective of protocols, will become visible. There is no reason to suppose that chief officers will feel any more comfortable with a PCC than with a police authority, particularly if the actions of holding the police to account appear to step over the boundary into interference with operational policing (Brain, 2010), whatever the provisions in the *Draft Protocol* (Home Office, 2011b).

There is often tension and always some residuum of hostility between those being assessed and those doing the assessing, and HMIC is no different from, say, Ofsted, in being resented for its inspections. There is a difference though between a more or less cordial professional distaste and the often visceral loathing which seems to characterise chief police officers' opinions of HMIC. The impression is also very strong that this dislike has intensified in recent years and seems to have to do explicitly with HMIC's 'fierce guardianship' of the public accountability of the police. HMIC is also criticised for trying to do two different things: assessing the 'efficiency and effectiveness' of a police force on one hand while on the other playing a role in the assessment and development of the chief officer team leading that force. Chief officer after chief officer returned to the charge that a separate professional organisation, not necessarily ACPO-related, should assess, promote and develop individual chief officers.

For its part, HMIC seems to be indifferent to the apparently adverse impact it has on chief officers and is steadfast in its determination to act 'in the public interest'. But indifference will not improve relations with chief officers that, under the surface at least, are strained and volatile. It cannot make for a productive working relationship if HMIC is seen as 'the Home Office's rottweiler' and if chief officers appear fearful of accountability and deviant in their attempts to duck responsibility to the public. Neither position is tenable for long. The criticism of HMIC cannot be dismissed as simply the jaundiced opinions of the disaffected or those who have most to fear. Very successful and highly respected chief officers voiced strong concerns to me, while Sir Denis O'Connor's literal shrug when I relayed those concerns was equally eloquent.

The Home Office is also regarded in a negative light by the majority of chief officers; indeed, a higher proportion of them disliked the Home Office's interference with policing and its exercise of power than felt negatively about HMIC. There has probably been an undercurrent of tension between chief officers and their political masters from the outset, but in recent years – possibly as a result of the very large amounts of criminal legislation passed by successive Labour administrations from 1997 – this has seemed to get stronger. There is near-universal disdain for the Home Office permanent officials who do not seem to understand policing, as well as for the short-term expediency of politicians. Again and again, chief officers stated that the Home Office 'did not listen' and that policy was sometimes made in spite of chief officers' opinions rather than as a result of them.

While ACPO sometimes has a consultative role in the framing of legislation, there is a strong feeling among chief officers that the Home Office too often makes policy off the cuff or as a knee-jerk response to political imperatives. The same indifference to chief officers' opinions was shown by the Home Office official interlocutor as was shown by HM Chief Inspector of Constabulary. While the 'great departments of state' can profess equanimity in the face of criticism, it cannot be comfortable for such officials to know that they are not trusted, just as chief officers may be dismayed when they realise how little their views seem to matter.

Part of the blandness of the 'official' responses has to do with the anonymity of the people laying the charges against HMIC and the Home Office, and it is of course easier for both HMIC and Home Office officials to dismiss criticism if it has no named origin. The point I made repeatedly to both organisations and to their spokespeople, as well as to the individual chief officers who spoke to me, was a simple one: such negativity needs to be addressed before it becomes corrosive. The remedy of greater consultation, of officials and inspectors listening more to the views of chief officers and the direct inclusion of chief officers in policy determination and in responses to public accountability, may go a long way to diffuse tensions and reverse the negative lights in which each holds the other. It is not simply the acidulated viewpoints of a few bruised individuals that we are considering here, but the representative and consistent opinion of a large body of very influential police officers.

FIVE

On the nature of experience and exclusivity: the police 'closed shop'

Interviewee 81: There must be something characteristic of policing which produces police leaders, rather than any old transferee from any old organisation. Policing isn't 'any old' delivery, it is hard-earned and hard-learned knowledge, and leaders should derive from that. I suppose I'm arguing against direct entry – which by a paradox I believe in – but what I mean is that whoever leads has to know the business well, whether that is public order, major crime or neighbourhood policing. You can't lead cops just because you are the best advocate of car insurance or chocolates.

There is in policing an exclusivity in terms of *understanding the job by having done it* that closely parallels the culture of the Armed Forces, where individual credibility can often depend on a judicious mixture of experience, track record, postings, 'hard' jobs and perceptions of that individual's achievements. Like soldiers, police officers tend to have little time for abstract theory and seldom pursue knowledge for its own sake, in the sense of 'pure' academic research. There are exceptions of course, but they are rare. What police officers tend to respond to is *experiential learning*, in which the application of practical knowledge to skill and thence to situation is highly regarded. There is a need for knowledge in policing: of the criminal law, of police procedure and police powers, and of the criminal justice system for instance, but these can often be subordinated to what 'works' in a given situation.[1] It follows from this that the police value those who have *applied* skills, such as forensic investigators or skilled interviewers, and correspondingly have little time for 'outsiders' who have not experienced policing in some way or who do not bring valued skills to bear on a situation.

---

[1] These observations are based on my experience over a period of 10 years of directing a training and development centre for police officers and implementing national and local learning strategies, and on military experience before that.

Moving from the attitude of the police in general to the attitudes of chief officers, it is not difficult to find the same exclusivity applied to police command, particularly if it concerns the risks around someone being appointed as a chief officer from outside:

> **Interviewee 39:** [...] within minutes, such a person would be gripping the rail in the Crown Court facing a charge of corporate manslaughter. Take covert armed surveillance: I have done it, and commanded it tactically, so I know what is involved. I know, for example, that after three days the team is exhausted and needs to be withdrawn, whatever the commander on the ground may say. How could someone coming in from outside have the first clue how to set the parameters for such an operation, let alone understand the implications of saying yes to a deployment in highly dangerous circumstances?

This chief officer evidently believes that any appointment to command which does not have experientially based knowledge of policing is dangerous, but the lines are drawn on a rather extreme basis. Lack of police experience does not necessarily preclude command of potentially lethal operations, as some ex-soldiers, now police officers, can testify. Another chief officer was a little more relaxed in his attitude to someone coming into police command from outside, but still made essentially the same 'life-or-death' point:

> **Interviewee 25:** Sixty per cent of this job is business management or project management, or chairing meetings or negotiation of one kind or another and anyone could do it with the right training and generic management experience. But 40% of the job is high-level risk management, sometimes literally involving life-or-death situations, and making the right judgement in those circumstances, such as a firearms deployment, comes with experience of doing policing, not from teaching, or commerce or anything else.

The same implacable scepticism about non-police commanders is behind this statement as lay behind the covert armed surveillance comment above. Chief officers often argue that the 'soft' bits of the job can be done by anyone with experience of managing projects or negotiating, but prior operational police experience is needed when command of a volatile situation is called for. It is a common argument, but one that is increasingly challenged. A prolific commentator on the police, Andy Hayman, a former Chief Constable of Norfolk and an ex-Assistant Commissioner at the Metropolitan Police, wrote this:

> The obvious argument against bringing in outsiders is that
> this new breed of chief constable would not be equipped
> to deal with operational matters – but they would be no
> different to a government minister making life and death
> decisions or to the chief executive of a health trust with
> no medical background having to deal with the impact
> of swine flu. In each case, such decisions are informed by
> advice from others who have more specialised knowledge.
> (Hayman, 2009)

It is not clear if Mr Hayman is relaying an idea that he espoused during
his service or whether this is something that he has come to accept
since leaving the police. The point he makes is resonant though: chief
officers have access to specialist advice in reaching operational decisions,
just like other occupations, and demanding that the chief officer has
requisite specialist knowledge him/herself seems unrealistic. To argue
otherwise suggests some sort of deliberate exclusivity; a point reinforced,
a little mischievously perhaps, by this chief officer:

> **Interviewee 9:** What is at work here is a very powerful
> protectionism, about which the police get highly emotional. That
> ought to be indication enough that we should try it!

There are times when the police collectively can be deeply conservative
(witness the response to Sheehy's proposed reforms in the 1980s)[2] and
they can be stubbornly resistant to change if they choose, as suggested
graphically in research by Barry Loveday (2005, 2008) for example,
but the sense of exclusivity suggested by the interviewee here indicates
a typical defensiveness which has to do with maintaining ACPO as
a species of 'closed shop'. In 2009, the former Health Minister and
briefly Home Secretary, Alan Milburn, chaired a panel which looked

---

[2] Sir Patrick Sheehy, a prominent businessman, was appointed in 1993 by the then
Home Secretary, Kenneth Clark, to chair a committee to look at police reform. The
recommendations of Sheehy's committee met vociferous and sustained opposition
across the police service, but particularly from ACPO and the Police Federation. Among
other proposals to reform the police, Sir Patrick suggested performance-related pay,
fixed term contracts, bonuses for chief officers and extending the retirement age to
60. The successor Home Secretary, Michael Howard, quietly shelved the proposals.
See Sheehy (1993); Terry Kirby 'Police resistance to reforms surprises Sheehy', *The
Independent*, 31 July 1993.

at access to the professions and concluded:

> [a] governing assumption [exists] in too many of our
> institutions that progress can be achieved on the basis of
> a limited pool of talent having access to a limited set of
> opportunities. Such elitism is unjust socially. And it can no
> longer work economically. (Milburn, 2009)

Those in the police who are opposed to the appointment of outsiders
are hostile to the idea that it might be thrust on them. Other chief
officers consider that the appointment of a non-police chief officer to
operational command is not inconceivable, just unlikely:

> **Interviewee 4:** We don't know [if it would work] because no
> one has done [it] in my working life. There's no logical reason why
> an eminent leader in another occupation shouldn't make a leader
> in the police, but it would be a long time coming and possession
> of the Chief Officer competencies alone would certainly not fit
> someone for operational command. The key thing which comes
> between aptitude and ability in police leadership is experience.

The experiential element is again emphasised and it is noteworthy that
this interviewee does not accept that the chief officer competencies
(which I examined in Chapter Three) are enough to describe or capture
the qualities needed to lead the police operationally; a point echoed
by another chief officer, who remarked:

> **Interviewee 47:** The relative ease with which my colleagues and
> I do the job is the product of more than 25 years' service: we've
> seen it and done it. An outside appointment would bring other
> experience to bear and would do things differently and maybe that
> difference is a threat which scares us a little bit.

The prospect of 'transverse' appointments from industry, the private
sector or elsewhere in public service at chief officer rank certainly causes
unease and a number of serving chief officers privately admitted to the
'threat which scares us a little bit', suggesting an unease which remains
hidden most of the time:

> **Interviewee 68:** Someone else doing your job better than you
> is probably a hidden nightmare for most of us, though I'm fairly
> confident that it would take a really exceptional person to come

into the service from outside and be able to deliver. Certainly, it would be interesting to see it tried, but no one is willing – not even in the Home Office – to take that kind of risk.

But this is not entirely true, because an 'outsider' (in the sense of his not having been a career police officer) was appointed with the rank of chief constable to head the British Civil Nuclear Constabulary (CNC) in 2007. One chief police officer welcomed the appointment:

Interviewee 24: I was pleased to see that civvy at the British Nuclear get the Chief's job. That really set the cat among the pigeons. He did the SCC [Strategic Command Course], you know.

The reference here is to Chief Constable Richard Thompson, who was the first 'civilian' ('civvy') for many years to be appointed directly to a chief constable post without first having come through the police ranks. The CNC polices the UK Atomic Energy Authority, the British Nuclear Group and other nuclear energy establishments in the UK, and protects nuclear materials in transit.[3] Mr Thompson indeed attended the Bramshill Strategic Command Course, but his extensive experience abroad as a diplomat in the Foreign and Commonwealth Office, evidently reassured those in the Civil Nuclear Police Authority making the appointment and in the Home Office/Department for Energy and Climate Change that he could do the job. We should not suppose that the CNC is somehow not real policing: all the security and investigative functions are invested in the CNC as they are in other police forces, but some chief officers have been apt to excuse, or even explain away Mr Thompson's appointment on the basis that it is highly specialist and not 'real policing' at all.

However, when Cumbria Constabulary had to deal with the series of fatal shootings and woundings by Derrick Bird in June 2010, the Civil Nuclear Constabulary was one of the forces which quickly assisted Cumbria in dealing with some 30 different crime scenes and in providing additional firearms officers to track the killer, who was armed with two powerful guns.[4] In that instance, the CNC was

---

[3] More detailed information is available from the CNC website: www.cnc.police.uk/; accessed 10 November 2010.

[4] See Fresco, A., O'Neill, S. and Wade, M. 'Cumbria Gunman Derrick Bird gave Chilling Warning of his Intentions', *The Times*, 3 June 2010, available from www.timesonline.co.uk/tol/news/uk/crime/article7143018.ece; accessed 3 June, 2010. Bird's final act was to shoot himself.

regarded as a police force able to provide 'mutual aid' like any other.[5] Its chief constable makes operational decisions and issues deployment orders, also like any other.

There are plenty of historical precedents for appointments as chief constable from outside the police; until the later part of the 20th century it was not at all uncommon for a distinguished soldier or sailor to take a chief constable post, often in shire forces but sometimes in city forces too. Most police forces have pictorial histories on display which show the early chiefs who came from the Army or the Royal Navy.

An example is Wiltshire Police which was founded in 1839. Its first chief constable of the then 200-strong Wiltshire Constabulary was Captain Samuel Meredith, Royal Navy, who served 31 years as Chief until 1870. He was succeeded by Captain Robert Sterne, Royal Navy, who served from 1870–1908 (38 years) as Chief. He was replaced by Lt. Col. Sir Hoël Llewellyn, chief constable from 1908–43 (37 years), and another army officer, Lt. Col. Harold Golden, led the force from 1946 until 1963.[6] Thus, for over a century, the post of chief constable of Wiltshire Police was an outside appointment from the Armed Forces. However, since the immediate post Second World War period, there have been very few non-police post holders in England and Wales[7] and even fewer military appointments. Mr Thompson is the sole appointee to command a police force from outside the service in the last 30 years. This is not to say that further such appointments could not be made, because there is no constitutional or legislative bar to non-police officers exercising command at chief officer rank, but it is unlikely that the same assumption that individuals could go immediately from military service to police service – would be made so glibly these days. Indeed, some chief officers argue that there would probably have to be restrictions on what outside appointees could do:

---

[5] There is policy precisely related to this; see *Mutual Aid Arrangements* www.homeoffice. gov.uk/.../consultations/rev-police-leadership-training/appendices?view=Binary; accessed 11 May 2011.

[6] Wiltshire is by no means untypical. I am grateful to Wiltshire Police's internal magazine *firstbeat*, December 2008/January 2009 edition, for information on its early chief constables. A further article by Charlotte Moorby entitled 'Celebrating 170 Years of Superb Service!' summarises the history of the force in the same edition (pp 14–15). See also Paul Sample's *The Oldest and the Best, a History of Wiltshire Constabulary, 1839–2003*, 2nd edn, 2003; available from www.wiltshire.police.uk/ index.php?option=com_docman&task=cat_view&gid=81&Itemid=100; accessed 12 May 2010.

[7] Indeed, chief constables now serve, averagely, between five and seven years in the rank, so the great longevity of years past is unlikely to be repeated.

Interviewee 64: I don't see why [external appointments] wouldn't work at ACPO – after all, lots of forces now have HR directors and finance directors at ACC level who are not police officers. They couldn't do police operations of course, and no sane chief constable would trust them as 'Gold', but until a few years ago, chief officers were expected to run personnel and training with no prior experience, and they had to rely on expert advice in the P&T [personnel and training] or HR [human resources] department. I actually don't see that that is very different from, say, taking the advice of a tactical firearms officer at an incident.

This echoes the point made above that chief officers making command operational decisions have access to and take into account, specialist advice, but goes on to note that chief officers with no experience of 'soft' skills such as those in human resources, finance or information services, nonetheless can lead them, often as first appointments. Seldom is the criticism of experiential unfitness in these equally specialist areas ever surfaced and it is tempting to argue that what is sauce for the goose is sauce for the gander. But Interviewee 64 clearly expects outsiders to have a very limited policing role, even with access to expert advice.

Another chief officer believed that the appointment of an outsider to any rank of chief officer was certainly possible even if the individual's activities would be limited, but the act of looking outside for candidates would neglect the talent already within:

Interviewee 89: They [outsiders] could do most of [a chief officer's job] apart from the operational command element. They would also have to work hard to develop the operational context and philosophical understanding which would enable them to make the right organisational decisions. Clearly those gaps could be filled and someone else could do the operational part of the job but why would you want to do that when you can employ someone with the right blend of operational experience with management and leadership skills? The dangers of going down this route should be clear for all to see in the way in which the Health Service has developed in recent years.

The favourite police analogy with the National Health Service is not exact here, since those brought into the NHS from outside have taken management roles, not operational roles. However, at least part of the reason that the Home Office and others are looking outside the police service for potential chief officers, is the relative dearth of candidates within. In Chapter One, I noted that chief officers generally did not like to travel far in search of promotion, with the result that some police authorities offer inducements to try to retain those already in post, though this is increasingly subject to scrutiny and challenge (O'Neill, 2009). The difficulty of increasing the pool of applicants for lead posts would be formidable if contenders were drawn only from within the police service. One insider commented

> **Interviewee 97:** it would be good if police authorities had a wider field from which to choose. This happens at ACC/commander level, but not often at selection for deputy and chief. There is a real need to do more, especially at the Strategic Command Course end and when prospective candidates apply for jobs.

It is hard to see how the improvement in processes recommended here will lead of itself to 'a wider field' of applications at deputy and chief constable levels, but Interviewee 97 went on to observe that:

> **Interviewee 97:** Operational policing is what [police officers] do and enjoy: it turns [them] on. But this is not needed at the top level and can lead to a shortfall in leadership skills and partnership work. The acquisition of business skills is some distance further off. The National College of Police Leadership will change all this over time but increased business skills are what are most urgent at the moment. There is an insularity about the police generally and about chief officers in particular, whilst the quality of thinking at the top is not as high as it could be.

A number of serving chief officers have commented on the need for aspirant chief officers to acquire business skills and this is already translating itself into components of the SCC. In an article entitled 'Free consultancy' in *Police Review* it was observed that candidates on the SCC now have to show that they 'can lead forces with cost effectiveness at the forefront of their minds' (Hitchcock, 2010, p 6). The head of Leadership Programmes at National Policing Improvement Agency (NPIA) and the then Director of the National College of Police Leadership, Deputy Chief Constable Alf Hitchcock, noted in the same article that

> [...] the new focus of the SCC is particularly on business skills and how you continue to deliver a high quality and

continuously improving service to communities in the context of reducing budgets.

This is all laudable and shows the responsiveness of the National College of Police Leadership in identifying 'new' core skills, but it is not addressing the essential conundrum, which is how the police can develop its own leaders of sufficient calibre to withstand pressures to import leaders from outside. Andy Hayman, in his article espousing external appointments to the police, also lights on the lack of chief officers with business skills:

> Being a modern chief constable is less about policing and more about being a business leader. We may have reached the point where an outsider from industry is better equipped to be a chief constable than a career officer, because they [sic] could be more objective in setting priorities and using resources. (Hayman, 2009)

It may indeed be that business skills are key components in the suite of abilities and attributes which the modern chief officer needs to have, but they will not be the only things. There will also be a need to develop and guide selected change processes in a financially constrained context, a requirement for objectivity about priorities, an ability to encourage and deliver policing engagement with local communities at the same time as providing larger and wider protective services, while enabling police officers themselves to move seamlessly between these two kinds of policing. Chief officers, as I have noted earlier, also require well-developed 'political' skills, negotiating capabilities of a high order and a clear capacity to formulate effective strategy. Generic policing skills do not seem to be needed at this level. There is even a school of thought that says operational skills have to be screened out or 'un-learned' at ACPO level, yet chief officers persist in their belief that credibility with lower ranks is important, as is the ability to make the 'right' operational decisions, and this then becomes an argument requiring chief officers to have come up through the ranks:

Interviewee 33: I've been on the ground and I can empathise with front-line officers in a way that someone without a policing background would find hard to do. I'm not talking about credibility, though that is an issue, I'm talking about being relied on to make the right decision in the right circumstances. Only experience and understanding of policing can make you do that.

One might expect the bulk of chief officers to agree with this robust assessment of what is wanted at command level in the police, but in fact there are plenty who anticipate multi-level entry, including to chief officer, as a part of inevitable change:

> **Interviewee 60:** […] there must be hundreds of people out there who could do this job as well as me. I think the best way to start this change process would be to open up all ranks to competitive entry.
>
> [Interviewer: All ranks?]
>
> Yes, all. Doing so will at least have the virtue of transparency, which the current promotion procedures do not have.
>
> [Interviewer: Can you elaborate?]
>
> Even if you pass OSPRE for sergeant or inspector, there is no guarantee that a force will promote you; and it may argue that there aren't enough vacancies or that you need experience in something else, when what it really means is that you personally are not wanted at that rank. Then, when you get to chief inspector, superintendent and chief superintendent, the selection process becomes absolutely baffling, very closed and not properly open to challenge. I know, I've been through it. So, going back to what I said just now: a competitive process of entry and promotion at all ranks would benefit policing and open it right up. Then we might really get the best available, instead of just the best-fitting, from within.

Interviewee 60 has captured a common affirmative response from chief officers in terms of opening up the police to different levels of entry. Table 5.1 shows the preponderant responses to my interview question about direct entry at different ranks.

Table 5.1: Opinion of multiple direct entry

	Number	Percentage
In favour	48	51%
Against	45	48%
Don't know	1	1%
Totals	**94**	**100%**

The data are very evenly balanced between those who accept that the police must change in this way and those who do not want to go down the multi-entry route. In retrospect it might have been helpful to ascertain whether this split in opinion was reflective of age and experience or whether 'pro' and 'anti' views were more generally distributed across the ACPO ranks, but such a determination will now have to await further research. Nonetheless, these data tend to undermine characteristically monolithic police responses in public to the notion of being able to join at ranks other than constable. More than half of the chief officers I spoke to seemed prepared, *at least in private*, to entertain multiple entry to police ranks. Despite this, the Policing Green Paper of 2008 appeared to set the then government's face against any entry mode other than at the bottom rank of constable.[8] As noted in Chapter One, the coalition government has talked openly about 'fast track' and multiple level entry to police ranks, to a general chorus of dismay in the police.[9]

Multiple entry does not answer the central question which sceptical police officers continue to ask and which is pointed exactly by this chief officer:

> **Interviewee 80:** It is the extent of operational experience (and I really emphasise this) that gives the police leader two things: (a) credibility with front-line officers and (b) the likelihood of making the right decision.

Credibility with 'front-line officers' is not predicated solely on the basis of what the chief officers had done in the past in operational policing (which was usually in another police force in any case) but is more to do with the perception by constables and sergeants whether the particular chief officer will bring them extra and more difficult work or whether they have a 'champion' on high who will guard their backs. The general impression which I have had from talking to front-line police officers over the course of the last 12 years is that the patrol sergeant or duty inspector is much more immediately their concern than an often remote chief officer from headquarters who comes into the station or out on patrol very intermittently. Indeed, a commentator on the police, Derek Barham, has directly stated that

> Any attempt to deviate from the [...] model progressing gradually from probationary constable to chief officer is

---

[8] See Chapter Two note 6.

[9] Reported by the BBC and available from www.bbc.co.uk/news/uk-12170502; accessed 1 February, 2011.

often denounced as being too radical for British policing. (Barham, 2010b, p 12)

which would be merely idiosyncratic were his comments not derived from a Metropolitan Police report called *Race and Faith Inquiry* which published its findings in July 2010 and concluded that

> [...] the traditional process of promotion is outdated, deters the highest calibre individuals from joining the police service and is a barrier to increasing diversity in the workforce. (Barham, 2010b, p 12)

Barham adds, probably not without some mischievousness, that

> [...] there is no need for an ACPO officer to have had any operational policing experience at all. (Barham, 2010b, p 12)

The decisions in short-term urgent operational situations which a chief officer may have to make include requesting mutual aid from other forces, authorisation of covert action, agreeing to deploy surveillance teams, ordering an armed response and implementing strategic road closure (for example in the event of flooding). However, one of the common 'received criticisms' of chief officers is about *long-term decisions* and how those officers (particularly ACCs) are no longer in post when the consequences or results of decisions made in the past emerge in the present. This is called 'butterfly policing' in some police forces which caricatures the ambitious chief officer as alighting on a policy or a decision and then quickly fluttering off to another without retaining any responsibility.

One widespread example of this in 2007–08 concerned the decision by a number of police forces to withdraw from actual or potential partnerships with universities to produce policing degrees (including two-year foundation [fd] degrees). Instead the forces linked with further education providers to follow a shorter 'artisan' National Vocational Qualification (NVQ) route, and the non-academic path was justified on the dual grounds of cost and applicability. However, a decision in January 2010 by the Learning Skills Council no longer to fund the NVQ for the police led to its rapid shelving by forces who did not want to have to fund the programme themselves. Those ACCs who, through their learning and development portfolios, had redirected their forces into the NVQ paths, had by this time either left their forces on promotion or had gone on to other things. In 2010–11, some of those same forces then turned back to universities to partner 'pre-joining' learning routes, where applicants to the police can self-fund initial training.[10]

One chief officer felt strongly that policing, even at the higher chief officer level, is not entirely about business processes and generic leadership skills but about the need to make hard operational decisions:

> **Interviewee 40:** It's a wretched myth that policing is easy and therefore anyone can do it. The opposite is true and very, very few can do policing well. Business is never about life and death but policing can be and that is why the tolerances are much higher. There's nowhere else to run when you're a chief constable and you have to make [...] decisions.

It's true that command decisions are exposed to scrutiny from many sides, not least from the police authority or the directly elected police crime commissioner or inquisitive media (which do not scruple to invoke the Freedom of Information Act in pursuit of their enquiries), but such decisions are usually about operational rather than strategic matters and it is comparatively rare for criticism to be levelled at chief officers for the quality of their strategic decision making.[11] This lends some weight to the rather cynical belief that some chief officers consistently duck their responsibilities in the long-term because there is no overall *national* police strategic plan to which learning and development, IT systems, human resource management, budgeting

---

[10] In 2010, ACPO, in association with the Home Office and the Association of Police Authorities, produced a report which noted that '[The Police] Service recruits 8,000 officers per year and most [forces] paid for them for six months to sit in a classroom and learn.' All this is a long way from the 'artisan' NVQ route espoused only three years previously: it is not surprising that many police officers look with jaundiced eyes on transient chief officers' experiments with learning programmes and their subsequent abrupt departures with work uncompleted.

[11] An exception concerns the implementation of a comprehensive online human resource enquiry system for the Metropolitan Police. An article by Sean O'Neill entitled 'Met Police Chief in Crisis Talks on Overdue, Over-Cost IT System' was published by *The Times* on 17 May 2010 and concerned, in O'Neill's words, 'A new computer system designed to deliver major financial savings for the country's biggest police force is running six months late and £10 million over budget [...]. The Metropolitan Police had planned to spend £38 million to overhaul its human resources department and save £15 million per year in office costs. But the latest estimate for the project is £48 million and no date has been set for when it will be ready.' (www.timesonline. co.uk/tol/news/uk/crime/article7128226.ece; accessed 17 May 2010)

and finance conform. HMIC, through a variety of thematic reports and initiatives,[12] has tried to impose some national consistency, as did NPIA, but neither achieved conspicuous success in herding these particular cats.

Another chief officer noted that there could be a tension between a strategic desire by the Home Office and others to open the ACPO ranks to outside competition, and the internal insistence on experience in the role:

> **Interviewee 79:** There are two or three in the wings as we speak [from outside policing], but a tyro with no knowledge of the police could not do the job as confidently and as well as someone with that knowledge and experience. I suppose it comes down to whether your need to refresh the service is greater than efficiently getting the job done.

This revisits the 'experience versus no experience' equation that I looked at earlier, and implies that any initiative to open up competition for chief officer ranks is merely a political exercise; whereas some chief officers think that it is much more a matter of the specific skills and attributes which an individual would bring to the task:

> **Interviewee 16:** it depends what that experience is. Policing isn't a set of tramlines which we make people fit into, sometimes the choices can be overwhelming. There must be [...] other people out there who could do what I do, but they bring different things to the job, as I bring my distinctive and individual gifts too, to whatever the task is.

This raises an important consideration: even if access to chief officer ranks is restricted to those who come from within the police service, the individuals concerned will not have homogeneous skills sets. They will have certain experiences in common but these are likely to be generic rather than specific and it would make very little sense for any promotions system to rely on identical experiential pathways. In very broad terms, it is still fairly unusual for someone who has spent a career almost entirely within the detective ranks to make it to chief

---

[12] For example *Training Matters*, 2002; *Getting Together* (on joint working) 2009; *E-Learning*, 2006 and *Safety Matters*, 2007; all (with many others) available in pdf format from: www.hmic.gov.uk/INSPECTIONS/Pages/ThematicInspections.aspx; accessed 17 May 2010.

officer. Equally, a police officer who has not engaged in operational duties since probation may not initially present the right 'profile' when seeking support for their application to the Police National Assessment Centre (as I noted in Chapter One).

However, those selected for development as chief officers present a wide variety of experiences, backgrounds and attainments, gained in many different areas of policing (Reiner, 1991). In other words, there is quite a broad 'church' of skills and attributes which chief officers bring to their roles, some of which have been gained in different parts of policing – not all of them front-line or operational. It must also follow that external candidates might equally bring a diverse range of attributes and skills to the job. Other than having moved up the ranks of the police and having shared the common experience of having been a police officer, it is difficult to isolate a 'chief officer factor' which is unique to policing and which disbars all other aspirants. There remains in police thinking a stubborn insistence that those in-police experiences are unique and not amenable to being replicated or learned:

> **Interviewee 67:** Would you trust a barrister to build a bridge? Well I bloody wouldn't. Why would you expect that a captain of industry could control something like the policing of the Olympics?

This officer's robustness is echoed by many: the invocation of other professions and industries suggests that policing is uniquely difficult (Blair, 2009, chapter 4) and, equally uniquely, only those within can understand it:

> **Interviewee 23:** I could do most of a top job somewhere else – except maybe in brain surgery. An accountant could probably do as good a job as me for 80% of the time – probably even better – but it's that remaining 20% which is entirely about understanding policing. That's what no outsider will have.

Perhaps the contrary view to this 'closed shop' opinion is best expressed by Andy Hayman, a chief officer who admits to having straddled both camps:

> Once I thought that it was a strength for a chief constable to have served at every rank in the force, because it developed an understanding and grounding for the job. But I am now not so sure. Someone rising through the ranks can develop their own prejudices or preferences – 'sacred cows' that may

affect their objectivity in planning, managing budgets and assessing priorities. Perhaps it would be better to parachute in an outsider who would not have that baggage – and the more varied their [sic] backgrounds the better. (Hayman, 2009)

Summary

The police seem evenly split between accepting the notion of multiple entry to the service and rejecting it. This is intensified with the debate about direct entry to ACPO ranks, where many police officers vociferously oppose the proposition; arguing that in order to command the police in operational situations, prior experience of policing is essential. Others argue that policing does not have such unique skill sets that they cannot be found elsewhere and that policing itself would actually be refreshed by direct entry from outside. There are precedents in history of appointing ex-military as chief constables, but only one instance of external appointment in modern times, even though that is held to be an exemplar appointment. The Metropolitan Police's *Race and Faith Inquiry Report* (MPA, 2010), also asserts that the police service itself suffers both in calibre and in diversity because of the 'traditional process of promotion' (cited in Barham, 2010b). It is probably the case that those opposed to multiple entry are speaking the loudest, whereas those prepared to try it are either quieter or more circumspect about saying so in public. The Home Office seems committed to ensuring that the internal selection system has a focus on the acquisition of business skills, but has not yet developed a policy for extending the options available from which chief officers can be recruited. In its turn, the coalition government may have resiled on the bald assertion in the 2008 Labour government Green Paper that entry to the police will only be through the constable rank.

Diminishing budgets are likely to dominate police command decisions for some years to come, but there is no insistence yet opening up the means of entry to the police or on any national command strategies across the service, even in 'soft skills' like human resource management, IT or learning and development, let alone any protocols for shared acquisition of equipment, vehicles or services. Such pooling of effort or resources continues to be largely bilateral and informal.

A national police force?

This leads me to consider another proposition recurrently favoured by politicians and some commentators about policing which continues to divide the chief officer ranks too: whether or not there should be a national police force. The questions posed in interview were: *What do you feel about the idea of a national police force in England and Wales? Is it feasible?*

One chief officer had mixed views:

> **Interviewee 79:** We have a 'distributed police system' which is locally based and locally accountable, so a national police force would entail constitutional change. Policing needs checks and balances as I said before and actually joint working at a local level is what the public seems to want. Local people want their police to be local too and would fear a force that didn't have to be accountable or responsive locally. However, amalgamated service provision (IT, vehicles, equipment, HR) is hard to resist on a national scale.
>
> [Interviewer: Is this a fear of the loss of autonomy by the police themselves?]
>
> Yes, a bit. No one likes or wants to be bypassed for some national decision.

'Locally based and locally accountable' policing is age old, deriving from the days of the local justice of the peace and the parish constable in the 14th century. A national police force, by contrast, has long been regarded as 'Continental practice', something done in France or the Netherlands, but not in the UK. Yet the Scottish police forces are independent of the rest of the UK, while in Eire, the *Garda Siochana* is an example of a national police force operating in a small locality but exercising central control. These examples, to some officers, act as a provocation:

> **Interviewee 34:** It's completely stupid. To what end? A national police force would be so easily dominated and used to ill effect by unscrupulous politicians. I look about and I don't see an impressive national model anywhere.
>
> [Interviewer: The *Garda Siochana*? Sweden? The Netherlands?]

> I said impressive. Those are only parish constables with a national title.

The 'constitutional change' which Interviewee 79 mentions above might be less profound than may appear. A simple Commons majority would see through a Bill which, though certain to be opposed in passage, would eventually clear the Lords and become law. The keys to the success of the creation of a national police force would probably be held by the media and by the ways in which public opinion responded to the presentation of the arguments, which might conceivably centre on the need to cope with terrorism or civil unrest (Blair, 2009, p 37). However, the attitude of the police themselves would be central to any debates. In 2004, Rick Naylor, then national chair of the Superintendents' Association, called for the abolition of the 43 'home' police forces of England and Wales, arguing that

> The existing structure of 43 autonomous entities aligned to boundaries which no longer reflect government structures in the regions, or the very local identities felt by individual communities has, we believe, outlived its usefulness. We have now reached the point where further significant improvement cannot be achieved without stepping outside structural arrangements. (Naylor, 2004)

Superintendent Naylor went on to suggest that '[a] logical solution would be a national police force deployed through a regional structure', which could be based on existing government regions in England and Wales. He knew that this would put him on a collision course with ACPO, whose national stance at that point was to oppose a national police force:

> We recognise that the proposal to create a national police force does not appear to sit comfortably with the received wisdom that British policing is best provided by local units allied to traditional boundaries. It is, however, our firm view that our proposal would provide precisely such a structure at the most local level and would simultaneously provide the consistency of approach which is so glaringly absent at the present time. (Naylor, 2004)

It is clear from this that it is by no means the case that the police service is unanimously hostile to the idea of a national police force, although a greater degree of resistance appears to exist among chief officers, whose views seem to be more polarised, than among the ranks below or their representative associations. Also, what chief officers told me in confidence may not be synonymous with any public utterance by the individual concerned. Political appetite for a national police force fluctuates, sometimes spurred by police resistance to a particular Home Secretary's cherished notion (UKBA, amalgamation, national ID cards), and sometimes because control of the police seems desirable to politicians in its own right. There is little in terms of intelligent commentary available to the researcher, but one good piece of work has been done by Edwards and Skidmore (2007) which proposes the abolition of the current 43 police forces in England and Wales, and their replacement with 'no more than a dozen regional' police forces. Such a development in turn might pave the way for a national force arising from the eventual amalgamation of the regional police forces.

One chief officer, alarmed by the prospect of a 'politicised' British police and drawing parallels with France, noted the frequency with which the notion of a national police force appeared and deprecated it strongly:

> **Interviewee 19:** This is a perennial, and I can tell you that there is no appetite for it in the police service. Look at the French experience: even a person as powerful as the Préfêt of an entire French department has to refer the tiniest and most trivial decisions to Paris for approval. If that happened here, we'd never get anything done. That's why you can't get anything accomplished on a bilateral level with the French – it's politicised to an intense degree. I'd hate to see that happen in British policing.

Another chief officer considered that a national police force would upset the traditional balance between the police, the politicians and the public:

> **Interviewee 50:** It would affect the traditional balances of power between the Home Secretary, the police authority and the chief constable. There would still be a local chief, but with much less power and it would be so much easier for Whitehall to tell the police what to do nationally; there'd be no scope for local initiatives, local solutions and local responses. If you want an impassive, remote and clinical police, go for the national model. You'd get efficiency, but the heart would have gone out of policing.

It is not clear from this why the local accountability would have to go simply because the police service became a national organisation, since it could still operate with a local police presence, as it does in the Netherlands. Yet it is a common opinion among some chief officers that moving to a national police model, centrally based, would adversely impinge on the delivery of local policing. There is little evidence to show this to be the case. Until 2005, when Neighbourhood Policing was introduced, the lack of understanding between police and public was endemic. The police glibly believed that they knew best, until HMIC produced its *Closing the Gap* report, which caused a quiet revolution in police thinking.[13]

There is a sense in which neighbourhood and community policing is the new 'flavour' in policing, and there is a concomitant belief that commitment to local engagement somehow rules out the creation of a larger stage, where issues can transcend the parochial and entail a more cooperative sharing of resources and skills. Such thinking inverts the argument that a national force would neglect local accountability. This chief officer, for example, was quite clear that there was no essential difference between national resources and national policing:

> **Interviewee 36:** Shared resources are the way ahead, and this is a way whereby smaller forces can continue to exist. What we need is a national collation of resources: everything from IT to helicopters, and forces will call upon such resources as they can utilise them. The police too should become national: it means that individual forces would keep their cap badges and their local touch and associations – just like a regiment in the Army – but that there would be unified direction, consistency and management. Then we could have proper leadership instead of parochialism. The police would also be powerful enough to see off any attempts at political control and interference. Ultimately, if we don't seize the initiative and do this, it will be taken away and done to us.

Another chief officer took the view, strongly to the contrary of fears that the 'local touch' will be lost, that a national police force:

> **Interviewee 30:** [is] the next logical step. The Army has done it: central command – local regiment. There would be huge savings

---

[13] *Closing the Gap* was written by Denis O'Connor in 2005 and, as I noted in Chapter Four, was a seminal document in bringing to wider attention the absence of meaningful contact or exchange of views between police and public.

---

and an altogether stronger entity would emerge which could easily resist the usual political 'divide and conquer' brigade.

The prospect of money savings, in a contemporary context of economic stringency, may serve to resurface the whole debate, but some chief officers are not convinced by economics alone:

> **Interviewee 67:** National policing has a very siren-like appeal but I'm not convinced it's either feasible or desirable. We need a guarantee of local involvement, though we don't necessarily need 43 forces run differently or indifferently. Might it save money? Possibly, but amalgamation cost a lot and went nowhere. We must be 20 years off a national police force, I'd guess – because there are plenty of national organisations for the police already with SOCA and NPIA.[14] It'll take a social convulsion of some dramatic kind to make politicians agree on a national force.

The possibility of 'social convulsion' caused by economic hardship should not be downplayed. Both the organisations cited by this chief officer as 'national' policing have disappeared in the wake of coalition government changes, and the new National Crime Agency (NCA) may well become 'national detective policing' in all but name.

We know that acquisitive crime often rises during a recession (see Tilley et al, 2007, and the British Crime Surveys)[15], and it is possible that a rise in other kinds of crime, including terrorism, crimes of violence and widespread disorder, might lead to renewed calls for a unified police approach. Certainly this chief officer thought that such a scenario was possible, and that a national police force would come:

---

[14] SOCA was the Serious Organised Crime Agency and NPIA the National Policing Improvement Agency (which included police training) until both were abolished by the incoming coalition government in 2010. Most of SOCA has been absorbed into the new National Crime Agency (NCA) as have parts of NPIA. ACPO has taken on responsibility for police leadership training from the NPIA.

[15] See *Acquisitive crime and plastic card fraud: Findings from the 2008/09 British Crime Survey – Supplementary Volume 3 to Crime in England and Wales 2008/09*; rds, Home Office April 2010, available from http://rds.homeoffice.gov.uk/rds/stats-release.html; accessed 26 May 2010. In fact, the latest BCS figures available at the time of going to press suggested that acquisitive crime (theft, robbery, burglary) were on the same downward trend as other crime types, bucking the usual trend of rising in a recession; see *Crime in England and Wales: Quarterly Update to September 2010*, 20 January 2011, London: Home Office Statistical Report 02/11; available from http://rds.homeoffice.gov.uk/rds/pdfs11/hosb0211.pdf; accessed 29 January 2011.

> **Interviewee 75:** […] but not immediately. As I have said to you, the culture and ethos of policing [now] is risk averse, backward looking and sceptical. We were all burned by the amalgamation debacle, and currently there is no appetite in policing or among politicians, for a national force. But there will be: let crime increase and society become uneasy, let the credit crunch intensify and unemployment increase, and the call for a national police force will be heard again.

Another chief officer spoke for many of his colleagues, perturbed by the proposition that size carries its own justification, when he argued that:

> **Interviewee 27:** […] big is not necessarily beautiful and we need to think very carefully before we abandon what has served us well for the past 175 years. […] There are inherent dangers in a national police force which in my view could threaten operational independence and threaten the tripartite relationship which has held policing in balance for so many years. It is not necessary to create a national service to deal with national issues.

This comment neatly encapsulates the three major reservations which many chief officers have articulated about the creation of a national police force: the loss of local responsiveness and accountability, the threats to the balance of power in the time-honoured tripartite relationship and the danger of political interference with the police. It may be the case that it is not necessary 'to create a national service to deal with national issues', but putting something on a national scale tends to be the default position for many matters surrounding crime and security. Indeed, the creation of the Serious and Organised Crime Agency (SOCA) came about precisely because organised criminality was seen to be moving beyond forces' and other groups' individual capabilities.[16]

---

[16] SOCA was the amalgamation of intelligence and operational responses, involving the National Criminal Intelligence Service and the National Crime Squad; incorporation of MI5's 'serious crimes team' and (the then) HM Customs & Excise Investigative Division followed. This is a persuasive example that actually 'national issues' very often call for national organisations to deal with them. However, following much criticism of its effectiveness, in July 2010, the incoming Home Secretary announced that SOCA would be abolished and its work taken over by a National Crime Agency (NCA). Certainly SOCA's record was mixed and attracted criticism from all sides, even from the Commissioner of the Metropolitan Police; see O'Neill, S. and Peddler, S. 'Long arm of law 'is not reaching Britain's most dangerous crime gangs', *The Times*, 12

Another chief officer thought that, although in 2006 amalgamation of police forces failed spectacularly (the first time it had been seriously considered since 1964), it has not gone away as an idea in politicians' minds especially when the economic arguments are now so powerful in favour of pooling resources:

> **Interviewee 15:** Oh I know there was all the hoo-ha about amalgamation, which was handled incredibly badly both by politicians and by the police themselves, but whilst amalgamation is not high on the agendas of the government or the opposition, it will be again in time. We can't justify our having separate and distinct sets of toys when the urgent need is to husband resources and make things go further. We still don't have inter-operable criminal databases, so how can chiefs justify this continued baronial structure?

Chief officers often express frustration that equipment ('separate and distinct sets of toys'), such as IT and communications, is often incompatible between forces and point to the continued existence of the 43 separate police forces in England and Wales as perpetuating the inefficiencies of autonomous ordering, duplication and specification of equipment. Some chief officers point to former national policing bodies which they believe have not acted with effectiveness and efficiency:

> **Interviewee 5:** SOCA is an example of a national body gone horribly wrong. Sir Stephen Lander[17] is the only person left in the world who thinks that SOCA is doing any kind of a job. National policing by the same token would do nothing. The whole thrust is local accountability.

The chief officer's views were echoed by another who agreed that:

> **Interviewee 26:** [...] SOCA is the perfect instance of a national structure, supposedly with a national and international remit, which has gone right off the rails. The example it sets makes me shudder: all that money and so little to show for it. Exactly the same would happen to a national police force. We'd waste millions and millions, only to have to dismantle the whole thing after five or 10 years.

July 2010, available from www.thetimes.co.uk/tto/news/uk/crime/article2640709.ece; accessed 28 July 2010.

[17] Sir Stephen Lander, formerly a Director-General of the Security Service (MI5), became chair of SOCA in 2004, stepping down in late 2009.

Now, if you were saying that policing needs a national strategy – that's different. There is absolutely no reason why we cannot have a coherent national strategy applied to the police function.

SOCA costs about £1.2 billion annually to run[18] and it is a recurrent argument in the wake of the ill-fated amalgamation of forces exercise in 2006, that drawing individual forces together in a national template could be equally expensive. Another chief officer counselled that SOCA should not be used as an indicative national model of policing:

Interviewee 70: Don't look to SOCA as an example of national policing. It's irretrievably broken.

[Interviewer: are there any national policing organisations which you think work well?]

Yes of course: NPIA worked some of the time, the national training organisation at Wyeboston,[19] ACPO itself. There are lots of examples of effective national bodies, but because one law-enforcement group with a limited remit functions adequately on a national basis, it does not mean that the whole of policing will. And here's a thought for you: if England, Wales and Northern Ireland did amalgamate as a single national force, where would that leave Scotland? Do you think they'd want to come in with us? Not a hope!

Scotland has toyed with the notion of creating a national police force, either as a separate 'crime-busting' force in addition to the eight existing forces, or through an amalgamation of the existing eight forces into one. Although Scotland functions autonomously in policing, there appears to be no appetite currently to create a national force.[20] The

---

[18] According to evidence given by Sir Stephen Lander and SOCA Director-General Bill Hughes in 2009 to the Commons Home Affairs Committee in which it was noted that criminal assets seized by SOCA in 2009 amounted to £78 million, while SOCA itself cost £1.2 billion, a ratio of 15 to 1; see www.dailymail.co.uk/news/article-1194977/Britains-FBI-Soca-spending-15-1-recovers-criminal-gangs.html; accessed 26 May 2010.

[19] In Lincolnshire. Wyeboston Lakes specialises in hi-tech crime and in covert police work, including intelligence gathering.

[20] See for example a report in November 2000 that the Scottish Justice Minister, Jim Wallace, shelved plans for a 'super ninth' police force ('National Police Force Bid Shelved after Accountancy Fears' reported in *The Evening News*, 6 November 2000, available from www.highbeam.com/doc/1P2-17882835.html; accessed 25 May 2010),

point however, is well made by Interviewee 70: a national police force is likely to be based on England and Wales, with the Police Service of Northern Ireland as an associate body. It would then be likely that Scotland would make its own national body of police in order to function efficiently with its neighbours, rather than continue with its eight autonomous forces. By contrast, when a Welsh National Force was suggested in 2006; public and police opposition was piecemeal, but several 'celebrities' voiced their concerns, which led to brief media coverage of the debate.[21]

As I noted above, there seems to be agreement, even among those who hold opposing views on the necessity for a national police force, that the current structure of 43 forces in England and Wales cannot endure for much longer:

> **Interviewee 82:** I'm against [a national police force] quite passionately, but at the same time I can see that we need rationalisation of forces. Forty-three separate [police forces] is completely insane and some independent commands are no bigger than London boroughs. It also means that there are too many tiers of command. The test for any chief executive is that he or she knows all the commanders; if you don't, your force is too big. If you're in each other's pockets, it's too small. A force of between 7,500 and 12,000 seems about right: small enough to care and big enough to cope.

One chief officer believed that if a national police force were to be a reality, it would have to overcome a reluctant police service and would probably have to be insisted on by those (presumably politicians and the media) who wanted it:

> **Interviewee 89:** There is a fundamental resistance to any such notion in the police itself. People would lose local accountability and probably lose status and position – at least further up the chain. The police service is deeply conservative and resistant to real change, so if there's ever an appetite for a national force, it would come from outside policing and would have to be imposed.

---

and Silvester, N. 'You will get Your Own FBI; National Police Force Planned for Scotland', *Sunday Mail* (Glasgow), 2001; available from HighBeam Research, www. highbeam.com; accessed 25 May 2010.

[21] Leading to the strange headline 'Our Future Looks Grim if we have a National Police Force; Astrologer Russell Grant's Prediction', *Daily Post* (Liverpool) 13 May 2006.

but this view is countered by another officer who remarked:

> **Interviewee 49:** I look around at my colleagues and peers, and all I can see, right to the horizon, is lots of feathered bums sticking up in the air, as all these ostriches bury their heads in the sand and croak out the mantra that local policing matters. Of course it does, but a national police force, properly funded, structured and overseen (overseen mind you, not politically interfered with) will deliver far more of value than 43 private kingdoms, more or less ruled by petty bureaucrats like me. [...] I'll see a national police force in my lifetime in policing, I'm certain of that, and just because it's national doesn't mean it's unresponsive to local issues, because the vast amount of policing delivery will still be at a local level, responding to local concerns. It's at the other end that the difference will be noticed.

Another chief officer had no reservations about the concept of a national police force and the way in which its creation would abolish 'petty kingdoms' and parochialism. One way that a national force would accomplish this, he believed, was that the ability of individual chief constables to scupper initiatives would be removed:

> **Interviewee 28:** I think that it is inevitable and a very good idea. We suffer from parochialism in the police service – lots of childish tantrums by chief constables undermine and sink initiatives not of their making. Getting 43 chief constables to agree takes huge effort for no result. Only external threats, impacting on their collective autonomy, make them think and act as one. A national police force would abolish all these petty kingdoms at a stroke, mine included, but I'd welcome it tomorrow.

There seems then to be some consensus that the current structure for England and Wales is in need of reform and this seems to involve slimming down the number of forces, while increasing the size of those which remain, either as 'super forces' or based on a regional model. Those who favour the notion of the national police force see this as the catalyst which will dismantle the 43-force structure and bring national consistency and closer coordination to bear:

> **Interviewee 66:** I'm a chief constable and I stand to lose my position and independence if a national police force is created so you may ask why I am in favour of it.

[Interviewer: OK, why are you?]

> Because it will work. Look; at the moment criminals, especially at level 3,[22] can exploit boundaries between police forces and we don't really have the capability for example to follow a criminal gang covertly from Merseyside to the Channel Tunnel. It would cross too many force frontiers and involve too much coordination. Somewhere along the way, we'd lose them. Now MI5 can follow terrorists, no problem; SOCA could probably follow their core nominals[23] but common or garden police forces can't – that's utterly inexcusable.

The same chief officer went on to note that there were national police organisations which had no difficulty in geographical coordination:

> **Interviewee 66:** If you look at something like [...] British Transport Police or HMIC you can see that central coordination is vital, but local application is where their policing or training or inspection most counts. I don't see why I can't continue to be the senior officer responsible for [this police force area] whilst at the same time being within a larger umbrella organisation to which I contribute officers and equipment, and from which I get officers and equipment, depending on the needs of the situation. It's hardly rocket science, is it?

The assertion that a national police force would be able to provide, in times of need, the requisite officers and equipment to deal with any situation, is a recurrent one and is not limited to those chief officers who feel disadvantaged in terms of vehicles, technology, equipment or numbers. Nor is it really about the massive collective use of force to counter social protest or criminality; it is much more about the proper allocation of resources to need at times of crisis. A number of chief officers cited the examples in 2008–09 of heavy flooding across the western and north western parts of the country, and the prolonged

---

[22] Under the National Intelligence Model, criminals are designated at three levels: local, inter-force/national and international. A drug dealer operating on a street corner would be a level 1 criminal; a drugs distributor in a region would be a level 2 and the drugs importer would be a level 3. The distinctions are rather blurred and inexact, as Giles Herdale and Peter Stelfox observe: 'There is considerable discussion within policing about how meaningful the three levels are in practice' (Herdale and Stelfox, 2008).

[23] A 'core nominal' is an habitual or lifestyle criminal who is regarded as a central or important catalysing figure in criminal undertakings. It is falling into disuse as a term.

and unexpectedly heavy snowfalls in 2009–10, where coordinated national police efforts would probably have yielded better dividends than overstretched single forces trying to cope on their own. This chief officer commented that such a national police force is:

> **Interviewee 36:** [...] feasible, necessary and probably coming within 10–15 years. There is a will for it outside policing and the political imperative for a national police force is high on the hidden agendas of all our potential masters. There are plenty within policing who support it too, especially those tired of the interminable bickering between forces and their ACPO teams. I haven't noticed that the Armed Forces suffer from being national, nor that we miss the old-style militias and yeomanry at county and shire level.

Another chief officer, with typical dry wit, observed that the creation of a national police force is probably good for neither citizen nor police officer, but on that basis alone, it would happen:

> **Interviewee 93:** I understand that to some it has a neatness and a precision and to politicians a real appeal because they could control the police much more easily. But is it good for the citizen? No, probably not. For the police themselves? No, probably not. Therefore a national police force is highly likely.

It is appropriate at this point, poised between those who oppose the concept of a national police force and those who support it, to look at the statistical responses to the question posed in interview. Chief officers were asked: *Do you support the notion of a national police force?* (Table 5.2).

Table 5.2: For and against a national police force

	Number	Percentage
Yes	30	35%
No	55	64%
Don't know	1	<1%
Totals	**86**	**100%**

Those who advocate the creation of a national police force, with the concomitant subordination of the currently autonomous chief officer's force within a national whole, are still in a minority – even if it is a substantial one. The bulk of opinion, nearly two thirds of those questioned, is opposed to the idea of an overriding national force, but it is not always easy to separate out whether this is to do with direct loss of power, status and influence or whether it is derived primarily from concerns about sustaining the tripartite relationship, or belief that the potential for overt political control of the police will be facilitated and enhanced by a national force, or advocacy that policing should only be locally applied and locally accountable (Krupicka, 2007).

Conclusions

Chief officers seem no different from most of the police population: many fear change and regard it with unease, particularly if it entails the importation of rivals and competitors from outside. The opposition to multiple-rank entry in policing is balanced between those who regard it as a breach of their professional knowledge and experience and those for whom it seems less of a threat and more of a refreshing challenge. The pivotal concern will be whether there is political will to open up the ranks of policing to outsiders and whether that will affect chief officers as well as the policing ranks below. At the moment, policing is a 'closed shop'; no one may enter except through the ground floor as a police constable and must work his or her way up through the ranks to make chief officer. It follows that the chief officers' shop is even more tightly closed. The single exception to this is sometimes dismissed as a specialist appointment rather than 'real' policing command. Whether or not that is true is not for me to judge, but if nothing else, the appointment has set a precedent and the extent to which it was greeted with hostility might say more about the unease of the critics than about the rightness or otherwise of the decision to appoint. The likelihood of fast-tracked direct entry has increased as a result of the coalition government's support in theory, though this may be some way from implementation.

The question whether or not there should be a national police force produced a less even balance of views, with fewer chief officers in favour, while a majority regarded the proposal in terms of detriment to, or downgrading of, their own positions of power and influence. Some saw it as inevitable because police efficiency demanded it, some thought it would come quickly, others that it was still far off, yet more believed with equal passion that it would never happen at all because there was no appetite for it in the police service. None of these factors may in fact be the catalyst. The creation of a national police force will *always* be an act of political will rather than a police initiative, and it is to the politicians that we should look for evidence of a mind-set in this direction. There is little discernible yet, though powerful arguments about economy, police efficiency and avoidance of duplication may yet bring the concept of a national police force back to political agendas. Then there will be plenty of police and public voices raised in protest, not least about the dangers of increased police susceptibility to political influence, as there have been with the directly elected police crime commissioner. Many chief officers will continue to deplore such a development in terms of erosion of 'local accountability'. What is perhaps most surprising about this sampling of police opinion has been the readiness and equanimity with which many chief officers contemplate the quite ground-breaking possibilities of both external appointments to ACPO and the creation of a single national police force, regarding them not as threats so much as challenges and opportunities for the future.

SIX

The future of policing

Interviewee 79: There has been a culture change in the last 10 years which I would urgently seek to reverse. The dominant theme now is 'what's in it for me?' rather than service for its own sake. This utter preoccupation with self has produced a quadrant of dilemmas: public, service, force and individual; but the individual dominates. The individual should be last, not first.

Interviewee 16: Decision making in the police is broken and needs urgent fixing, the National Police Board notwithstanding; policy making is also at an all time low.

Interviewee 49: You have to be careful what you wish for in this game: if we ask for more, we have to show tangible difference. This new government will not be easy to manipulate and as a police service we have to know where we are going. So, the short answer to what urgently needs changing in the police is that we need to know what direction we are going in and how it will be afforded in these financially tight times.

Interviewee 93: These really are stirring times, and it's exciting to be at or near the top in policing when they are happening. So much is up in the air: the Policing Pledge is dead and buried, so how is performance to be assessed? Forces are facing 20%-25% cuts in budget, new threats to security loom and the Olympics are just around the corner, and over it all and dominating the entire police agenda, is answering the question: What are the police about? Do we need them? If we do, in what shape? Local or national? Private or public? Warranted or not warranted? Profession or trade? Graduate or artisan? Armed or unarmed? Very exciting times; not for the fainthearted, that's for sure.

Police officers like to talk about policing, and chief officers are no exception to this general observation. They enjoy discussing the nature of the job and its ramifications, the criminal justice system, engagement with the public, the difficulty of investigating crimes, the nature of 'criminal society' and the character of public order; even the political changes which affect policing. They find endless fascination in the job and virtually endless satisfaction in its execution, not to mention indulgence in endless arguments about the efficacy of equipment and uniform. There are downsides to this widespread enthusiasm for the role of chief police officer, of course, and deep frustrations, such as those about the number of forces (Chapter Five), or the directly elected police crime commissioners (PCCs) who will hold chief constables to account (Chapter Four), as well as axes to grind and special pleadings to indulge, like calls for a return to Peel's Principles (Bloy, 2010). They are fully alive to the dilemma that Robert Reiner noted: 'Good policing may help preserve social order: it cannot produce it' (Reiner, 2010, p xiv).

The general sense though, as will be seen in the pages which follow, is of people who are stimulated by what they do, reflective about the nature of the task they have taken on, and philosophical about whether anything will improve as a result. Chief officers can be resolute in the face of criticism and utterly focused on the outcomes of policing operations and initiatives, but they can also complain at length about how misunderstood the police service is and how difficult the tasks are that they are given, and, as we have seen above in Chapter Four, their tolerance of what they see as interference with their operational independence (from no matter what source that 'interference" comes) is very low indeed. There are perennial complaints about scarcity of resources and 'doing more with less', along with a new realism about the resources now available for policing in a time of economic stringency and shrinking budgets.

This final chapter looks ahead to what chief officers believe to be the challenges facing policing over the next decade. The themes emerged in response to these questions: *What things need urgent changing in policing? How would you change them?*

This is an opportunity for us to engage with officers who have made policing their life's work and who have undergone transformative experiences in arriving at their present positions. Chief officers are mostly positive and thoughtful people, uneasy about some things they see which suggest that the old certainties about society are disappearing (see Reiner, 2010, p 239) and occasionally conservative about internal change, acutely aware of 'the ambivalence surrounding the police task in a liberal democracy' (McLaughlin, 2007, p 53), while enthusiastic about developments such as neighbourhood policing, forensic science and the quality of new recruits coming into the service. Most too have a deep and abiding affection for the police service. Their opinions are important, not only because collectively they understand policing so thoroughly, but also because they are instrumental in determining what shape policing will take for the next generation, and, as Tim Newburn has pointed out, there are 'many possible futures' in policing (Newburn, 2003, p 707).

The future of policing may be akin to the dystopia that Robert Reiner sees: far more closely linked to the divided and feral society we have created than to any kind of 'policing' that may be on offer or in current favour (Reiner, 2010, p 257), or it may approximate more to the view of politicians, that society's ills are curable through individual constraint and communitarian effort, modulated through the police 'cutting crime' (Fresco, 2010). Chief officers are not analytical sociologists/criminologists like Reiner or Newburn, but pragmatic leaders, dealing with 'the politics of now'. Their views on what policing needs must inevitably be seen within their own contexts, and we would be wrong to suppose that they can give us a coherent societal world view, much less that they have the answers to the choice

> between some form of social democracy and, at best, the barbarism of high crime rates, and a fortified society.(Reiner, 2010, p 258)

At the same time, we must be aware, as Robert Reiner has so perceptively observed, that

> Police and policing cannot deliver on the great expectations now placed on them in terms of crime control. (Reiner, 2010, p 256)

In the pages that follow, I have grouped together chief officers' opinions when they coincide or intersect or are fundamentally opposed, but it is worth remembering that these are idiosyncratic people whose views are highly individualistic and therefore the range of views and thoughts expressed in the following pages are characteristic of the range of personalities within ACPO and their views necessarily are of 'a more turbulent, disorderly social world' (Reiner, 2010, p 255). The other perennial point to make is that the opinions confided to me in closed sessions may not necessarily be those which the same chief officers would espouse in public or on the record.

A number of chief officers believe that policing itself needs a fundamental reappraisal in the context of the whole criminal justice system, perhaps through the medium of a royal commission. One chief officer passionately desired an objective external assessment of what the police are expected to do and wanted an enquiry into the rationale for some of its ancillary functions and support groups, such as police community support officers (PCSOs) and special constables. He was exercised by the lack of definition in these respective functions, what seems like political 'knee-jerk' reactions to events and believed that a royal commission would provide some objective analysis of what policing is and where it should go:

> **Interviewee 70:** We desperately, desperately need a royal commission on the police. The last one was in 1964[1] and it will take us away from having to jump to the latest 'theme of the day' from the Home Office. I think the Policing Pledge was a good idea, but I think the raft of measures will remain, not go away, and so we only add to our burdens. What the fuck are we doing in policing? We don't know what to do with PCSOs and Specials [special constables]. We don't know what society wants any more.

Another chief officer also called for a royal commission, deploring the 'short-termism' of both politicians and fellow chief constables and sharply endorsing the view that part of the problem was that successive governments did not seem to know what they wanted from policing. The implication is that policing has drifted away from any public consensus about its functions. The officer was adamant that this consensus had to be recovered – to 'refresh policing' – but observed that the impetus needed to search for agreement about what policing should be and how it should be done, had to come from outside the police service itself:

> **Interviewee 9:** The real problem is lack of longevity. There is a maximum five years' view, whether it's from chief officers or from the politicians. The government doesn't know what it wants policing to be – does it want single patrol? Does it really want discretion? A royal commission would completely refresh policing – the population of the UK could have a say in what police forces it has, and we could ask properly what the country wants from its police. The lead has to come from outside the police ranks and the whole thing has to be handled objectively.

---

[1] In fact the last Royal Commission on the Police sat for nearly two years from 1960, reporting in 1962. The Police Reform Act, derived in part from the findings of the Royal Commission, passed into law in 1964.

This is a view commonly expressed by chief officers and is of a piece with a common complaint that policing cannot supply solutions to society's ills if society does not articulate what it wants policing to be. That is not helped, or at least is harder to focus, when there is increasing blurring between 'private' and 'public' policing, such as may be seen in 'the extended police family' which includes PCSOs, other police volunteers and special constables. Newburn noted sagely a few years ago that

> Undoubtedly, the future of policing is one that is likely to be characterised by the increasing visibility of a broad, and perhaps broadening, range of providers of policing and security services. (Newburn, 2003, p 210)

This observation lends weight to some chief officers' comments that 'public' policing needs clearer definition, distinguishing it from largely unaccountable 'private' policing (Button, 2002), which may be difficult to achieve by the service alone (Neyroud, 2003, p 579). The perception that there should be external, objective assessment of policing was echoed by another chief officer who was keen that policing be completely opened to scrutiny in the context of a review of the whole criminal justice system. It is not enough to look at the police in isolation, even though in broad terms they 'pump-prime' the whole criminal justice system by presenting alleged offenders at court. Instead, the justice process itself should be the subject of review:

Interviewee 88: I've heard calls for a royal commission on the police and I think that's absolutely right. It must look at the police and address where it is going and the context of the criminal justice system. We're the 'gateway' to that whole process.

[Interviewer: What do you mean by 'gateway'?]

The criminal justice system doesn't operate unless the police put people into it. The police have to detect reported crime, identify probable offenders, interview and then charge suspects and bring them to court through the [Public][2] Prosecution Service, before any barrister or judge has done anything at all. Crude but largely

---

[2] The Director of Public Prosecutions, Keir Starmer, announced in 2009 that the Crown Prosecution Service was to be amalgamated with other prosecution services, including that for HM Revenue & Customs, and would be called the Public

> true. Now, have a royal commission on the police and this would have a real impact. It's more than 40 years since the last one, so it would be very timely, very needed.

It is clear that the concept of a royal commission is invoked because the interviewees believe that any review of policing/criminal justice that is called for needs to be objective, impartial, thoroughgoing and involve the views of a wide spectrum of public, professional and academic opinion. The police is only one voice in all of this and cannot be its own judge and jury. A legally led and constituted, government-supported and evidentially wide-ranging royal commission would provide, these chief officers argue, precisely the debate about *form, function* and *future* that policing appears to need to recover its direction and to reaffirm its purpose (Newburn, 2003, p 718).

The comments examined above can stand for quite a spread of chief officers' views that some sort of fundamental reappraisal of policing is needed. Their private opinions have found reflection in some public utterances by eminent police officers, including the current President of ACPO, Sir Hugh Orde, who called for a new royal commission on the Police when he was interviewed on the BBC Radio 4 *Today* programme on 23 March 2010. The interview was afterwards reported by John Ozimek in these terms:

> Sir Hugh reckons we are long overdue a fundamental review of the way that England and Wales are policed. The last such review took place in 1962 – and as far as he is concerned, a lot has changed since then. Police face new challenges – from cyber-crime to international terror. [...] Sir Hugh envisages a major strategic and structural review of policing in the UK, and the best time to carry out such an exercise is now – before some crisis forces knee-jerk change on the police force. All aspects of policing should be under review, save one: the operational independence of chief constables. (Ozimek, 2010)

The special pleading for operational independence is predictable (and I looked at the controversy about this in some detail in Chapter Four), but Sir Hugh's 'official' views received support from an unexpected

---

Prosecution Service (PPS). The name change has been slow to catch on, and many police officers and the media still refer to the CPS.

source. Sir Ian Blair, former Commissioner of the Metropolitan Police, speaking at a symposium entitled Future of Policing was reported to be

> [...] worried that the last review of policing was set up during an era that pre-dated even the threat posed by Irish Republican terrorism – and he pointed out that there had been vast technological and social changes since.
>
> He believed that there needed to be 'a situation in which policing is assessed again for the 21st century' [and] added: 'We have not had a review in a holistic way since 1962. Then the police did not have radios. There was no internet and no terrorism.'[3]

There is some limited consensus, it would appear, that a royal commission or something akin is needed to address the difficulties around purpose and function in which policing finds itself. What are these difficulties? One chief officer was sure that the police had lost focus on what they were there to do because of the plethora of numeric and quantitative targets set by performance regimes that cut across 'real policing' (which he defines as catching criminals, echoing Home Secretary Theresa May (Fresco, 2010)). Further, the familiar observation recurs that the whole of the criminal justice system, not policing alone, should be included in the commission's remit:

> **Interviewee 31:** I genuinely think that policing is in a crisis. [...] We're too focused on what the law-abiding citizen wants and can make too much of it. One way to reassure is in showing that you can catch criminals and they can't get away with what they do. The courts don't always help with that. One of the best things to happen to criminal justice in recent times was the Auld report[4] which took

---

[3] 'ACPO head calls for police service overhaul', 23 March 2010, *Police Oracle*, available from www.policeoracle.com/news/ACPO-Head-Calls-For-Police-Service-Overhaul_22643.html; accessed 4 June 2010.

[4] Lord Justice Auld's *Report on Criminal Justice* in 2001 led to widespread local reforms. Many 'summary' offences were made subject to Fixed Penalty Notices (fines) instead, which did away with police records for minor offences, and people went to court only if they wanted to plead not guilty. This more than halved the number of cases brought before magistrates and streamlined a process which at one time threatened to overwhelm the criminal justice system, at least at the 'petty' level. See *A Review of the Criminal Courts of England and Wales* by Lord Justice Auld, 2001, a pdf file of the report is available from www.criminal-courts-review.org, accessed 1 April 2009. The site is now maintained merely as an archive by the Ministry of Justice but it is worth

> loads of stuff away from magistrates' courts and replaced it with fixed penalty notices and fines. We need something like that for the whole of criminal justice including the police and we need it urgently.

However, some chief officers are not at all convinced that a royal commission was the answer. Some argued that there is such uncertainty around policing that it imperils the tripartite relationship, especially as successive Home Secretaries have sought to influence police authorities (or replace them) to the detriment of chief constables' independence of action. The advent of the directly elected police crime commissioner (PCC) is likely to intensify political pressure on the police, which is not the same as saying that the police themselves are 'politicised' (see Neyroud, 2003, pp 578–9). There may be a need for some sort of review to address these issues, but there are also reservations about whether a royal commission was the right machinery:

> **Interviewee 5:** We have to address deep uncertainty in the constitutional arrangements around policing: the so-called 'tripartite relationship' is misshapen – there is too thin a line from the Home Secretary to the police authority sometimes at the expense of the operational independence of a chief constable. I'm not convinced that a royal commission would be the answer. That in 1962 made some progress, but Douglas Hurd was right when he said something to the effect that 'nothing grows in the arid shade of a royal commission'.[5] It takes too long to report. What we need is a big positional statement on policing which will come from an open and detailed debate. There's no doubt that policing is in crisis: what matters is what we can do about it.

Precisely what constitutes the 'crisis' in policing varies in minor detail from one interlocutor to another, but there is broad agreement that it embraces a perception of widespread disrespect for the police and the law generally, the rise of dysfunctional groups, such as inner-city gangs, the inability of the criminal justice system to deter people from crime

---

noting that the Auld Report also led directly to a government White Paper and to some provisions in the Police Act 2002.

[5] Sir Trefor Morris, former HMCIC, in a written submission to the Parliamentary Select Committee on Home Affairs, (Appendix 6 of Evidence), February 2002, observed '"Nothing grows in the arid shadow of a Royal Commission" said Douglas Hurd, then Home Secretary, when he was being pressed to have such an examination of the police service in the late 1980s.' Available from: www.publications.parliament. uk/pa/cm200102/cmselect/cmhaff/612/612ap08.htm; accessed 16 June 2010.

and the general ponderous ineffectiveness of the system in bringing offenders to justice; the difficulty in securing the support of the public, generally hostile or critical media coverage of policing compounded by high-profile errors or misjudgements by the police; the attrition of crime and public fear of crime, and the degree to which the police are overseen and subject to 'interference' (debated by McLaughlin, 2007, pp 80–1, for example). One chief officer summed it up like this:

> **Interviewee 33:** Look, there has never been such a time when people thought less of the police than now – and so much of it is our own fault. We've even started to alienate the law-abiding, not to mention the dispossessed, the vulnerable, the victims, the courts and the rest of the justice system, the public and the journalists, while criminals just laugh at us knowing that when they reoffend they'll get off lightly and can hide behind Human Rights' legislation anyway. You've judges who don't want to send people to prison, juries who won't convict and lawyers who will use every trick in the book to bamboozle or confuse witnesses. We're utterly pissed off by it: imagine how victims and witnesses feel!

Another chief officer believed strongly that the politicisation of the police has gone so far that a royal commission would not now serve any useful purpose, and that some other means of enquiry would have to be adopted, though those things that are broken are less the outcomes of processes and more to do with selfishness and lack of moral principle:

> **Interviewee 84:** Policing is too politicised now for a royal commission to make any difference, and it's not likely to serve a purpose anyway. [...] You despair really. [...] We have become disconnected from Peel's Principles,[6] such as public confidence in the police. What we have now is 'status creep' where people move to the job[s] with the most kudos; the basic role of prevention of crime and patrol is at the very bottom of the food chain.

---

[6] Sir Robert Peel, 1778–1850, was responsible, when Home Secretary in 1829, for the introduction in London of the 'new' police; the forerunner of all other civil police forces in Britain. He formulated nine Principles of Policing and the one referred to here is : '(7) To maintain at all times a relationship with the public that gives reality to the historic tradition that the police are the public and that the public are the police, the police being only members of the public who are paid to give full time attention to duties which are incumbent on every citizen in the interests of community welfare and existence' (see Hurd, 2007; Bloy, 2010).

Crime prevention (the cumulative effect of which leads to and supports crime *reduction*) has been the 'Cinderella' of policing probably since its inception by Robert Peel in 1829, and the reasons for this are not hard to seek. It is entirely human to want to be involved in a dramatic emergency response, or to engage in a high-profile investigation or to experience the adrenaline rush involved in the apprehension of a serial offender. These actions are preferred by most police officers at all ranks to the largely unseen or low-profile 'delayed gratification' of thwarting the would-be criminal by making crime too risky or difficult to undertake. One chief officer remarked wryly in interview with me that '*there are no headlines in crime prevention*', which sums up a common police response: preventing crime is worthy, even laudable; but it is not exciting or noticeable (Clarke, 1980).

When Peel advanced his 'Nine principles of policing' (Hurd, 2007; Bloy, 2010), he noted from the outset that 'the police exist to prevent crime and disorder', an emphasis on a primary purpose that has abraded over time. At the same time, because 'the police are the public and the public are the police' (principle 7), there has to be a genuine and close engagement between the police and the public, such that there is confidence in the ability of the police to promote 'the interests of community welfare and existence'. What this chief officer is saying is that policing needs to return directly to Peel's *principles* and therefore to resonate with the new emphasis on re-engagement with and endorsement by the public.

Another chief officer took up the suggestion that there has been a disconnection between police and public:

> **Interviewee 50:** I think that this [question] is really, really interesting. I think policing has really lost its way and that no-one knows or cares what society wants its cops to be. There is huge confusion in society at large and within politics about what I call the freedom equation: what parts of your liberty will you give up or surrender in exchange for safety and freedom from being a victim of crime? Will you allow Draconian policing in exchange for your insistent safety or would you prefer a balance of controls on your life? It's very difficult and very urgent and so far we're not even having the debate! It has got to come from people outside the police – perhaps through something like a royal commission. That can be dangerous territory though – no-one can guarantee what might emerge from a really thoroughgoing enquiry into the police.

The question of balancing individual freedom against collective security, while raised here in a very contemporary context, harks back to the problems which Peel had to deal with when introducing to a sceptical House of Commons the notion of a civil police force. Then, a Select Committee commented in 1827 that

> It is difficult to reconcile an effective system of police with that perfect freedom of action and exemption from interference, which are the great privileges and blessings of society in this country. (Hurd, 2007, p 71)

That Peel overcame the widespread belief that police would be a threat to freedom, and established the Metropolitan Police is something for which we can be grateful, but even he had to wait two more years, until 1829, for the legislative time to be right and the circumstances for his Bill to be propitious (Hurd, 2007, pp 101–2) before he could persuade the political parties to give his innovations a chance. Even then, his 'new police' were unpopular and derided for a number of years. There is a sense in which chief officers believe now that relations between police and public are not as good as they could be and that policing has too low a status in society, even that 'no one knows or cares what society wants its cops to be'. Such unpopularity runs the risk of forcing the police into a defensive frame of mind, which some chief officers seem only too ready to adopt as a stance in the face of criticism.

The comments from Interviewee 50 are reflected in the comments of another, somewhat disaffected officer, who argued that the need for fundamental reappraisal of the police is self-evident, but that the lead from within the ACPO ranks is lacking. One salient point the chief officer makes is that policing is not simply about upholding the law:

> **Interviewee 98:** We need an all-embracing debate about what policing is and what society wants from its police – we can't have that debate on our own, and it would need a neutral to organise and chair such a debate. But policing is a bit lost and confused about what it is supposed to be and I see no visionaries in the service who will take the lead of giving us purpose and meaning. Preventing and detecting crime is not enough, it's not even a description which covers more than a part of policing. There's so much more than just applying the law – there's protecting the weak and holding the ring between antagonists to name two other important things we do. But this is what we need the debate about: should there be a limit on the social responsiveness of a police service?

It is clear from many comments that if the debate were widened to include the whole of the criminal justice system, not just the Police service, it is likely that there would be substantially greater numbers of chief officers in favour. This does not amount to a full consensus for a royal commission, rather that there should be open and 'all-embracing' debate about policing, in the context of the criminal justice system and society as a whole. One chief officer repeated the opinions made familiar above, but went on to express unease with the criminal justice process:

> **Interviewee 64:** The current major and urgent need for change is actually within the whole of the criminal justice system not simply in policing.

This is of importance in the debate about whether society cares about its criminal justice system, and therefore its police, or not. Evidence seems to indicate that people *do* care and, in recording public anxieties about crime and crime outcomes, successive British Crime Surveys underline this.[7] Indeed, the piloting of 'virtual courts' in parts of London during 2009 and 2010 suggests that some attempt is also being made to speed up the turnover of cases in the criminal justice system (see Caless et al, 2010, pp 358–60). That said, we do not yet have 'holistic' community courts which deal with repeat offenders any more than we have a criminal justice system which deals adequately with repeat victimisation (Lamm Weizel, 2005; Nicholas and Farrell, 2008).

One chief officer was specific about what should be considered and who should be involved in any 'public colloquium' about the police and the wider criminal justice system:

> **Interviewee 34:** We urgently need to articulate the future of policing and to hold a very public colloquium in which all shades of opinion and expert witness can be heard. I do not mean a royal commission, but I do mean something official, something urgent and something all-embracing, which looks at policing in all its manifestations and at the whole nexus of relationships with stakeholders. It's not just the public which needs a say (although it

---

[7] The British Crime Survey (BCS), primarily of people who have been victims of crime, is conducted annually. The BCS base is around 40,000 but it has been subject to some criticism for the smallness of this sample, the omission of crimes of violence from the survey and the apparent partiality of what it records (victims' views rather than those of the public at large); see Farrall et al (1997).

may be the most important component), but the criminal justice system, the judiciary, lawyers, the [P]PS,[8] prison service, probation service and so on; so that policing as the way into the CJS is properly considered. The whole public/private policing debate is needed too.

The rise of 'private policing', in which a form of policing and security is provided to those who pay, by largely unregulated and often unaccountable organisations and private companies, is a very contemporary phenomenon that has provoked some intense debates, principally among academic commentators (for example Button 2002, 2007; Wakefield, 2003). The issues involved are not simply about the rich being better able to purchase security – through 'gated communities' and the like – or the regulation by commercial interests of access to public spaces (which are often more to do with social inequality or the arrogant commercialisation of amenities than with policing); but also the continued expansion of the 'wider policing family'. PCSOs, the growth of police staff in areas such as crime scene investigation and the burgeoning of police staff volunteers and the increased numbers of special constables have blurred 'official' policing boundaries, so that what defines a police officer has become steadily more ambiguous (see Jones and Newburn, 2005, pp 737–9). Some chief officers have told me that the time is approaching when the only distinguishing feature of a police officer will be possession of the warrant card and the consequence of that will be the use of the 'public' police only to enforce compliance or to deal with widespread social disorder. That would indeed be a long way from Peel's original conception, and would dismay most of the current generation of chief officers as well.

Some officers seemed discomfited by what they saw as the size of the problems confronting policing, but warmed to their theme like this interviewee, who decried the 'muddled amateurism' of much current policing:

> **Interviewee 67:** Oh, where to start? We continually default to what we're comfortable with in policing, and this covers everything from police uniform to relations with the media. There is too much in the way of muddled amateurism still. We need a proper professional structure, complete graduate entry and promotion dependent on skills and training, open selection processes above chief inspector, an end to risk aversion and development of adequate relations with the public. People will always resent the police

---

[8] [Public] Prosecution Service.

> except when they need us to hold the ring or sort out a problem, but we're crap at explaining ourselves – and that stems from the muddled amateurism which I see all around me all the time. We need cleverer cops, cops with PhDs as well as with street skills, and we're as far from getting any of this as I am from becoming commissioner of the Met. It'll never bloody happen.

This is quite a catalogue and the views expressed here cover a 'wish list' spectrum that perhaps few other chief officers would sign up to in total, even though 'muddled amateurism' is a recurrent complaint among many of them. ACPO is distinguished by the near ubiquity of degrees held by its members; but if the definition of a profession entails 'graduate entry', then policing is some way from attaining such status (even in chief officer ranks). The nature of a profession is more than this of course, requiring some extensive body of specialist knowledge, self-regulation and high qualification for entry.[9] None of these things is yet wholly characteristic of policing. There are, so far, only parts which have restricted and specialist areas of knowledge (homicide

---

[9] Interestingly, the Australian Competition and Consumer Council, at a conference in 1997, endorsed a description of a profession by John Southwick as

> A disciplined group of individuals who adhere to high ethical standards and uphold themselves to, and are accepted by, the public as possessing special knowledge and skills in a widely recognised, organised body of learning derived from education and training at a high level, and who are prepared to exercise this knowledge and these skills in the interest of others. Inherent in this definition is the concept that the responsibility for the welfare, health and safety of the community shall take precedence over other considerations.

We may not feel able to accept this objectively as a definition (which is why I call it a 'description'), but it does outline some characteristics of policing, though perhaps the 'widely recognised, organised body of learning derived from education and training at a high level' is still missing. Another attempt to codify 'professional' was proffered in 2004 by Cruess et al:

> [A]n occupation whose core element is work based upon the mastery of a complex body of knowledge and skills. It is *a vocation in which knowledge* of some department of science or learning or the practice of an art founded upon it *is used in the service of others*. Its members are governed by codes of ethics and profess a commitment to competence, integrity and morality, altruism, and the promotion of the public good within their domain. These commitments form the basis of a social contract between a profession and society, which in return grants the profession a monopoly over the use of its knowledge base, the right to considerable autonomy in practice and the privilege of self-regulation. (my italics)

investigation is one such); the police do not themselves regulate their membership and there are no formal entry requirements, though all applicant police officers must pass the police initial recruitment (PIR) test. Much more emphasis is actually placed on the attainment of National Occupational Standards during 'probation' which embrace both behaviours and skills (see Chapter Three), than on formal entry qualifications. As I noted in Chapter One, the possession of a degree and probably a postgraduate HE Diploma, characterise the qualifications of officers serving in chief officer posts. They may not have had them when they came into the police as constables, but they pretty much have them by the time they seek appointment to ACC posts. We should note additionally that Peter Neyroud's *Review of Police Leadership and Training* recommends that applicants to the police first complete a 'pre-joiner's programme' in which they study and attain some of the basic competencies for a constable. He recommends partnerships between police forces and academic providers to deliver this, and one likely outcome is that entry to the police in the future may be governed by the possession of a 'police practice' diploma, which a year's further study could convert to a degree. The police may become, de facto, a graduate entry profession, governed by Neyroud's recommendation of a 'chartered police institute' (Neyroud, 2011, pp 12–19)

Another chief officer chimed with some of the observations about 'muddled amateurism', asking whether policing was based on knowledge or on skills, and suggesting that the national debate about policing, which so many chief officers seem to want, must include what qualifications there should be in policing. What became a professional qualification for a police officer would very much depend on how the police service saw itself:

> **Interviewee 98:** We need to know who and what we are. Is policing a profession such as medicine or the law or is it a blue-collar job akin to an assembly line worker? Until we know what we are, we can't say what we need to know. *[...]* We need to be clever to catch clever criminals. Therefore we should be attracting graduates much more systematically than at present. There should be additional reward for possessing a good related degree (I don't

---

The question remains vexed: there is little in the way of a substantial body of learning which is peculiar to the police (except perhaps investigative 'doctrine'), and policing as a whole does not regulate its members or their qualifications as a profession does. Perhaps the best one may conclude is that policing is 'a profession in parts', and that the chief officer ranks come closest to what other professions look like.

mean in geography or urban planning, but law, criminology, forensic science; things like that) or we should more systematically fast track bright graduates. If this is where the debate on the future of policing should be, then we do not want anything to do with NVQs [National Vocational Qualifications]. If we are not artisan, we do not need artisan qualifications, but intellectual ones like good degrees. If we are artisan, we need an officer direct entry, like the Army.

There seems little internal appetite for any return to 'officers/other ranks' divisions in the police service, and the commentator here seems to assume a single common entry system, where more 'systematic' recruitment of graduates may include 'a good related degree'. The essential point is that policing has not yet had the debate about whether it is 'artisan' or 'intellectual'; that is, whether it is skills or knowledge based (see the discussion in Chapter One and work by commentators such as McLaughlin, 2007 or Neyroud, 2011). Until the police service has that debate, it seems, recruitment may continue to be incoherent.

One chief officer was robust in calling for change and suggested that graduate entry should be adopted as the norm, while making the familiar point that, by the time individuals reached chief officer rank, they were entering a de facto graduate profession:

> **Interviewee 14:** Policing should be a graduate profession if we ever want to be taken seriously, and not a trade. Too many dismiss the need for intellection in a police officer, yet too many are quick to say the police are unintelligent. They're not thick, but they're often inarticulate. What's needed as an urgent national policy is that we become a degree profession and link up with universities: there's too big a gap between ACPO and the rest of the police.

Another chief officer suggested that the ambiguity around the artisan or intellectual status of police officers arose from ACPO's own apparent double standards:

> **Interviewee 62:** The whole vexed question of what constitutes a qualification in policing needs to be revisited. What we have currently is, frankly, a mess. We don't know if we're a trade or a profession and no one in the top echelons of policing seems able to make a decision about NVQs or degrees. Yet almost all the ACPO members have degrees! If there could be a clearer indicator of what route policing needs to go, I don't know of it.

This debate has some way still to run, and I did not detect enough in the way of consensus from those chief officers I interviewed to justify a separate 'official' debate or colloquium about whether policing is 'a trade or a profession'. There is though a strong current of opinion and belief that a debate must be had about what policing is and where it is going. As we have seen, some think that the best medium to manage this is a royal commission; others want something quicker and less formal. All seem agreed that the spectrum of opinions consulted must be as wide as possible and must engage with the public, while there is a substantial body of chief officer opinion which argues that it is not just policing that should be discussed in depth but the entire criminal justice system. In the latter case, a royal commission might be the right machinery, embracing legal argument and making formal enquiries, but there is also a case for something like a parliamentary committee enquiry instead, which might accomplish similar tasks in a shorter time frame.

Other future factors

Chief officers were also exercised about the public image of the police and how it seemed dominated by negativity. One listed things that had gone wrong in recent years and which had generated hostile media coverage of policing and which in turn led to criticism of how the police behave towards the public:

> **Interviewee 18:** I don't know how you do it but we need to address the current negativity about the police. A host of things have gone wrong – from the shooting of de Menezes in 2005 to Bob Quick's resignation, to the death of Ian Tomlinson at the G20 summit[10] – all of which impact adversely on the police. The more

---

[10] Jean Charles de Menezes was a Brazilian electrician who was shot dead in July 2005 by anti-terrorist police who had mistakenly identified him as one of a group of Muslim extremists who were intent on exploding suicide bombs in London. The resultant enquiry and criticism of the Metropolitan Police contributed to the lack of trust in Sir Ian Blair's leadership and his subsequent departure (see links at www.ipcc.gov.uk/en/Pages/the_stockwell_investigation.aspx, accessed 22 July 2011; and www.guardian.co.uk/uk/2008/dec/12/de-menezes-verdict; accessed 25 July 2010).

Assistant Commissioner Bob Quick resigned in April 2009 when he was photographed entering Downing Street with classified papers on display that gave details of an impending counter-terrorist operation, which had to be brought forward as a result (see Dodd and Batty, 'Police Chief Bob Quick Steps Down over Terror

reluctant we are about being open and transparent, or the more reticent we are about what happened, the more the criticism and distrust will mount. Too many people feel that they cannot trust the police at the moment and we've simply got to turn that around. Neighbourhood policing is one positive way, but that's local and parochial. The real key is the hostility of the media, which thrive on bad news stories about the police. We need to influence [...] the media and this is something we need to do quickly.

Some chief officers seem to have an uncomfortable relationship with the media, but equally some of their colleagues are more relaxed about dealing with questions from journalists. The points being made by this chief officer are about trust and profile: the news media present the police in particular ways and are the primary sources for most people's perceptions of the police, including their efficiency and legitimacy (Chermak et al, 2006. Few police, either chief officers or the ranks below, receive any formal training in handling the media and too often the police default position is 'no comment' or defensiveness (Mawby, 2002), or an attempt to manage the newsworthiness of an incident, which is not always successful given how powerful the media influences are (Dubois, 2002).

Many forces use media spokespeople (often ex-journalists themselves) to front for any story or issue, but some chief officers believe that this is actually to the detriment of training senior police officers to handle the media positively (see Chapter One). What has to be remembered is that sustaining media relations calls for considerable skill and investment; merely 'influencing' is not enough, and can actually be counterproductive (Cooke and Sturges, 2009). Therefore, while the points raised by Interviewee 18 are important, the solution might be more complex than he suggests. We might note too that the examples he uses are all derived from the Metropolitan Police. Many chief officers resent the assumption that shortcomings in the Metropolitan Police necessarily reflect the condition of policing elsewhere in England and Wales, and they point to the different conditions, tensions and crime types in their forces. However justified this irritation with the MPS may be, it is beside the point. It is rather the high-profile nature of the cases

Blunder', 9 April 2009; report available from www.guardian.co.uk/uk/2009/apr/09/bob-quick-terror-raids-leak.

Ian Tomlinson died shortly after being seen to be hit by riot police in London in April 2009, at a time of protest against the economic problems being discussed by world leaders at the G20 meeting.: www.bbc.co.uk/news/uk-england-london-10723274; accessed 25 July 2010.

cited and their ability to run as critical stories in the media for days at a time which do the real damage. It seems unlikely that the public will want to make distinctions between crowd control techniques at the G20 in London and tactics for policing a picket line in Greater Manchester or Birmingham, if the outcomes are similar violent confrontations. Whether chief officers like it or not, these examples tarnish the whole police, provoking one chief officer to remark:

> **Interviewee 47:** It is not just the incessant bad publicity which causes the long-term damage: people actually don't expect the police always to get it right. What's really damaging is our reluctance to admit our own fault, to acknowledge our errors. That's what caused the problems about de Menezes and others – no one stood up and said 'Yes, right, we screwed up. Sorry.' These things happen, but we get defensive and fortress-minded, don't we? Afraid to admit mistakes, afraid of litigation, afraid of publicity.

The often negative publicity about the police, ranging from the London examples cited by Interviewee 18, to the investigation of the Soham murders in Cambridgeshire,[11] and gun crime in Nottinghamshire, can also make the police reluctant to express any pride in their service. It is therefore a refreshing change to hear a chief officer noting that received opinions about the police need to be seen in context:

> **Interviewee 27:** There is nothing fundamentally wrong with the police service. It just needs nurturing and developing rather than reforming. Sixty per cent of the public think we are doing a good or excellent job. Whilst we need to improve on that position, some of those who criticise us (e.g., politicians, the media, etc) enjoy significantly lower levels of public trust and confidence and they should perhaps look at themselves first before they seek to reform policing.

Tim Newburn, among others, has drawn attention to the fact that criminologists can become fixated on what is new and developing in policing, rather than what is constant (see Newburn, 2003, p 707), and

---

[11] This was the investigation into the murder of two girls, Holly Wells and Jessica Chapman, both aged 10, by primary school caretaker Ian Huntley in the village of Soham in August 2002. The subsequent police investigation revealed that Humberside Police had suspicions of Huntley's sexual predation but had not passed them to Cambridgeshire Police when checks were being carried out on Huntley's application to the school (see Bichard, 2003).

in the analysis of police shortcomings or errors, or flawed judgments, it is perhaps all too easy to lose sight of those things the police do well. It is quite possible that continuous, external, media-reported criticism of the police builds a public perception that the service is broken and needs reform, while police officers themselves are not loth to draw attention to problems and difficulties; so that comments such as those from Interviewee 27 above help to show that negativity about the police is not universal. Such positive sentiments are also endorsed by this chief officer:

> **Interviewee 81:** It's depressing that so many can be so negative about this job. What we need to stress is what we've already got: tradition, history, transparency, the investigation process, collaboration. There are so many things we do well, so many strengths in the police service, that to seek always after novelty and change runs the risk of forgetting the stable things, the things which make the police what they are – like the copper's helmet. We very rarely say what we want to hold on to.

Some chief officers believe that the future will probably embrace a national police force (the arguments for and against which, as espoused by chief officers themselves, I examined in Chapter Five). A precursor to any national structuring of the police might be the pooling of resources, so that equipment and vehicles, or uniforms and personal protection could all be purchased centrally. One chief officer thought that working in this way on a 'national partnership scale' would bring massive benefits:

> **Interviewee 92:** Shared resources, shared services: we must align with our partners on a major scale. If we can do it at the neighbourhood policing level and really make partnerships work, then the argument to do so at a national level is overwhelming. At such a level, the purchasing power alone would be enormous and could ensure that the police have the very best equipment and transport, as well as aligning with departments of state to get a coherent grip on things like child abuse and domestic violence. [...] Of course, as soon as the police speak with one voice, there will be politicians trying to shout louder and to take that voice under control. Resisting the attempts by others to dominate the police, whilst at the same time retaining the democratic systems of governance as well as local accountability, will be the real challenges of the future. And we should be addressing them now.

This strikes a chord with a number of chief officers who seem to believe that the grip on the police service by politicians is getting stronger. This was exemplified for many in the wake of considerable political (and media) criticism of the police's handling of an investigation into the Conservative MP Damian Green in 2009.[12] The outcome was an embarrassing climb-down by the police and the Public Prosecution Service, as well as by the incumbent Home Secretary who approved the police investigation in the first place. Other suggestions that MPs were above the law followed in an investigation of alleged misappropriation of public funds and expenses, when the MPs involved pleaded parliamentary privilege.[13] Not surprisingly, this produced a strong response from some chief officers:

> **Interviewee 33:** I'm astonished that the right of the police to arrest and question an MP was challenged. OK, the debate about expenses and MPs' fitness for public office [took] over, but there should never be any suggestion that somehow MPs are above the law, or members of the House of Lords cannot be questioned like any other citizen. It's abundantly clear that the Home Secretary wants to control chief constables, but I worry that this means political interference not legal regulation. Policing must resist being a pawn of the political playmaker [...] it's the thin end of a nasty wedge.

The issue here is not specifically related to the Home Office, which I examined in Chapter Four, but rather to the many political initiatives which can affect policing on 'law and order' platforms or through pledges made by political parties when in opposition or in party manifestos published in advance of a general election. One chief officer

---

[12] See, for example, 'Damian Green: I was Threatened with Life Imprisonment by the Police', *The Guardian*, 17 April 2009, available from www.guardian.co.uk/politics/2009/apr/17/damian-green-arrest-leaks-inquiry; accessed 14 June 2010. The arrest of Mr Green, then Shadow Home Secretary, arose from an investigation by the Metropolitan Police into the leaking of information from the Home Office (he was the recipient of leaked documents). Politicians were particularly outraged that police were allowed to search the MP's office in the House of Commons and to seize papers. The DPP decided that the case would not succeed at court and dropped the prosecution, largely because the material leaked was not classified.

[13] See for example BBC news report 'Ex Labour MPs and Tory Peer Lose Expenses Ruling', 11 June 2010, available from http://news.bbc.co.uk/1/hi/politics/10293475.stm; accessed 14 June 2010. Some of those involved in the 'expenses scandal', both Commons and Lords, were tried and sentenced to prison terms in early 2011.

thought that the policing future was less about the grand designs, large political initiatives and manifesto pledges, and more about honing the 'work in progress' within the police service, which the police largely should be left alone to get on with:

> **Interviewee 27:** Those things which we need to do to improve (for example, the introduction of a more citizen-focused style of policing, the implementation of neighbourhood policing, better local engagement with the public, improved partnership with local authorities and other agencies, internal cultural change, building an improved service ethos, improving leadership and supervision, improving technology, improving efficiency and effectiveness, cutting back office costs through rationalisation and sharing, tackling serious and organised crime more effectively, etc.) are all what could be described as work in progress and by and large we just need to be left to get on with them. We are constantly being bombarded with central initiatives many of which are peripheral to our core business and largely based on short-term funding which divert us from our core business and achieve little long-term benefit.

Many chief officers would recognise and respond to this observation that the police should be left to do what they do best, and not be encumbered by or burdened with 'central initiatives' which 'are peripheral to [...] core business'. However, the logic of this position can provoke the perennial complaint that the police always act as if they know best. It was thinking that they did which drove the original wedge between police and public, and allowed the public's fear of crime to rise while recorded crime actually went down. It was precisely this that made the police respond to neighbourhood concerns with puzzlement and an inability to deal effectively with anti-social behaviour and petty vandalism (see Edwards, 2005, chapter 15, for example).

One chief officer noted how corrosive it could be to police/public relations if there was no engagement and how the police 'need to be there' ready and able to respond to what people want:

> **Interviewee 65:** The most important thing to change is the police belief that they know best in every situation. They don't. Sometimes the patronising 'don't worry your dear little head about it' can make the public wince (and me), so talking down to people is thoroughly mistaken. The new emphasis on 'citizen focus' is absolutely right because people know what scares them – including the media – and we need to be there and on that wavelength, able to respond.

The police service has learned (slowly) to listen and to respond to the concerns of communities; even though the response is not yet all that it could be. To argue that 'central initiatives' have no part to play in the evolution of policing is to deny the need for policing to move forward and to develop. Certainly, intelligence-led policing and PCSOs would have been still-born as initiatives had the police service as a whole refused to accommodate them.

To be fair, Interviewee 27 is not arguing for a stolid indifference to political imperatives, but for the very understandable need for policing to be allowed to get on with the job without unnecessary interference. There is nothing wrong with this, provided that such a stance is not used as an excuse to stifle progress or to refuse to be receptive to new ideas. Chief officers often comment that they and their forces suffer from 'initiative fatigue' where those who don't understand policing very well want to impose solutions on what they perceive as problems, without necessarily taking responsibility for what subsequently happens. An example often cited was the suggestion by the then Prime Minister Tony Blair in 2002 that police officers could take those on whom a penalty notice for disorder had been levied to an ATM where the requisite fine could be paid at any time of the day or night.[14] As many police officers pointed out at the time, very few of those who offended actually had bank accounts or credit cards, so the 'Islington initiative' of on-the-spot cash for fines was doomed from the outset.

All chief officers could probably cite other such instances, and I can sympathise with their impatience of half-baked or woolly notions of this kind, as well as of the promotion of an endless round of similar initiatives– what they call 'reinventing the wheel'. That said, it is surely not sensible always to endorse a 'Nanny knows best' approach to local or petty crime? People know what frightens them; it merely frustrates them when the police don't listen or appear to assume that local concerns are not important or unreal. Robert Peel and his first police commissioners understood only too well in 1830 the temptation on the part of the police to assume that reassurance is all about being seen to act rather than about more subtle evidence that policing is working:

---

[14] See the BBC report 'Blair Defends Truancy Crackdown', 29 April 2002, available from http://news.bbc.co.uk/1/hi/uk_politics/1958325.stm; accessed 16 June 2010, and www.telegraph.co.uk/comment/personal-view/3622354/Tony-Blairs-instant-justice-will-make-criminals-of-us-all.html; accessed 20 May 2011.

> [...] the test of police efficiency is the absence of crime and disorder, and not the visible evidence of police action in dealing with them.[15]

Many chief officers have noted here and elsewhere that it is important to respond to people's fear of crime, immoderate and exaggerated though it sometimes is. It's preferable to listen than to ignore, and if part of the future of policing is about engagement with citizens and prompt response to their concerns, then the characteristic of the warranted police officer will be that s/he leads and coordinates local efforts to create a secure neighbourhood,[16] while at the same time retaining a more specialist capacity to provide 'protective services' such as the investigation of serious crime and the prevention of violence.

Summary

Chief officers have real concerns about the future of policing and where the service is going. They worry that policing will be hijacked by politicians or that the present 'muddled amateurism' will persist. Some call for a royal commission to undertake a politico-judicial review of the function of policing and to engage with a wide spectrum of views about where policing should go and how it should be determined and described. Others deprecate the characteristic slowness of royal commissions to report and point to the speed with which policing can change. Others want a wide-ranging debate about policing but not a formal legal mechanism; others still want any review of policing to be part of a wider-ranging enquiry into the whole criminal justice system, perhaps using the medium of a parliamentary select committee enquiry. There are special pleas for the police to be left alone to get on with the job, and for police officers themselves to try to re-engage positively with the news media to try to reverse what is seen as an implacably negative approach to the work of the police. This negativity, chief officers argue, inevitably adversely affects how the public regards the police and makes engagement with communities harder than it should be.

---

[15] Peel's principle 9, see footnote 7.

[16] As is already happening in some neighbourhood policing teams where a regular police officer oversees the work of special constables, PCSOs, other wardens, Neighbourhood Watch volunteers and other local partnerships, including those with 'civilian' statement takers. The supervisory responsibility entailed in these kinds of tasks has yet to be reconciled with the NOS-defined role of constable, but it is, like so many initiatives in community engagement, a 'work in progress'. See Caless, 2010 (chapter 6).

These views, from people who care deeply about policing and who, collectively, have an unparalleled experience and understanding of policing, are worth listening to. However, can there be too much fundamentally wrong with a police service that insistently calls for an objective review of what it does, especially when the calls are led by those in charge of that service?

General conclusions

As always, of course, what chief officers told me in the privacy of confidential discussion may be very different from any public utterances they may make. Without exception, the chief officers who spoke to me did so with honesty and forthrightness, confident that I would not betray the trust they showed in talking to me in the first place. I hope that they, as well as you the reader, believe that these glimpses into the private thoughts, enthusiasms, fears, unease, frustrations, satisfactions, achievements and despair of chief officers has been illuminating. Certainly, it has been for me an experience of continual enlightenment and understanding. I may not have been able to function, as one chief officer hoped,[17] as a 'champion' of the police throughout this exploration of the world of the 'top cop', but by being even-handed, I trust that those who spoke to me will feel that they have been well served.

It seems axiomatic that it is not easy to become a chief officer. Not only is there a requirement, at the moment at least, for a substantial track record at all or nearly all the ranks from constable to superintendent, but also the aspirant needs a high-achieving profile, an unequivocal recommendation from line manager and chief constable and must show potential to meet the 12 ACPO competencies for chief officers. These things will be enumerated and evidenced in application to the national gateway, Senior Police National Assessment Centre, success in which gives access to the Strategic Command Course (SCC). This programme stretches and extends aspirant chief officers, and provides – as they themselves have indicated – unparalleled networking opportunities and contacts which will last throughout their ACPO careers. 'Graduating' from the SCC is no guarantee of a post because candidates have to apply for advertised vacancies and appointments are in the gift of police authorities, with chief constables as members of the interview panels. The directly elected police crime commissioner will presumably share this appointment process with chief constables once police authorities

---

[17] See Introduction.

have disappeared, but there is little detail available yet to the outside enquirer about how the new arrangements will work, despite the government's publication of a *Draft protocol* (Home Office, 2011b).

What is also obscure is what proportion of SCC 'graduates' fail to obtain appointment at all. Such evidence as exists seems to indicate that eventually, virtually all police officers who get through the SCC obtain posts as ACCs. If that impression is objectively true, then there needs to be greater rigour in the appointments process. It cannot be healthy for the police service that attendance on a learning programme like the SCC practically guarantees employment. Data are lacking in the public domain and the whole area of chief officer appointment would benefit from greater transparency and perhaps some independent professional assessment, for example by the Chartered Institute of Personnel and Development or the Chartered Management Institute. I do not mean to imply that the process of appointment is in any way suspect or unethical, but independent commentators like me otherwise have no way of knowing whether it is as good as it could be.

Once appointed, chief officers face arduous workloads and long hours. To some extent, this continues the conditions under which the police service, or at least those of inspector rank and above, labours. To that is added a characteristic culture, superficially similar to that of junior hospital doctors, in that 'being there' in the workplace is an almost unquestioned assumption. ACCs and other chief officers work 70 hour weeks routinely and research has suggested that there is a correlation between such excessive work time and illness, particularly coronary illnesses. The public profile of chief officer entries on force websites suggests more of a work–life balance than probably is the case in reality, but it is no surprise that chief officers should adopt a persona or mask: such 'fronts' are common to operational leaders in all walks of life. Privately however, chief officers admit to fears about their tenure in the job, the intrusiveness of oversight, intense rivalry with their peers and some nervousness about being seen to be omnicompetent.

There is some confusion whether or not there is a discrete phenomenon called a *police leader*, or whether the generic skills of leadership may be applied to policing as to commerce or other forms of public service. That ACPO has taken over police leadership programmes from NPIA may give encouragement to those who believe that transformational leadership is the only viable default position, while those who argue for 'situational leadership' will also make their voices heard. The 12 ACPO competencies as they stand have very little about them which is unique to policing; it is the *application* of those generic competencies to the work of chief officers in commanding their forces which is more specialised. At the same time, it would be timely to revisit the competencies and ascertain if they actually reflect the daily reality of work as a chief officer, and if they do not, to revise, reduce or refine them. Certainly, there is a groundswell of opinion among chief officers themselves that policing command does not lend itself readily to leadership templates and that, depending on circumstances, chief officers move through a spectrum or range of leadership 'hats', which they may wear according to the demands of the situation. (That said, such responses are not unique to policing and can be found in many professional occupations from teaching to town-planning.) There is little clarity between management and leadership in policing at present and there seem to be few opportunities for chief officers truly to be transformational in how they lead.

There is an impression from the opinions expressed about police authorities (and latterly the PCC), HMIC and the Home Office, that chief officers dislike oversight and have low opinions of those tasked to oversee the police. Closer examination suggests that it is the interference with operational independence which causes most uneasiness. Some chief officers were at pains to point out to me that accountability is part of proper democratic control of the police function and they had no problem with having to justify and explain what they do. What sometimes upset them was the expectation that they could continue to deliver the same outcomes with demonstrably fewer resources, and that they should tolerate encroachment on the way in which they disposed of those resources in tactical and operational activities. It is more than mere resentment of the 'muddled amateur', rather it seems to be a determination to keep policing free of political and other vested interest interference. How far chief officers will be successful in resisting influence and impact – particularly in the person of the PCC – is anyone's guess, but the guile and resourcefulness of some police officers in dealing with their police authorities should not be underestimated when the latter are replaced in 2012 by the PCCs. Relations between chief officers and HMIC/Home Office look as though they will remain fraught – at least under the surface – until all sides are prepared to acknowledge and work through the rifts and strains in their relationships.

There is some (privately expressed) appetite for multi-level entry into the police service and a general and tangible shift in principle from the traditional 'closed shop' mentality of entry only in the rank of constable. At the same time, there is a solid and substantial weight of police opinion against the creation of a national police force, though some chief officers argue cogently for pooled resources and a national approach to equipment, uniform and logistics in the police service. Many seem to believe that the route to a national force will be through regionalised and collectivised steps, beginning with a reduction in the number of 'home' forces. What characterised chief officers' responses to the topics of multi-level entry and a national police force was the openness with which many seemed prepared to consider the prospects, and the seriousness with which they embraced change. As always, of course, privately expressed opinions may not match public utterances.

There is a common thread among chief officers when looking to the future of policing that there needs to be some form of thoroughgoing debate about the relationship between policing and society that goes beyond functions within the criminal justice system alone. Many chief officers called for an independent forum (royal commission, parliamentary committee, judicial enquiry) to assess formally and fundamentally what society wanted its police to be. Others suggested that a return to Peel's Principles would be a starting point, particularly as current assessment of the police task seems confined, in the person of the Home Secretary at least, to the reduction of crime and thus ignoring what chief officers believe to be the many other complex functions of policing. There is optimism about the future of the police, even within the context of reduced budgets, resource 'squeeze' and reductions in the workforce, and chief officers seem to believe, privately anyway, that crime is set to rise again. If that happens of course, the demand for increased resources will again be heard, and there is some suggestion that chief officers are positioning themselves to take advantage of any perception that law and order are breaking down. Perennial topics for debate, but not yet for resolution, include whether or not the police should be a profession and self-regulating, and whether a prerequisite of that status would be graduate entry. Several pointed to the structuring of the chief officer ranks as evidence both of a closed shop and of de facto graduate entry. Some chief officers, as well as outside commentators, have called for degrees to be required for the ranks of inspector and above,[18] which might entail, perhaps, an 'officer/other ranks' split which was once before attempted (unsuccessfully) by Lord Trenchard in the 1930s. Peter Neyroud's *Review* recommendation for the creation of a 'chartered police institute' is a possible way forward, as is a parallel

---

[18] Richard Stone in his report on the 10 years since the MacPherson Inquiry into the death of Stephen Lawrence, suggested that degrees be mandatory for the police service, later saying that they should be required for inspectors and above. See *Police Review*, 27 February, 2009, p 4; the report itself is available through the Equality and Human Rights Commission (2009).

recommendation for the growth in 'pre-joiner' partnerships with FE colleges and universities (Neyroud, 2011).

No-one can be long in the company of chief officers of police without acknowledging that, overwhelmingly, they are thoughtful, judicious, intellectually curious, decisive people with great experience across the whole spectrum of policing, and that they think in very original ways about crime, criminals, criminal justice, society, politics and ethics. They also exhibit the prejudices popularly associated with their positions, by being suspicious of politically motivated change, cautious about criminological theories of offending and resistant to media pressures to change their priorities. There is a chief officer 'culture', as there is a 'police canteen' culture, and it can sometimes reinforce risk aversion or perpetuate stereotypes – particularly in received opinions about the Civil Service and the media.

At the same time, very many chief officers are delightful companions, dry, incisive, witty, hugely knowledgeable, ironic and rueful by turns, who exhibit considerable patience when being asked 'damn fool questions'. I'm grateful for that patience and I'm glad to have met them. In the sense that we perhaps get the police we deserve, my final conclusion is that we are probably well served by the police we have, which is not to say that reform of police function and purpose is not overdue. But that would be another book.

Police leaders and resignations

In 2008, Sir Ian Blair, then Commissioner of the Metropolitan Police, resigned and there was a consequent sigh of relief throughout policing. He had clung to office for so long that his tenacity had become an embarrassment, and that had threatened the public's often fragile respect for the police. When Sir Paul Stephenson, Blair's successor, resigned on 17 July 2011, citing the 'distraction' which criticism of him would cause the Met, there was, by contrast, considerable dismay and regret. Actually, his action is typical of the man; his honesty and strong sense of public probity would not have allowed him to continue if he felt that he had himself become the story.

The Independent Police Complaints Commission (IPCC), known in policing as 'the 20/20 hindsight brigade', is investigating allegations against the former Commissioner, so it is probably premature to come to any conclusions about the ethics of the relationship between police leaders and senior editorial staff at the now defunct *News of the World*, as it also may be about the wider question of newspapers paying police officers for information. Assistant Commissioner John Yates has also resigned (18 July), citing similar reasons to Sir Paul's for his departure, after a week of heavy pressure and publicity. Two former chief officers at the Metropolitan Police, Andy Hayman and Peter Clarke, are also in the frame for the IPCC to look at.

This all seems to lend substance to media claims that policing is in crisis and that the police are led by inept, malign or naïve people. But there are some things we would do well to bear in mind: first, the Met is not the police. It likes to think it is sometimes, because it has some national roles, but policing is more than what happens in London. The second point is that policing goes on, whoever is at the top. Someone will step in and mind the shop, while the police go about their daily, routine, necessary and unglamorous tasks. The third point to make is that none of the allegations against any of the police leaders is yet proved and the cloud of speculation may be as evanescent as mist before sunrise.

The final point is this: when I did my research a year or so ago on chief police officers, what came across most strongly to me was that people at the top of policing cared very much about the image of the police and about how the public perceived them. It really matters to them that they are trusted and that people can rely on their fairness and neutrality. This relationship is not something that any good cop would willingly put at risk and we would be daft to join the current feeding frenzy engendered by the media and politicians – neither of which trades comes anywhere near policing in the public's sense of moral worth.

Bibliography

ACPO, *A People Strategy Framework for Policing in England and Wales 2008-13*, 2008, London: National Policing Improvement Agency (NPIA).

ACPO, 'Statement of Purpose', 2009, www.acpo.police.uk/About/AboutACPO.aspx; accessed 15 May 2011.

ACPO (Association of Chief Police Officers), *Final Response to the Government's Green Paper, From the Neighbourhood to the National*, 2008, London: ACPO.

ACPO, Home Office and the Association of Police Authorities, 'The Insight Programme – A 10 Year Workforce. Model and Plan', 2010, *Police Review*, 19 March 2010, p 23.

ACPO/Skills for Justice, *Twelve Competencies for a Chief Officer*, 2003, HO circular 27/2003, London: Home Office.

Adlam, R., 'Governmental Rationales in Police Leadership: an Essay Exploring Some of the "Deep Structure in Leadership Praxis"', 2002, *Policing and Society*, vol 12, no 1, pp 15-36.

Adlam, R., 'Nice People, Big Questions, Heritage Concepts', 2003, chapter 2 in R. Adlam and P. Villiers (eds) *Police Leadership in the 21st Century: Philosophy, Doctrine and Developments*, 2003, Winchester: Waterside Press.

Adlam, R. and Villiers, P. (eds), *Police Leadership in the 21st Century: Philosophy, Doctrine and Developments*, 2003, Winchester: Waterside Press.

Akers, R. and Sellers, C., *Criminological Theories: Introduction, Evaluation, and Application*, 4th edn, 2004, Los Angeles, CA: Roxbury Publishing Company.

Alderson, J., *Policing Freedom*, 1979, London: Macdonald and Evans.

Alderson, J., *Law and Disorder*, 1984, London: Hamish Hamilton.

Alderson, J., 'Police leadership', 2003, in Adlam and Villiers (eds) *Police Leadership in the 21st Century: Philosophy, Doctrine and Development*, pp 56-67.

APA (Association of Police Authorities), *Police Performance Management: Practical Guidance for Police Authorities*, 2006, London: Home Office/APA.

APA, *Accountability in Action – Police Authorities Adding Value*, 2007, London: APA.

APA, *Engaging, Consulting and Informing Communities: How to Review and Develop Police Authority Strategies*, 2008a, London: APA.

APA, *The Police Authority Role in Neighbourhood Policing: Ensuring Sustainability*, 2008b, London: APA.

APA, *What is a Police Authority?*, 2009, www.apa.police.uk/APA/About+Police+Authorities; accessed 16 February 2010.

APA, *Police Authorities: A Quick Guide*, 2010, London: Home Office/APA.

Audit Commission/HMIC, *The New Performance Landscape for Crime and Policing*, 2009, www.auditcommission.gov.uk/communitysafety/audit/policeinspection/Pages/policeinspectionframework.aspx; accessed 16 February 2010.

Auld, Lord Justice, *A Review of the Criminal Courts of England and Wales* (The Auld Report), 2001, www.criminal-courts-review.org, accessed 1 April 2009.

Barham, D., Leading article on promotion, *Police Review*, 16 April, 2010a, p 12.

Barham, D., 'Multi-point of Direct Entry', *Police Review*, 20 August, 2010b, p 12.

Barling, J., Slater, F. and Kellaway, E., 'Transformational Leadership and Emotional Intelligence: an Exploratory Study', 2000, *Leadership And Organisational Development Journal*, vol 21, no 3, pp 157-61, www.emeraldinsight.com/Insight/viewPDF.jsp?contentType=Article&Filename=html/Output/Published/EmeraldFullTextArticle/pdf/0220210304.pdf; accessed 4 March 2009.

Baron, A. and Armstrong, M., *Human Capital Management: Achieving Added Value through People*, 2007, London: Kogan Page.

Bass, B., *Leadership and Performance Beyond Expectation*, 1985, New York: Free Press.

Bass, B., *Transformational Leadership: Industrial, Military and Educational Impact*, 1998, Mahwah, NJ: Laurence Erlbaum.

Bauld, R., Brough, P., and Timms, C., 'Work–life and the Influence of Time Demands and Flexible Employment Policies', *Proceedings of the 8th Australian Psychological Society Industrial and Organisational Conference*, 2009, Sydney, Australia, pp12–16, www.allworthjuniper.com.au/8th_IOP_Conference_Proceedings.pdf; accessed 22 July 2011.

BBC, *The Secret Policeman*, 2004, http://news.bbc.co.uk/1/hi/magazine/3210614.stm, accessed July 2006.

BBC, 'Ministers defeated in Lords over police reforms plan', 2011, www.bbc.co.uk/news/uk-13368514; accessed 11 May 2011.

Bebbington, S., 'Setting Standards', *Police Review*, 3 July 2009, pp 18-21.

Bebbington, S., 'Fast Track', *Police Review*, 5 February 2010a, pp 18-19.

Bebbington, S., 'HMIC Accused of Forcing Hands Over Welsh Chief's Appointment', *Police Review*, 8 October 2010b, p 4.

Bebbington, S. 'Flexible Friends', *Police Review*, 12 March, 2010c, pp 18-19.

Bellingham, Z., 'Respect for Authority', *Police Review*, 29 October 2010, pp 22-3, 25.

Bennis, W., 'On Becoming a Leader,' 1989, cited in Long, M., 'Leadership and Performance Management', 2003, in T. Newburn (ed) *Handbook of Policing*, Devon: Willan Publishing, pp 628-54.

Bennis, W. and Thomas, R., *Geeks and Geezers: How Era, Values and Defining Moments Shape Leaders*, 2002, Boston, MA: Harvard University Press.

Bettison, Sir N., "I'm Not Worth £213,000", *The Times*, 12 April 2010.

Bichard, Sir M., *The Bichard Inquiry Report*, 2004, HC653, London: The Stationery Office.

Blair, I., 'Leadership that Learns', 2003, in R. Adlam and P. Villiers (eds.), *Police Leadership in the 21st Century, Philosophy, Doctrine and Developments*, Winchester: Waterside Press, Chapter 12, pp 169-173.

Blair, Sir I., *Policing Controversy*, 2009, London: Profile Book.

Blair, Sir I., Speech at the Future of Policing Seminar, PoliceOracle. com, 24 March 2010.

Bloom, N., Kretschmer, T. and Van Reenen, J., *Work Life Balance, Management Practices and Productivity*, 2006, London: AIM (Advanced Institute of Management Research).

Bloy, M. 'Sir Robert Peel's Nine Principles of Policing', in *A Web of English History*, April 2010, www.historyhome.co.uk/peel/laworder/9points.htm; accessed 4 June 2010.

Bosely, S. 'Too Much Overtime is Bad for Your Health, says Study', *The Guardian*, 11 May 2010, www.guardian.co.uk/society/2010/may/11/overtime-heart-risks-research; accessed 12 May 2010.

Boyle, A., *Trenchard, Man of Vision*, 1962, London: Collins, Chapters 19 'Police Reformer' and 20 'Police Administrator'.

Brackett, D., *Holy Terror: Armageddon in Tokyo*, 1996, New York: Weatherhill.

Brain, T., 'You're Fired!', *Police Review*, 22 October, 2010, pp 26-7.

Brough, P. and Biggs, A., 'Occupational Stress in Police and Prison Staff', in J. Brown and E. Campbell (eds) *The Cambridge Handbook of Forensic Psychology*, 2009, Cambridge: Cambridge University Press, pp 707-717.

Brough, P. and O'Driscoll, M., 'Work, Family Conflict and Stress', in A. Antoniou and C. Cooper (eds) *A Research Companion to Organizational Health Psychology*, 2005, Cheltenham: Edward Elgar, pp 346-65.

Bryman, A., *Leadership and Organisations*, 1986, London: Routledge and Kegan Paul.

Burns, J., *Leadership*, 1978, New York: Harper and Row.

Button, M., *Private Policing*, 2002, Devon: Willan Publishing.

Button, M., *Security Officers and Policing; Powers, Culture and Control in the Governance of Private Space*, 2007, London: Ashgate.

Bynum, R., 'Transformational Leadership and Staff Training in the Law-Enforcement Profession', 2008, *Police Chief*, vol 72, no 2, pp 72-5, 77-8, 80-1.

Cabinet Office, *Security in a Global Hub: Establishing the UK's Border Arrangements*, 2007, London: Cabinet Office; www.cabinetoffice.gov.uk/media/cabinetoffice/corp/assets/publications/reports/border_review.pdf; accessed 10 May 2010.

Caless, B., *'Presenteeism' and the Long Hours' Culture Among Chief Officers of Police*, 2005, a confidential research paper for the Chief Constable, Kent Police.

Caless, B., *Work–Life Balance in the Police*, 2006, Maidstone: Kent Police Authority.

Caless, B., '"Numties in Yellow Jackets": hostility to the PCSO', 2007, *Policing: A Journal of Policy and Practice*, vol 1, no 2, pp 187-95.

Caless, B. (ed), Bownas, J., Simpson, M., Spruce, B. and Underwood, R., *Blackstone's Handbook for the Special Constabulary*, 2010, Oxford: Oxford University Press.

Calvert, E., Russell, H. and O'Connell, P. J., *Reconciling Work and Family Life: Workplaces, Occupation and the Experience of Work–Life Conflict*, 2009, Dublin: ESRI.

Carr, T., *Authentic Leadership: The Competencies Senior Women Need in Order to be Successful*, 2007 Guildford, Surrey: eve-olution/enguage.

Carswell, D., 'Police Authorities Association Despises You', January 2009, www.talkcarswell.com/show.aspx?id=368; accessed 16 February 2010.

Caswell, C., 'Police Governance', *Police Oracle*, 1 July 2010, www.policeoracle.com/news/Timeframe-for-Governance-Changes-%91Realistic%92_24797.html; accessed 12 May 2011.

CCJS (Centre for Crime and Justice Studies), *Ten Years of Criminal Justice under Labour: An Independent Audit*, January 2007, London: King's College.

Centrex, *Leading for those We Serve: The Police Leadership Qualities Framework (PLQF)*, 2006, Bramshill Police Staff College Leadership Academy, quoted in Coliandris, G. and Rogers, C., 'Linking Police Culture, Leadership and Partnership-Working', 2008, *Police Journal*, vol 81, no 2, pp 111-125.

Chan, J., 'Damage Control: Media Representation and Responses to Police Deviance', *Law Text Culture*, vol 2, no 1, pp. 36-60.

Chermak, S., McGarrell, E. and Gruenewald, J., 'Media Coverage of Police Misconduct and Attitudes Toward Police', 2006, *Policing: An International Journal of Police Strategies & Management*, vol 29, no 2, pp 261–81.

Church, A. and Bracken, D., 'Advancing the State of the Art of 360-Degree Feedback', 1997, *Group and Organizational Management*, vol 22, pp 149-66.

Civitas, 'The Nine Principles of Good Policing', 2010, www.civitas.org.uk/pubs/policeNine.php; accessed 9 June 2010.

CJS (Criminal Justice System), 'Virtual courts', 2008, http://frontline.cjsonline.gov.uk/_includes/downloads/guidance/better-use-of-technology/20081003_Virtual_Court_Factsheet.pdf; accessed 9 June 2010.

Clarke, A., '"You're nicked!" Television Police Series and Definitions of Law and Order' (1992), in Strinati, D. and Wragg, S. (eds) *Come On Down? Popular Media Culture in Post-War Britain*, 1992, London: Routledge, pp 232-53.

Clarke, R., '"Situational" Crime Prevention: Theory and Practice', 1980, *British Journal of Criminology*, vol 20, no 2, 136-47.

Clements, P., *Policing a Diverse Society*, 2006, Oxford: Oxford University Press.

Cockcroft, T. and Beattie, J., 'Shifting Cultures: Managerialism and the Rise of "Performance"', 2009, *Policing: An International Journal of Police Strategies and Management*, vol 32, no 3, pp 526-40, www.emeraldinsight.com/Insight/viewPDF.jsp?contentType=Article&Filename=html/Output/Published/EmeraldFullText Article/Pdf/1810320307.pdf; accessed 29 January 2010.

Cohen, L. and Felson, M., 'Social Change and Crime Rate Trends: A Routine Activities Approach', 1979, *American Sociological Review*, vol 44, no 4, pp 588-608.

Coliandris, G. and Rogers, C., 'Linking Police Culture, Leadership and Partnership-Working', 2008, *Police Journal*, vol 81, no 2., pp 111-25.

Conway, N. and Briner, R., *Understanding Psychological Contracts at Work: A Critical Evaluation of Theory and Research*, 2005, Oxford: Oxford University Press.

Cooke, L. and Sturges, P., 'Police and Media Relations in an Era of Freedom of Information', 2009, *Policing and Society*, vol 19, no 4, December, pp 406-24.

Covey, S., *Seven Habits of Highly-Effective People*, 1989, London: Simon & Schuster.

Cowley, R. and Todd, P., *The History of HM Inspectorate of Constabulary: the first 150 years, 1856-2006*, 2007, London: HMIC.

Crawford, C., (Chief Executive of the Metropolitan Police Authority (MPA)), *MPS Approach to Talent Management and Succession Planning*, 14 January 2010, www.mpa.gov.uk/committees/cep/2010/100114/04/?qu=HPDS&sc=2&ht=1; accessed 10 March, 2010.

Crime in England and Wales: Quarterly Update to September 2010, 20 January 2011, London: Home Office Statistical Report 02/11; http://rds.homeoffice.gov.uk/rds/pdfs11/hosb0211.pdf; accessed 29 January 2011.

Cruess, S.R., Johnston, S. and Cruess, R.L., '"Profession": a Working Definition for Medical Educators', 2004, *Teach Learn Med*, Winter, vol 16, no 1, pp 74-6, www.ncbi.nlm.nih.gov/pubmed/14987179; accessed 12 June 2010.

Defence Academy of the United Kingdom, www.da.mod.uk/colleges/jscsc/jscsc-library/artwork/hugh-montague-trenchard/first-viscount-trenchard; accessed 23 June 2009.

Denning, Lord, *R v. The Commissioner of Police for the Metropolis, ex parte Blackburn*, 1968, QB 138, p 136, cited in McLaughlin, E., *The New Policing*, 2007, London: Sage, p 181.

Denston, L., 'Senior Police Leadership: Does Rank Matter?', 2003, *Policing: An International Journal of Police Strategies and Management*, vol 26, no 3, pp 400-18.

De Stickere, R., *The History of Recruiting and Training Senior Officers in Police Forces in England and Wales*, 1988, Hampshire: Bramshill Police Staff College.

Dhani, A. and Kaiza, P., *Police Service Strength England and Wales, 30 September 2010*, 2011, London: Home Office Statistical Bulletin, 27 January 2011, http://rds.homeoffice.gov.uk/rds/policeservicestrength/03.11; accessed 28 January 2011.

Digman, J., 'Personality Structure: Emergence of the Five-Factor Model', 1990, *Annual Review of Psychology*, vol 41, pp 417-40.

Dobby, J., Anscombe, J. and Tuffin, R., *Police Leadership: Expectations and Impacts*, 2004, Home Office Online Report No. 20/04, London: Home Office.

Drodge, E. and Murphy, S., 'Interrogating Emotions in Police Leadership', 2002, *Human Resource Development Review*, vol 1, no 4, pp 420-38.

DTI (Department of Trade and Industry), *The Essential Guide to Work–Life Balance*, 2001, www.dti.gov.uk/work-lifebalance/publications.html; accessed 14 January 2010.

Dubois, J., 'Media Coverage of Organized Crime – Police Managers' Survey', 2002, *Trends in Organized Crime*, vol 7, no 4, June, pp 29-54.

Eagly, A. and Johannesen-Schmidt, M., 'The Leadership Styles of Men and Women', 2001, *Journal of Social Issues*, 57, pp 781-97.

Eagly, A. and Johnson, B., 'Gender and Leadership Styles: a Meta-analysis', 1990, *Psychological Bulletin*, no 108, pp 233-56.

Edwards, C., *Changing Policing Theories for 21st Century Societies*, 2005 edn, Sydney, NSW: Federation Press.

Edwards, C. and Skidmore, P., *A Force for Change, Policing 2020*, 2007, London: Demos Publications, also www.demos.co.uk/publications/aforceforchange; accessed 25 May 2010.

Edwards, R., 'Police £5,000 Worse Off in Move to Cut Overtime', *The Daily Telegraph*, 13 August 2010, www.telegraph.co.uk/news/uknews/law-and-order/7942152/Police-5000-worse-off-in-move-to-cut-overtime.html; accessed 16 August 2010.

Electoral Commission, *Frequency of Voting and Attitudes towards Voting*, 2001, www.ipsos-mori.com/researchpublications/researcharchive/poll.aspx?oItemId=1236; accessed 20 February 2010.

Equality and Human Rights Commission, *Police and Racism: What has been Achieved 10 Years after the Stephen Lawrence Inquiry Report?*, 2009, www.equalityhumanrights.com/news/pre-june-2009/commission-reports-on-police-and-racism-ten-years-on-from-the-macpherson-inquiry; accessed 12 May 2011

ESDS (Economic and Social Data Service), *British Crime Survey*, 2010, www.esds.ac.uk/government/bcs/; accessed 9 June 2010.

Fahy, P. 'Making of the Modern Leader: Proposals for Identifying and Developing the Senior Officers of the Future', 2008, *Policing Today*, vol 14, no 1, February, pp 17-18.

Farrall, S., Bannister, J., Ditton, J. and Gilchrist, E., 'Open and Closed Question', *Social Research Update*, University of Surrey, Summer 1997, http://sru.soc.surrey.ac.uk/SRU17.html; accessed 10 June 2010.

Flanagan, Sir R., *HMIC Annual Report, 2004-2005*, 2005, Chapter 2, www.hmic.gov.uk/SiteCollectionDocuments/Annual%20Reports/ARP_20040401.pdf; accessed 23 February 2010.

Ford, R., 'Police Stations and Courts Could Close in Cost-Cutting Measures', *The Times*, 24 June 2010, www.thetimes.co.uk/tto/news/uk/crime/article2570271.ece; accessed 24 June 2010.

Foster, J., Newburn, T. and Souhami, A., *Assessing the Impact of the Stephen Lawrence Inquiry*, 2005, Home Office research study, 294, London: Home Office, www.homeoffice.gov.uk/rds/pdfs05/hors294.pdf

Foti, R. and Hauenstein, N., 'Pattern and Variable Approaches in Leadership Emergence and Effectiveness', 2007, *Journal of Applied Psychology*, 92, pp 34-55.

Fresco, A., 'Cuts Signal End of "Gold-Plated" Policing, Sir Hugh Orde Warns', 2010, *The Times*, 30 June, www.thetimes.co.uk/tto/news/uk/article2579175.ece; accessed 30 June 2010.

Friedman, M., *Type A Behavior: Its Diagnosis and Treatment*, 1996, New York: Plenum Press.

Gattrell, V., 'Crime, Authority and the Policeman State', 1990, in F. Thompson (ed) *The Cambridge Social History of Britain, 1750-1950*, vol 3, Cambridge: The University Press.

Gibson, A. and Villiers, P., *Leading for those we Serve*, 2007, NPIA/Home Office, www.npia.police.uk/en/docs/PLQFLeadingForThoseWeServe.pdf; accessed 2 January 2009.

Gillen, T., *Performance Management and Appraisal*, 2nd edn, 2007, London: CIPD.

Godfrey, B., 'Peel, Sir Robert', 2008, in T. Newburn and P. Neyroud (eds) *Dictionary of Policing*, Devon: Willan Publishing pp 191-2.

Godfrey, B. and Paul, L., *Crime and Justice, 1750-1950*, 2005, Devon: Willan Publishing.

Golding, B. and Savage, S., 'Leadership and Performance Management', 2008, in T. Newburn (ed) *Handbook of Policing*, 2nd edn, Devon: Willan Publishing, pp 725-59.

Goldstein, H., 'Improving Policing; a Problem-Oriented Approach' *Crime and Delinquents*, 25 April 1979, pp 236-58.

Goleman, D., 'Leadership that Gets Results', 2000, *Harvard Business Review*, March/April, pp 78-90.

Goleman, D., Boyatizis, R., McKee, A., *The New Leaders: Transforming the Art of Leadership into the Science of Results*, 2002, New York: Little, Brown & Co.

Goleman, D., Boyatizis, R., McKee, A., *Primal Leadership: Realizing the Power of Emotional Intelligence*, 2002, Boston, MA: Harvard Business School Press.

Goleman, D., 'What Makes a Leader?', 2004, *Harvard Business Review*, January, vol 82, no 1, pp 82-91.

Goudriaan, H., Wittebrood, K., and Nieuwbeerta, P., 'Neighbourhood Characteristics and Reporting Crime: Effects of Social Cohesion, Confidence in Police Effectiveness and Socio-economic Disadvantage', 2006, *British Journal of Criminology*, no 46, pp 719-42.

Gove, M., 'If Crime's on the Up, Your Chief Constable Must Explain Why or be Sacked', 2005, *The Times*, 15 March , www.thetimes.co.uk/tto/law/columnists/article2042724.ece; accessed 21 June 2010.

Graef, R., *Talking Blues*, 1990, London: Collins Harvill.

Greer, C. and McLaughlin, E., '"Trial by Media": Policing, the 24-7 News Media Sphere and the "Politics of Outrage"', 2011, *Theoretical Criminology*, 15, 1, pp. 23-46.

Grint, K., 'Learning to Lead: Can Aristotle Help Us Find the Road to Wisdom?', 2007, *Leadership*, vol 3, no 2, pp 231-46.

Grosman, B., *Police Command: Decisions and Discretion*, 1975, Toronto, Canada: The Macmillan Co. of Canada Ltd. [Copy in Bramshill Library, Access no 0007839/3DAA].

Gwent Police Authority, *Protocol Governing the Relationship Between Gwent Police Authority and Gwent Police*, 2009, www.gpaweb. demonweb.co.uk/pa/publications/protocolpoliceauthority%20 and%20police.pdf

Halford, A. with Barnes, T., *No Way Up The Greasy Pole: A Fight against Male Domination in the British Police Force*, 1993, London: Constable and Trans-Atlantic Publications.

Hannagan, T., *Management: Concepts and Practices*, 2nd edn, 1998, London: Financial Times/Prentice Hall.

Hansard, 'Police Responsibilities and Rewards' (Sheehy Report), *Proceedings of the House of Commons*, 28 October 1993, vol 230, Columns 975-89: London HMSO, http://hansard.millbanksystems.com/ commons/1993/oct/28/police-responsibilities-and-rewards#1993-10-28T15:30:00Z; accessed 4 June 2010.

Hansard, "Police Reform and Social Responsibility Bill" debate, *Proceedings of the House of Lords*, 11 May 2011, columns 895-932, London: TSO, www.publications.parliament.uk/pa/ld201011/ ldhansrd/text/110511-0001.htm#11051171000299; accessed 17 May 2011

Hartfield, C., MacVean, A., Grieve, J. and Phillips, Sir D. (eds), *The Handbook of Intelligent Policing*, 2008, Oxford: Oxford University Press.

Hayman, A. 'Would Outsiders Make Better Chief Constables?', 2009, *The Times*, 7 December, www.timesonline.co.uk/tol/comment/ columnists/guest_co ntributors/article6946579.ece; accessed 13 May 2010.

Hays, K., Regoli, R. and Hewitt, J., 'Police Chiefs, Anomia, and Leadership', 2007, *Police Quarterly*, vol 10, no 1, pp 3-22.

Hazell, R., *Police and Constabulary Almanac*, 2009, Dartford, Kent: R. Hazell and Co.

Heffernan, W., 'Three Types of Leadership', 2003, in R. Adlam and P. Villiers, (eds) *Police Leadership in the 21st Century: Philosophy, Doctrine and Development*, Winchester: Waterside Press, pp 134-45.

Heidesohn, F., 'Gender and Policing', 2003, in T. Newburn (ed) *Handbook of Policing*, Devon: Willan Publishing.

Herdale, G. and Stelfox, P., 'National Intelligence Model', 2008, in T. Newburn and P. Neyroud (eds) *Dictionary of Policing*, Devon: Willan Publishing, pp 173–174.

Hersey, P. and Blanchard, K., 'Life-Cycle Theory of Leadership', 1969, *Administrative Science Quarterly*, 16, pp 321-38.

Hetherington, P., 'Extremists Could Commandeer New Police Authorities, Councillors Warn', 2008, *The Guardian*, 8 December, www.guardian.co.uk/society/2008/dec/08/elected-police-authorities-emergency-services-local-government-councillors; accessed 16 February 2010.

Hill, C. and Jones, G., *Strategic Management Theory: An Integrated Approach*, 9th edn, 2010, Mason, OH: Southwestern Cengage Publishing.

History and Policy, www.historyandpolicy.org/papers/policy-paper-16.html; accessed 21 April 2010.

History of Home Office from The National Archives website, www.ndad.nationalarchives.gov.uk/AH/2/detail.html; accessed 23 February 2010.

Hitchcock, A., 'Leading from the Front: the National Police Leadership College', 2009, *Police Professional*, no 169, 9 July, pp 17-18.

Hitchcock, A., 'Free Consultancy' in *Police Review* 12 March 2010, p.6

HMG Green Paper, *Police Reform*, 2008, http://police.homeoffice.gov.uk/publications/police-reform/green-paper-chapters; accessed 10 March 2009.

HMIC, *Delivering the Policing Pledge – Early Findings*, 2009, London: HMIC, http://inspectorates.homeoffice.gov.uk/ hmic/inspections/thematic/policing-pledge-early-finds.pdf?view=Binary; accessed 15 November 2009.

HMIC, *Police Governance in Austerity: HMIC Thematic Report into the Effectiveness of Police Governance*, HMIC Zoë Bellingham, 2010a, London: HMIC.

HMIC, *Valuing the Police: Policing in an Age of Austerity*, 2010b, July, London: HMIC.

HMIC/Audit Commission, *Learning Lessons: An Overview of the First Ten Joint Inspections of Police Authorities by HMIC and the Audit Commission*, March 2010, London: HMIC, www.hmic.gov.uk/SiteCollectionDocuments/Individually%20Referenced/PAI_NFS_20100315.pdf; accessed 5 May 2010.

Home Affairs Committee of the House of Commons, *The Work of the Home Office*, 2009, Oral Evidence given by Rt. Hon. Alan Johnson MP, Secretary of State, Sir David Normington, Permanent Secretary Home Office, and Constable Adrian Parsons, Kent Police, 15 December, www.publications.parliament.uk/pa/cm/cmhaff.htm; accessed 21 April 2010.

Home Office, *Recruitment and Selection of Chief Police Officers: Guidance on Appointment Procedures*, 2002a, HO Circular 60/2002, London: Home Office.

Home Office, *Fixed Term Appointments for Senior Police Officers*, 2002b, HO Circular 68/2002, London: Home Office.

Home Office, *Performance and Development Reviews (PDRs), for chief police officers*, 2003, HO Circular 27/2003, London: Home Office.

Home Office, *Police Leadership: Expectations and Impact*, 2004a, London: Home Office.

Home Office, *Review of the Selection and Appointments Process of Independent Members of Police Authorities*, 2004b, London: Home Office.

Home Office, *Guidance on the Gender Equality Duty in the Police Service*, 2007, London: Home Office, http://police.homeoffice.gov.uk/publications/equality-diversity/agenda-equality-police-service2835.pdf?view=Binary; accessed 3 February 2010.

Home Office, *Green Paper, From the Neighbourhood to the National: Policing our Communities Together*, 2008, London: Home Office.

Home Office, *Assessment of Women in the Police Service*, 24 February 2010a, http://library.npia.police.uk/docs/homeoffice/assessment-women-police-service.pdf; accessed 22 June 2011.

Home Office, *Policing in the 21st Century: Reconnecting Police and the People*, July 2010b, London: The Stationery Office; www.homeoffice.gov.uk/publications/consultations/policing-21st-century/policing-21st-full-pdf; accessed 27 July 2010.

Home Office, *Crime in England and Wales: Quarterly Update to September 2010*, 20 January 2011a, London: Home Office Statistical Report 02/11; http://rds.homeoffice.gov.uk/rds/pdfs11/hosb0211.pdf; accessed 29 January 2011.

Home Office, *Draft Protocol for Elected Police Crime Commissioner*, 2011b, London: Home Office, www.homeoffice.gov.uk/publications/police/police-commissioners-protocol; accessed 15 May 2011.

Home Office/ACPO/APA, *Setting Local Policing Plan Priorities and Assessing Performance Within APACS: Interim Good Practice Guidance for Police Authorities and Police Forces*, 2008, London: Home Office/ACPO/APA.

Hooper, A. and Potter, J., *Intelligent Leadership: Creating a Passion for Change,* 2000, London: Random House.

Hough, M. and Maxfield, M., *Surveying Crime in the Twenty-First Century,* 2007, Devon: Willan Publishing.

Hunsley, J., Lee, C. and Wood, J., 'Controversial and Questionable Assessment Techniques', 2004, in S. Lilienfeld, J. Lohr and S. Lynn (eds) *Science and Pseudoscience in Clinical Psychology,* New York: Guildford Publishing, pp 39-76.

Hurd, D., *Robert Peel: A Biography,* 2007, London: Weidenfeld & Nicolson.

Innes, M., 'What's Your Problem? Signal Crimes and Citizen-Focused Problem-Solving', 2005, *Criminology and Public Policy,* vol. 4, no. 2, pp 187-200.

IPSOS MORI, *Local Elections Turnout,* 2000, www.ipsos-mori.com/newsevents/ca/ca.aspx?oItemId=368; accessed 20 February 2010.

Irving, B., *Reassurance Policing – Making It Happen: A Summary End-Of-Programme Report on Implementation Management,* 2005, London: The Police Foundation and Pembroke College.

Jewkes, Y., *Media and Crime,* 2004, London: Sage.

Johnston, I., *President's Speech,* 16 September 2008, to Superintendents' Association Annual Conference at Carden Park, www.policesupers.com/news/full.asp?id=77&news=345; accessed 12 July 2010.

Jones, A., 'Future Proof', *Police Review,* 8 May 2009, pp 38-9.

Jones, T. and Newburn, T., *Policing after the Act: Police Governance after the Police and Magistrates' Courts Act 1994,* 1997, London: Grantham Books.

Jones, T. and Newburn, T., 'The Transformation of Policing? Understanding Current Trends in Policing Systems', 2005, in T. Newburn (ed) *Policing: Key Readings,* Devon: Willan Publishing, pp 733-50.

Jung, C., 'Psychological Types', 1971 (1921), in *Collected Works of C. G. Jung,* Volume 6, Princeton, MA: Princeton University Press, see para 91.

Kakabadse, A. and Dainty, P. 'Police Chief Officers: a Management Development Survey', 1988, *Journal of Managerial Psychology,* vol 3, no 3, pp 1-45.

Kamsteeg, F., Meerholz, K. and Ybema, S., 'Ethnographying Police Identity Formation, Tales from Street and Management Cops', 2010, '5th Annual Ethnography conference, Queen Mary, University of London, 1-3 September, www.liv.ac.uk/managementschool/ethnography_conference/papers2010/Kamsteeg.pdf; accessed 4 November 2010.

Kingshott, B. 'Women in Policing: Changing the Organizational Culture by Adopting a Feminist Perspective on Leadership', 2009, *Criminal Justice Studies*, vol 22, no 1, pp 49-72.

Kirby, T., 'Police Resistance to Reforms Surprises Sheehy', 1993, *The Independent*, 31 July, www.independent.co.uk/news/uk/resistance-by-police-to-reform-surprises-sheehy-the-inquiry-chairman-outlines-his-case-for-changing-conditions-to-terry-kirby-1488245.html; accessed 24 May 2010.

Krupicka, B., *Police Reform, Governance and Democracy*, 2007, London: Emerald Publishing Group.

Lamm-Weizel, D., *Analyzing Repeat Victimization: Problem-Oriented Guide for Police*, Problem-solving Tools Series 4, 2005, Washington DC: COPS/US Department of Justice.

Leishman, F. and Mason, P., *Policing and the Media: Facts, Fictions and Factions*, 2003, Devon: Willan Publishing.

Lewis, S., 'Restructuring Workplace Cultures: The Ultimate Work-family Challenge?', 2001, *Women in Management Review*, vol 16, no 1, pp 21-9.

Long, M., 'Leadership and Performance Management', 2003, in T. Newburn (ed) *Handbook of Policing*, Devon: Willan Publishing, pp 628-54.

Loveday, B., 'The Challenge of Police Reform in England and Wales', 2005, *Public Money and Management*, vol 25, no 5, pp 275-81.

Loveday, B., 'Police Authorities', 2008, in T. Newburn and P. Neyroud (eds) *Dictionary of Policing*, Devon: Willan Publishing.

Loveday, B. and McClory, J., *Footing the Bill: Reforming the Police Service*, 2008, Policy Exchange, www.policyexchange.org.uk/publications/publication.cgi?id=66; accessed 26 July 2010.

Loveday, B. and Reid, A., *Going Local: Who Should Run Britain's Police?*, 2003, London: Policy Exchange.

Loveday, B., Williams, S. and Scott, P., 'Workforce Modernization in the Police Service: Prospects for Reform?', 2008, *Personnel Review*, vol 37, no 4, pp 361-74.

Lustgarten, L., *The Governance of the Police*, 1986, London: Sweet & Maxwell.

Maccoby, M., *The Leaders We Need and What Makes Us Follow*, 2007, Boston, MA: Harvard Business School Press.

MacPherson, Sir W., *Report of an Inquiry into the Investigation of the murder of Stephen Lawrence*, 1999, London, Parliament, Cmd. 4262.

Mason, P. (ed.), *Criminal Visions: Media representations of Crime and Justice*, 2003, Devon: Willan Publishing.

Mawby, R., 'Continuity and Change, Convergence and Divergence: the Policy and Practices of Police-Media Relations', 2002, *Criminology and Criminal Justice*, vol 2, no 3, pp 303-24.

McGuire, C., Magin, K. and Friedman, R., 'Best Practices in New Employee Orientation: Developing and Retaining a Motivated, Engaged Workforce', 2009, *ICF International*.

McLaughlin, E., 'The Permanent Revolution: New Labour, New Public Management and the Modernisation of Criminal Justice', *Criminal Justice*, 2001, vol 1, no 3, pp 301-318.

McLaughlin, E., *The New Policing*, 2007, London: Sage Publications Ltd.

Middleton, J., *Beyond Authority: Leadership in a Changing World*, 2007, London: Palgrave Macmillan.

Milburn, A., *Unleashing Aspiration – The Final Report of the Panel on Fair Access to the Professions*, July 2009, Institute for Career Guidance, www.icg-uk.org/article607.html; accessed 10 November 2010.

Miller, H., Watkins, R. and Webb, D., 'The Use of Psychological Testing to Evaluate Law-enforcement Leadership Competences and Development', 2009, *Police Practice and Research*, vol 10, no 1, pp 49-60.

Mills, H., Silvestri, A. and Grimshaw, R., *Police Expenditure 1999-2009*, 2010, Centre for Crime and Justice Studies; London: King's College and the Hadley Trust, www.crimeandjustice.org.uk/opus1777/Police_Expenditure_embargo.pdf; accessed 24 August 2010.

Ministry of Justice, 'Straw: Virtual Courts Deliver Swift Justice', 2009, www.justice.gov.uk/news/newsrelease270509a.htm; accessed 9 June 2010.

Ministry of Justice, *Provisional Quarterly Criminal Justice System Performance Information – December 2009*, May 2010, www.justice.gov.uk/publications/docs/quarterly-cjs-performance-stats-q3-09-10c.pdf; accessed 9 June 2010.

Mortimore, R., *Local Elections: Why No-one gives a Monkey's*, IPSOS/MORI, 2002, www.ipsos-mori.com/newsevents/ca/ca.aspx?oItemId=306; accessed 20 February 2010.

MPA (Metropolitan Police Authority), *Race and Faith Inquiry Report*, 2010, London: MPA.

Myers, Isabel Briggs, with Peter B. Myers, *Gifts Differing: Understanding Personality Type*, 1980, various editions to 1995, Mountain View, CA: Davies-Black Publishing.

Natarajan, M., *Women Police in a Changing Society: Back Door to Equality*, 2008, Aldershot, Hampshire: Ashgate.

National Archive, HO 242: *HM Inspectorate of Constabulary: Reports, Papers and Minutes, 1856,* http://yourarchives.nationalarchives.gov.uk/index.php?title=Home_Office_Inspectorates; accessed 23 February 2010.

Naylor, R., 'Time for a National Police Force?', 2004, speech to Superintendents' Association Annual Meeting, reported as 'Superintendents in Controversial Call for Creation of National Police Force' in *The Birmingham Post,* 16 August, www.highbeam.com/doc/1G1-120690303.html; accessed 25 May 2010.

Neville, Dame E., 'Leading Act: Debate on the Quality of Police Leaders', 2003, *Police Review,* 18 July, pp 26-7.

Newburn, T., 'The Future of Policing', 2003, in T. Newburn (ed) *Handbook of Policing,* Devon: Willan Publishing, pp.707-21.

Newman, M., *Emotional Capitalists: The New Leaders,* 2008, Chichester: John Wiley and Sons.

Neyroud, P., 'Policing and Ethics', 2003, in T. Newburn (ed) *Handbook of Policing,* Devon: Willan Publishing, pp 578–602.

Neyroud, P., 'Foundation for Leadership', 2010, *Police Professional,* Issue 221, 9 September, pp 12-13.

Neyroud, P., *Review of Police Leadership and Training,* 2011, London: Home Office.

Nicholas, L. and Farrell, G., 'Repeat Victimization', 2008, in T. Newburn and P. Neyroud (eds) *Dictionary of Policing,* Devon: Willan Publishing, pp 239-41.

Nolan, Lord., *Standards in Public Life: First Report of the Committee on Standards in Public Life* (1995) Cm2850, London: HMSO.

NPIA, *The Police High Potential Development Scheme* (HPDS), 2009, www.npia.pnn.police.uk/en/8563.htm; accessed 6 July 2010.

NPIA, 'Diploma in Policing' the revised IPLDP qualification, Version 1.4, March 2010a, www.npia.police.uk/en/docs/IPLDP_FAQs_v1_4_March_2010.doc; accessed 6 July 2010.

NPIA, Strategic Command Course, 2010b, www.npia.police.uk/en/2211.htm; accessed 6 July 2010.

O'Connor, Sir D., *Closing the Gap,* HMIC report on Policing, 2005, London: The Stationery Office.

O'Driscoll, M., Brough, P., and Kalliath, T., 'Stress and Coping', 2008, in C. Cartwright and C. Cooper (eds) *The Oxford Handbook of Organizational Well Being,* Oxford: Oxford University Press, pp 237-66.

O'Neal, M., *Type A Personality: A Look Inside the Mind of an Alpha Male,* 2009, www.authorsden.com/categories/article_top.asp?catid=35andid=49846; accessed 15 January 2010.

O'Neill, S., 'Police Chief Takes Home Office to Court over Secret Culture of "Irrational" Cuts', 2009, *The Times*, 28 May.

O'Neill, S., 'Cleveland Police Chief Sean Price's £200,000 Pay and Perks Package', 2009, *The Times*, 7 July, www.timesonline.co.uk/tol/news/uk/article6652909.ece; accessed 10 November 2010.

O'Neill, S., 'Cameron to Tell Police Chiefs They Must Do More with Less', 2010, *The Times*, 21 June, www.thetimes.co.uk/tto/news/politics/article2565017.ece; accessed 21 June 2010.

Ortmeier, P. and Meese, E., *Leadership, Ethics and Policing: Challenges for the 21st Century*, 2009, Upper Saddle River, NJ: Prentice Hall.

O'Shea, P., Foti, R., Hauenstein, N. and Bycio, P., 'Are the Best Leaders both Transformational and Transactional? A Pattern-oriented Analysis', 2009, *Leadership*, vol 5, no 2, pp 237-59.

Ozimek, J., 'Police Reject Tory Plans for Elected Chiefs', 2010, *Policing*, 24 March, reproduced in *The Register*, March 2010, www.theregister.co.uk/2010/03/24/tory_police_clash/; accessed 4 June 2010.

Patterson, D., 'Be an Effective Leader', *FBI Law Enforcement Bulletin*, vol 78, no 6, June 2009, pp 14-18.

Pearman, R. and Albritton, S., *I'm Not Crazy, I'm Just Not You: The Real Meaning of the Sixteen Personality Types*, 1996, Mountain View, CA: Davies-Black Publishing.

Pellew, J., *The Home Office 1848 –1914: From Clerks to Bureaucrats*, 1982, London: Heinemann Educational Books, pp 122-44, http://yourarchives.nationalarchives.gov.uk/index.php?title=Home_Office_Inspectorates; accessed 26 February 2010.

Phillips, Sir D., Caless, B. and Bryant, R., 'Intelligence and its Application to Contemporary Policing', 2007, *Policing: a Journal of Policy and Practice*, vol 1, no 4, pp 438-46, Oxford: Oxford University Press.

PNAC, *Assessment Exercises*, 2009, Appendix B, pp 13-16 of the NPIA document: www.npia.police.uk/en/docs/SPNAC_Reasonable_Adjustment_Policy_2009.pdf; accessed 12 July 2010.

PNAC (Police National Assessment Centre), 'Application Booklet', 2010, www.npia.police.uk/en/docs/SPNAC2010ApplicationForm.doc; accessed 12 July 2010.

Pointon, I., 'Commission Impossible', 2010, *Police Review*, 23 July, pp 18-19.

Police Oracle, 'ACPO Head Calls for Police Service Overhaul', 23 March 2010, *Police Oracle*, www.policeoracle.com/news/ACPO-Head-Calls-For-Police-Service-Overhaul_22643.html; accessed 4 June 2010.

Police Reform Working Group, *'A Force to be Reckoned With': A Policy Report*, 2009, Centre for Social Justice, www.centreforsocialjustice. org.uk/default.asp?pageref=266; accessed 25 May 2010.

Politics, 'Budgets and Finance for Police Authorities', 2009, www. politics.co.uk/briefings-guides/issue-briefs/policing-and-crime/ police-funding-\$366697.htm; accessed 16 February 2010.

Raine, J., 'Best Value', 2008, in T. Newburn and P. Neyroud (eds) *Dictionary of Policing*, Devon: Willan Publishing, pp 14-15.

Read, T. and Tilley, N., *Not Rocket Science? Problem-solving and Crime Reduction*, 2000, Home Office Crime Reduction Research Series, Paper no 6, London: Home Office, http://rds.homeoffice.gov.uk/ rds/prgpdfs/crrs06.pdf; accessed 25 June 2010.

Reiner, R., *The Blue-Coated Worker*, 1978, Cambridge: Cambridge University Press.

Reiner R., *Chief Constables: Bobbies, Bosses, or Bureaucrats?* 1991, Oxford: Oxford University Press.

Reiner, R., 'Police and the Media', 2008, in T. Newburn (ed.), *Handbook of Policing*, 2nd edn, Devon: Willan Publishing, pp 313-339.

Reiner, R., *The Politics of the Police*, 4th edn, 2010, Oxford: Oxford University Press.

Reith, C., *A New Study of Police History*, 1956, London: Oliver and Boyd.

Research, Development and Statistics (RDS), *Stepping Up: Making the Move to ACPO: A Review of the Demands and Attractions of ACPO Level Roles and the Way the Police Service Manages Talent into those Roles*, 2010, London: Home Office.

RDS, *Response from the Home Office – December 2008*, 2010, London: Home Office, http://rds.homeoffice.gov.uk/rds/pdfs08/consult-bcsu16-response08.pdf; accessed 9 June 2010.

RDS, *Consultation on the British Crime Survey Extension to Cover under 16s*, 2010, London: Home Office, www.homeoffice.gov.uk/ publications/science-research-statistics/research-statistics/crime-research/hosb0211/hosb0211?view=Standard&pubID=864175; accessed 12 May 2011.

Reuss-Ianni, E., *Two Cultures of Policing*, 1984, New Brunswick, NJ: Transaction.

Rolph, C., *Report of the Royal Commission on the Police*, 1962, British Journal of Criminology, vol 3, pp 177-9.

Rose, D., 'Junior Doctors Desert the NHS', 2010, *The Times*, 6 September, www.thetimes.co.uk/tto/health/news/article271 5136.ece; accessed 6 September 2010.

Rowe, M. and Garland, J., 'Have You Been Diversified yet? Developments in Police Community and Race Relations Training in England and Wales', 2003, *Policing and Society*, vol 13, pp 399-412.

Royal Commission on the Police, *Final Report*, Cmnd 1728, 1962, London: HMSO, available from the Open Library (OL14805963M) at: http://openlibrary.org/books/OL14805963M/Royal_Commission_on_the_Police_1962; accessed 4 June 2010.

Russell Group, summarised at www.russellgroup.ac.uk/home; accessed 12 May 2011.

Savage, M., Watson, R. and Sherman, J., 'Lib Dem Rebellion Scuppers Tory Policing Plans', *The Times*, May 11 2011, www.thetimes.co.uk/tto/news/politics/article3016317.ece?CMP=EMCeb2; accessed 12 May 2011.

Savage, S., Chapman, S. and Cope, S., *Policing and the Power of Persuasion: The Changing Role of the Association of Chief Police Officers*, 2000, London: Blackstone Press.

Schafer, J., 'Developing Effective Leadership in Policing: Perils, Pitfalls and Paths Forward', 2009, *Policing: An International Journal*, vol 32, no 2, pp 238-60.

Schulz, D., *Breaking the Brass Ceiling: Women Police Chiefs and Their Paths to the Top*, 2004, Westport, CT: Praeger.

Scott-Lee, Sir P., 'Report on Chief Constable Michael Todd', 2009, *Police Oracle*, 10 February, www.policeoracle.com/news/Report-On-Chief-Constable-Michael-Todd_18432.html; accessed 12 May 2011.

Senior Police National Assessment Centre (PNAC), *Senior PNAC, Results and Analysis Report*, Executive Summary, November 2009a, NPIA, www.npia.police.uk/en/docs/SPNACResultsandAnalysis ExecSummary2009.pdf; accessed 12 July 2010.

Senior PNAC, 'Senior PNAC Presentation: Overall Result', 2009b, www.npia.police.uk/en/docs/SPNACPresentation2010.pdf; accessed 12 July 2010.

Sheehy, Sir P., *Inquiry into Police Responsibility and Rewards*, 1993, Cm 2280, London: HMSO.

Sigurdsson, J. and Dhani, A., *Police Service Strength 14/10, England and Wales, 31 March 2010*, 22 July 2010, London: Home Office, http://rds.homeoffice.gov.uk/rds/pdfs10/hosb1410.pdf; accessed 22 July 2010.

Sigurdsson, J. and Mulchandani, R., *Police Service Strength 2009, England and Wales*, 2010, Home Office Statistical Bulletin 03/10, London: Home Office.

Sigurdsson, J. and Mulchandani, R., *Police Service Strength, England and Wales, 30 September 2009*, 28 January 2010, 03/10, London: Home Office, http://rds.homeoffice.gov.uk/rds/pdfs10/hosb0310.pdf; accessed 21st July 2010

Silverman, D., *Doing Qualitative Research*, 2000, London: Sage Publications.

Silvestri, M., *Women in Charge*, 2003, Devon: Willan Publishing.

Silvestri, M., '"Doing" Police Leadership: Enter the "New Smart Macho"', 2007, *Policing and Society*, vol 17, no 1, March, pp 38-58.

Smith, C., *Providing the Future Chief Officers of Police*, 1990, Association of Chief Police Officers (ACPO), [Bramshill Ref.: 3DHB ASS O/S].

Southwick, J., 'Australian Council of Professions' View', during proceedings of a joint conference on competition law and the professions, Perth, April 1997, www.accc.gov.au/content/index. phtml/itemId/277772, accessed 12 June 2010.

Stallion, M. and Wall, D., *The British Police: Police Forces and Chief Officers, 1829-2000*, 1999, Police History Society, Bramshill, Hampshire, UK.

Stein, S., Papadogiannis, P., Yip, J. and Sitarenios, G., 'Emotional Intelligence of Leaders: a Profile of Top Executives', 2009, *Leadership and Organisational Development Journal*, vol 30, Iss: 1, pp 87–101.

Tilley, N., Robinson, A. and Burrows, J., 'The Investigation of High-Volume Crime,' 2007, in T. Newburn, T. Williamson and A. Wright (eds) *Handbook of Criminal Investigation*, Devon: Willan Publishing, pp 226-54.

Van Vellsor, E. and Ascalon, E., 'Role and Impact of Leadership Development in Supporting Ethical Action in Organisations', 2008, *Journal of Management Development*, vol 17, no 2, pp 187-95.

Virtanen, M., Ferrie, J., Singh-Manoux, A., Shipley, M., Vahtera, J., Marmot, M. and Kivimaki, M., 'Overtime Work and Incident Coronary Heart Disease: The Whitehall II Prospective Cohort Study', 2010, *European Heart Journal*, vol 31, no 9, European Society of Cardiology, http://eurheartj.oxfordjournals.org/content/early/2010/05/04/eurheartj.ehq124.full.pdf+html; accessed 12 May 2011.

Visser, F. and Williams, L., *Work–Life Balance: Rhetoric Versus Reality?*, Independent report commissioned by UNISON, 2006, London: The Work Foundation.

Wakefield A., *Selling Security, The Private Policing of Public Space*, 2003, Devon: Willan Publishing.

Walker, A., Flatley, J., Kershaw, C. and Moon D., *Crime in England and Wales, 2008-2009*, 2009, London: Home Office, www.homeoffice.gov.uk/rds/pdfs09/hosb1109vol1.pdf; accessed 22 February 2010.

Wall, D.S., 'The Ideology of Internal Recruitment: the Chief Constables of England and Wales and the Tripartite Arrangement', 1994, *British Journal of Criminology*, vol 34, no 3, Summer, pp 322-38.

Wall, D.S., *The Chief Constables of England and Wales: The Socio-Legal History of a Criminal Justice Elite*, 1998, Aldershot: Dartmouth.

Wankhade, P. and Brinkman, J., *'New Public Management' and Leadership: Whether there is any Contingent Relationship between Leadership Style and Performance Status*, 2007, www.ipa.udel.edu/3tad/papers/workshop5/Wankhade.pdf; accessed 1 February 2010.

Weber, M., *The Theory of Social and Economic Organizations*, translated by A. Henderson and T. Parsons, 1947, New York: Free Press.

Weisburd, D., Mastrofski, S., Greenspan, R. and Willis, J., *The Growth of Compstat in American Policing*, 2004, Police Foundation Reports, www.policefoundation.org/pdf/growthofcompstat.pdf; accessed 12 February 2010.

WestMarland, L., *Gender and Policing*, 2002, Devon: Willan Publishing.

Williams, C., 'Britain's Police Forces: Forever Removed from Democratic Control?', 2003, *History and Policy*, www.historyandpolicy.org/papers/authors.html; accessed 17 February 2010.

Wright, A., *Policing: An Introduction to Concepts and Practice*, 2002, Devon: Willan Publishing.

Wright, A., Alison, L. and Crego, J., 'The Current State of Police Leadership Research', 2008, in L. Alison and J. Crego (eds) *Policing Critical Incidents: Leadership and Critical Management*, Devon: Willan Publishing, chapter 4.

Appendix

This is the questionnaire that formed the basis for all the interviews.

Top Cops

Questionnaire for chief officers

1. Would you describe your role as 'baron', 'boss', 'bobby', 'bureaucrat' (Reiner 1991) or as something else?

    What is your current role?

    How would you describe your leadership style? Is it, for example, transactional, or transformational, or facilitative, or situational, or a blend depending on circumstances or something else entirely?

2. How do you develop people? Are the same opportunities available now as you had, or are they better or worse?

3. Can you estimate roughly what proportions of your time you spend on
    * Relations with your police authority, or similar oversight body
    * Performance management and targets
    * Relations with HMIC and the Home Office/political parties
    * Public relations and reassurance issues
    * Police command and directing
    * Duty as 'Gold' command or its equivalent?

4. How did you become a chief officer? Deliberate and planned ambition? Happy accident? Someone's influence? Mentoring? Other?

5. How do you get people to follow you?

6. Has leadership in the police changed since you joined? How? What has stayed the same?

7. What is your view of the practice of ACPO spokespeople for business areas? What is yours (in general terms if you wish)? How important is it? How much of your time does strategic national work of this kind occupy?

8. How would you describe your relationships with your peers, both inside and outside the force or organisation in which you serve?

9. What ambitions remain for you in policing? What about outside policing?

10. How secure in the job do you feel? Is it ever a case of 'uneasy lies the head that wears a crown' or not?

11. What things need urgent changing in policing? How would you change them?

12. What is your view of multiple direct entry to the police (including to chief officer)? What is your view of the government's avowal in its 2008 Green Paper to stay with 'constable entry only' into the police?

13. Could someone without your experience (indeed, with no experience of the police at all) still do your job?

14. If you had your time over again, would you be a police officer? If yes, why? If no, equally, why?

15. What do you feel about the idea of a national police force in England and Wales? Is it feasible?

16. How would you describe your relationship with your police authority or other oversight body?

17. Can you describe your relationship with HMIC?

18. Can you describe your relationship with the Home Office?

19. What do you do to 'balance' your life outside policing? Does it work (do you feel, therefore, that your life is in balance?)?

20. What would you like to be your legacy to policing?

21. Have you any other observations, comments or opinions?

Index

Page references for footnotes are followed by *f*